Global Justice

METAPHILOSOPHY

METAPHILOSOPHY SERIES IN PHILOSOPHY

Series Editors
Armen T. Marsoobian
Brian J. Huschle

Global Justice

Edited by

Thomas W. Pogge

Copyright © Blackwell Publishing 2001

First published, with the exception of chapter 7, as
Metaphilosophy, Vol 32, No. 1/2 2001

Reprinted 2003

Blackwell Publishing
108 Cowley Road
Oxford OX4 1JF, UK

Blackwell Publishing Inc
350 Main Street
Malden, Massachusetts 02148, USA

British Library Cataloguing in Publication Data has been applied for

Library of Congress Cataloging-in-Publication Data has been applied for

ISBN 0–631–22712–1 (pbk)

Typeset by Cambrian Typesetters, Frimley, Surrey
Printed and bound in Great Britain
by MPG Books Ltd, Bodmin, Cornwall

This book is printed on acid-free paper

Contents

1

INTRODUCTION: GLOBAL JUSTICE

THOMAS W. POGGE

This collaborative project was stimulated by two independent invitations. One, from Gertrude Lübbe-Wolff, suggested that I organize a seminar on international justice at the Bielefeld Zentrum für interdisziplinäre Forschung (ZiF), of which she is the president. The other, from Armen Marsoobian, suggested that I guest-edit a special double issue on philosophical cosmopolitanism for *Metaphilosophy*, of which he is the editor. It seemed clear that each of these ideas would benefit greatly from being combined with the other.

In the event, two supportive patrons did not suffice to launch the project. To finalize ZiF funding for the seminar, I wrote a brief proposal. It sketched my organizational ideas for a three-day seminar in June 2000 as well as some of the main disagreements among alternative moral approaches to the design and assessment of foreign policies and the global institutional order, focusing especially on disagreements about the moral significance of national borders. This proposal, however, did not find favor with the ZiF's external reviewers, who, deliberating through the fall of 1999, concluded that the interesting and controversial problems of global justice arise not at the level of moral values and principles, but about their balancing and application. The topic calls for economists and lawyers more than for philosophers and political theorists, or so they found. With this negative verdict, the project seemed dead on January 5, 2000.

But forty-eight hours later, it had sprung back to life through the remarkably quick and unbureaucratic intervention of Joel Rosenthal, who offered that all travel costs would be paid by the Carnegie Council for Ethics and International Affairs, of which he is the president. With most of the cost covered in this way, the ZiF could offer to take care of food and lodging. With three supportive patrons, the project was back on track.

Even though the mailing of invitations was already several months behind the initial schedule, I took a couple of days to think about the reviewers' reaction. These reflections changed not only the invitation letter, but also my chapter for the conference as well as, indirectly, some of our discussions.

There is indeed widespread agreement on some basic values relating to global justice. With some minor variations, people are against oppression, hunger, and grinding poverty, and in favor of development and human rights. But the reviewers are nevertheless quite wrong to conclude that the interesting questions must therefore concern implementation. The deep and consequential disagreements, actually, are not about these more technical matters but about responsibilities. This point is well illustrated by the 1996 World Food Summit in Rome, organized by the U.N. Food and Agriculture Organization (FAO). At the summit 186 governments joined to condemn it as "intolerable that more than 800 million people throughout the world, and particularly in developing countries, do not have enough food to meet their basic nutritional needs." Having endorsed this declaration, the U.S. government then went out of its way to explain that "the attainment of any 'right to adequate food' or 'fundamental right to be free from hunger' is a goal or aspiration to be realized progressively that does not give rise to any international obligations." Many who signed the declaration, approved it, or drew hope from it reject the U.S. statement as a grave moral error. This is a disagreement at the level of moral values and principles, and a consequential one at that: Currently, fully one-third of all human deaths, some 18 million annually, are due to poverty-related causes.

One lesson from this paradigmatic disagreement is evident: Thinking about global justice must not be confined to the exposition and justification of goals, values, and ideals, but must be extended to the question of obligation. This extension has been a central concern of Onora O'Neill's work, exemplified once more in her contribution to the present volume. Thinking about responsibilities in a global setting is especially important and especially challenging in a global context where massive harms are often caused by the conduct of many agents who, individually, do not seem to contribute enough, or to know enough about their contributions, to deserve serious moral criticism. Yes, we ought to make a major effort to stop hunger, AIDS, and global warming. But there are millions of agents, related to these problems in many different ways, and there is no institutional division of labor in place. How then should each of these agents reflect on its own role and determine its obligations? What moral principles can lead us to successful coordination, to fulfilling our collective obligations?

This question looks bound to produce important and interesting discussions and responses. But the response that, in our world, wealthy and powerful states have no obligations at all in regard to starvation abroad does not seem to merit careful consideration. Who could seriously believe this? Well, a moral skeptic, perhaps. But the U.S. government does not subscribe to moral skepticism. On the contrary, it is rather more fond of appeals to morality than most. So what is one to do with its "interpretive statement" on the Rome declaration?

Considering the statement's content alone, one may be tempted to ignore it as wildly implausible. But the statement was issued by the most powerful agent on Earth. It is likely to make a huge difference in human terms whether the U.S. government and its allies hold and act on the principle that affluent states have no obligations in regard to starvation abroad. So it seems urgent to engage the official U.S. position on world hunger.

Yet how can one seriously and responsibly engage a moral view that is absurd, even perverse, on its face? One might reason by example, as people often reason with teenagers. Suppose the United States is involved in negotiating an International Monetary Fund loan and conditions attached to it. Do you really think that the United States has no obligation at all to consider how alternative sets of conditions would foreseeably affect the incidence of hunger in the prospective debtor country? Or suppose the United States is involved in drafting particular trading rules within the World Trade Organization. Do you really believe that the United States has no obligation to give any weight at all to how the alternatives would foreseeably impact the ability of the world's poorest and most vulnerable populations to meet their nutritional needs? One might add: Do you really believe that the American people, whom the U.S. government is representing, would on reflection endorse affirmative answers to the two preceding questions? Such questioning may change the mind of a teenager or even – who knows? – the mind of a government official. But it is hardly intellectually challenging work. A chapter criticizing the official U.S. position on world hunger is likely to resemble a leaflet more than an intellectually serious normative argument. It is not very interesting to write, not very interesting to read, and, since it will also not have any real effect, likely to be a little embarrassing within an academic context.

It is perhaps not surprising, then, that the discourse intellectuals produce about the moral principles of politics, and of international politics in particular, is often rather strange and remote, rather "academic," as they say. Since speaking truth to power, for all the noble sound of this phrase, is not intellectually exciting, we rather speak truth to one another. We develop complex conceptions of global justice that, though generally continuous with the moral convictions of ordinary people, are worlds apart from the foreign policies and global institutional arrangements that our elected leaders are forging in our names. We recognize this distance, of course, but we prefer to focus on the much smaller intra-academic gaps, which we can hope to overcome through reasonable argument. And we tend to shy away from questions of responsibility and implementation, which would lead us onto mildly embarrassing terrain. Any plausible way of realizing any of our conceptions of global justice would assign tasks to the developed states that go far beyond anything their leaders might conceivably accept. Effective reduction of hunger and severe poverty worldwide, for example, would require a real effort costing perhaps as much as $230 billion annually (1 percent of the affluent countries' gross national product) for several years. When the FAO, after the Rome summit, asked all developed states, together, merely to provide an extra $6 billion annually for modernization of agriculture in the developing countries, the United States commissioned a study designed to show that $2.6 billion would be enough to reach the summit target of halving hunger by 2015. Again, one is at a loss how to engage such a view. Should one say that, in view of 18 million poverty-related deaths annually, it would not be so bad if the FAO's request led to faster achievement of the target? Should one add that the target itself is grotesquely unambitious – taking nineteen years to eradicate only half the hunger problem while envisioning some 200 million poverty-related deaths in the interim? Or should one just ignore the U.S. government's position in favor of some more serious intellectual work?

These reflections raise the issue of the role and responsibilities of intellectuals. Should we think about our role in consequentialist terms – perhaps defending the U.S. position in its essentials in order to gain credibility with the powers that be, which might then permit us to improve that position at the margins? Or do we have an obligation to make clear to citizens how dramatically their own moral views differ from those officially set forth in their behalf? Should we highlight and discuss, for instance, the more questionable policies their governments pursue and defend in their name, such as the U.S. government's official denial of any obligation to give weight, in its decisions and policies, to foreigners' rights to adequate nutrition?

More interesting and also quite important may be the task of *explaining* the relevant policies of the developed Western states as well as the divergence of the moral views expressed by their governments from those of most ordinary citizens. For example, why are these governments doing so very little toward the eradication of severe poverty abroad even while they are prepared to spend billions on other humanitarian initiatives, such as the NATO bombing of Yugoslavia? And why do most citizens of those countries acquiesce in these priorities? There are obvious cynical answers to these questions. One such answer is that helping the world's poorest populations emerge from poverty tends to strengthen their states and thus to weaken our own, while bombing Yugoslavia tends to reinforce the existing power hierarchy. Another answer is that citizens are interested in violence perpetrated by evil foreigners, which gives us opportunities to express moral outrage and condemnation, and opportunities also to play the noble roles of protector and peacemaker; but we are far less comfortable thinking about malnourished children, who just die, anonymously, all over the developing world, at the rate of tens of thousands every day.

There is surely some truth in such cynical explanations. But one also feels that they do not give the whole story. There are likely to be aspects of our moral thinking that tend to blind us to our responsibilities in regard to global poverty and tend to reconcile us to the moral priorities our governments express in their declarations, in their foreign policies, and in the way they shape the global institutional order. If so, political philosophers could make an important contribution by identifying and critically examining these aspects of ordinary moral thinking.

These were some of the thoughts with which we started our essays and our discussions in Bielefeld. Other issues were discussed as well, of course, as the following essays amply illustrate. Most of these essays have been considerably revised in light of our debates, to which several other participants, besides the authors, also contributed greatly: Hilary Bok, Amanda Dickins, Kerstin Haase, Andrew Kupers, Lukas Meyer, Markus Pins, Katja Vogt, and Kerstin Zyber. We are grateful to them all, as well as to our three sponsors and the chief administrative organizer Marina Hoffmann, for helping to make possible so productive and rewarding an event. Finally, we are grateful to the editorial staff of *Metaphilosophy*, including Armen T. Marsoobian, Brian J. Huschle and Suzanne Solensky.

2

PRIORITIES OF GLOBAL JUSTICE

THOMAS W. POGGE

As I look back on the post-Cold War period, the greatest surprise for me is that the affluent states have done so very little toward eradicating global poverty. This is surprising because the conditions for a major effort seemed exceptionally favorable. The fading of the Soviet bloc gave the developed states greatly enhanced opportunities to incorporate their moral values and concerns into their foreign policy and into the rapidly developing international institutional order. It also enabled these high-income countries to cut their military expenditures as a share of gross domestic product (GDP) by about 46 percent, from 4.1 percent of GDP in 1985 to 2.2 percent of GDP in 1998, according to the United Nations Development Programme (UNDP 1998, 197; UNDP 2000, 217), and thereby to reap an annual peace dividend of currently roughly $420 billion.[1] Maintaining healthy economic and technological growth throughout the period, the developed states thus had both the power and the funds to make a major effort toward poverty eradication.

However, no such effort took place. The developed states, during the same period, actually cut their official development assistance (ODA) as a share of gross national product (GNP) by about 27 percent.[2] They have also reduced their allocations to multilateral development efforts, revised Part XI of the 1982 United Nations Convention on the Law of the Sea to the disadvantage of developing countries, and imposed onerous terms of trade on the latter in the context of the Uruguay Round.

To be sure, developed states have been more willing to appeal to moral values and to use such appeals in justification of initiatives – such as the NATO bombing of Yugoslavia – that would have been unthinkable during the Cold War. But these appeals only heighten the puzzle. If it makes sense to spend billions and to endanger thousands of lives in order to rescue a million people from Serb oppression, would it not make more sense to

[1] This is 1.9 percent of their current aggregate GDP of over $22 trillion (UNDP 2000, 209).

[2] From 0.33 percent of GNP in 1987/88 to 0.24 percent of GNP in 1998 (UNDP 2000, 218).

spend similar sums, without endangering any lives, on leading many millions out of life-threatening poverty?

To appreciate the force of this question about priorities, one must know some of the salient facts about global poverty. About one-quarter of all human beings alive today, 1.5 billion, subsist below the international poverty line,[3] "that income or expenditure level below which a minimum, nutritionally adequate diet plus essential non-food requirements are not affordable" (UNDP 1996, 222). This level is specified in terms of one 1985 U.S. dollar per person per day at purchasing power parity (PPP).[4] Due to inflation in the intervening years, this level now (year 2000) corresponds to an annual per capita income of $581 PPP or to an annual per capita income of $145 at current exchange rates.[5] So households in the poorest quartile cannot afford, per person per year, whatever basic necessities can be bought for $581 in the United States or for $145 in the average poor country. Such severe poverty has consequences: 790 million persons are not adequately nourished, while one billion are without safe water and 2.4 billion without basic sanitation (UNDP 2000, 30); more than 880 million lack access to basic health services (UNDP 1999, 22); about one billion are without adequate shelter and two billion without electricity (UNDP 1998, 49). "Two out of five children in the developing world are stunted, one in three is underweight and one in ten is wasted."[6] One-quarter of all children

---

[3] World Bank 1999, 25. Because life expectancy among the very poor is much lower than average, far more than a quarter of all human lives – and deaths – occur within the poorest quartile. Conventional methods of measuring the extent of poverty may thus distort what is morally significant by assigning lower weight to the poor in proportion to their lower life expectancy. Suppose, for example, as is approximately true, that the poor live, on average, half as long as the nonpoor. The number of lives and deaths in the poorest quarter would then be twice the average number of lives and deaths in the other three quarters: two-fifths versus three-fifths. Forty percent of all human lives and deaths would occur among the poor, even while these poor, at any given time, make up only 25 percent of the world's population. This distortion affects most conventional statistics I cite in this essay, though not of course the statement that one-third of all human deaths are due to poverty-related causes.

[4] World Bank 1999, 276. The international poverty line is being newly specified this year by replacing the purchasing power of $1 in the United States in 1985 with the purchasing power of $1.08 in the United States in 1993 (World Bank 2000, 17). But inflation between 1985 and 1993 in the United States was not 8 percent, but over 34.3 percent (<http://stats.bls.gov/cpihome.htm>). The revision thus lowers the international poverty line by 19.6 percent and thereby conveniently reduces the widely publicized number of global poor without cost to anyone. (In response to my inquiry about this, the World Bank has written me that this revision is justified by the fact that the prices of what the poor consume, and especially of basic foodstuffs, have risen more slowly than other prices.) Still, even after the revision, this number is still 1.2 billion (World Bank 2000, 17 and 23; UNDP 2000, 4).

[5] This last figure takes account of the fact that in the poor countries only about twenty-five cents, on average, are said to be needed to buy local currency that has as much purchasing power as one dollar has in the United States. Thus, the World Bank converts China's GNP per capita of $780 to $3,291 PPP, India's $450 to $2,149 PPP, Indonesia's $580 to $2,439 PPP, Nigeria's $310 to $744 PPP, and so on (World Bank 2000, 274–75).

[6] U.N. Food and Agricultural Organization (FAO), at <http://www.fao.org/focus/e/sofi/child-e.htm>.

between the ages of five and fourteen, 250 million in all, work outside their family for wages, often under harsh conditions, in agriculture, construction, textile or carpet production, for instance, or as soldiers, prostitutes, or domestic servants.[7] These children do not receive much of an education, and most of them, if they survive long enough, are likely to join the currently one billion illiterate adults (UNDP 2000, 30).

Severe poverty causes not only massive underfulfillment of social and economic human rights, such as the "right to a standard of living adequate for the health and well-being of oneself and one's family, including food, clothing, housing and medical care."[8] Severe poverty and economic inequality also contribute significantly to the underfulfillment of civil and political human rights associated with democratic government and the rule of law. Desperately poor people, often stunted from infancy, illiterate, and heavily preoccupied with the struggle to survive, can do little by way of either resisting or rewarding their local and national rulers, who are therefore likely to rule them oppressively while catering to the interests of other (often foreign) agents more capable of reciprocation. The income and staying power of such rulers often depend less on their poor subjects than on a small local elite or on a few foreign companies and governments, to whom they can sell the country's natural resources and from whom they can obtain grants and loans and weapons. Such rulers have little need for popular support, and many of them use torture, restrict freedom of expression, and perpetuate their rule by force.

Severe poverty is by far the greatest source of human misery today. Deaths and harms from direct violence around the world – in Chechnya, East Timor, Congo, Bosnia, Kosovo, Ethiopia and Eritrea, Rwanda, Somalia, Iraq, and so on – provoke more publicity and hand-wringing. But they are vastly outnumbered by deaths and harms due to poverty. In 1998, some 588,000 deaths were due to war; other homicides and violence caused some 736,000 more. Starvation and preventable diseases, by contrast, claimed about 18 million human lives, thus causing about one-third of all human deaths.[9] The few years since the end of the Cold War have seen over 200 million deaths due to poverty-related causes.

Reducing severe poverty abroad is not easy, of course, but it is generally much easier than reducing violence abroad. Attempts to stop violence often involve violent means (as in the bombing of Iraq and Yugoslavia),

---

[7] World Bank 1999, 62. The International Labor Organization (ILO) reports that "at least 120 million children between the ages of 5 and 14 work full time. The number is 250 million, or more than twice as many, if we include those for whom work is a secondary activity" (<http://www.ilo.org/public/english/270asie/feature/child.htm>).

[8] Universal Declaration of Human Rights, §25.

[9] World Health Organization 1999, Table 2. The total number of human deaths in 1998 was 54 million, or 148,000 per day. Among these, "worldwide 34,000 children under age five die daily from hunger and preventable diseases" (United States Department of Agriculture 1999, iii).

often provoke violence (as in Kosovo), and may also serve as precedents that encourage further and perhaps dubious violent interventions. Such attempts are therefore often associated with significant moral and economic costs, which are difficult to measure even *ex post*, let alone to predict *ex ante*. Inaction in the face of violence abroad is thus often the right choice or at least a choice that has strong and morally significant reasons in its favor. Attempts to reduce poverty do not face such problems. There is so much severe poverty in so many different countries that one can find plenty of places where money can be effectively spent, especially on local goods and services: on enabling poor people to afford more and better foodstuffs and shelter, on financing more and better schools and basic health services, or on improving the local infrastructure (safe water, sanitation, electricity, road and rail links). When such projects are under-taken with the genuine aim of effecting enduring progress in the world's poorest regions – rather than with the aim of buying political support from their rulers or from domestic exporters – they are generally far more cost-effective at saving and improving human lives than so-called humanitarian interventions are. And they do not, in any case, run substantial risks of worsening the situation. Many have thought Western inaction in the face of the Rwandan genocide a clear-cut indication that we simply do not care about the victims we are abandoning to their fates. In that case, however, one might still adduce the complexities and time pressures of a rapidly developing situation as a (weak) excuse. No such excuse is available for our long-standing decision to tolerate the massive death toll from starva-tion and preventable diseases, the reduction of which would involve lower costs and much lower risks to ourselves.[10]

Consider foreign aid. Net ODA provided by the United States was under $9 billion in 1998. This amount is less than half a percent of the federal budget,[11] $32 per U.S. citizen.[12] It corresponds to 0.10 percent of U.S. GNP (versus 0.21 percent under Ronald Reagan in 1987/88) – the lowest among members of the Organization for Economic Cooperation and Development (OECD), which, in the same period, have reduced their aggregate net ODA from 0.33 percent of their combined GNPs to 0.24 percent or $52 billion (UNDP 2000, 218). The allocation of such funds is, moreover, governed by political considerations: Only 21 percent goes to the forty-three least-developed countries (UNDP 2000, 218), and only 8.3

---

[10] There used to be the argument that eradicating hunger now would lead to more wide-spread hunger in the future. But this argument is now thoroughly discredited by the realiza-tion that eradication of poverty tends to entail an often dramatic decline in birth rates.

[11] "The U.S. Agency for International Development (USAID) administers America's foreign assistance programs, which account for less than one-half of 1% of the federal budget" (<http://www.info.usaid.gov/pubs/cp98/progprview.htm>).

[12] The United States has sharply reduced its contributions to other international antipoverty programs as well (<www.brown.edu/Departments/World_Hunger_Program/hungerweb/HN/Articles/WFS/EDIT2.html>), though not to the World Food Program.

percent is spent on meeting basic needs.[13] The OECD countries together thus spend $4.3 billion annually toward meeting basic needs abroad – 0.02 percent of their combined GNP, or 0.8 cents per day for each person in the poorest quartile.

One might think that these low and shrinking ODA allocations are due to the recently ascendant belief that poverty reduction is best achieved through private investment and free markets. But this is not how our governments themselves explain their policies – most elaborately, perhaps, in connection with the World Food Summit in Rome, organized by the U.N. Food and Agriculture Organization (FAO) in November 1996. Its principal achievement was this pledge by the 186 participating governments:

> We, the Heads of State and Government, or our representatives, gathered at the World Food Summit . . . reaffirm the right of everyone to have access to safe and nutritious food, consistent with the right to adequate food and the fundamental right of everyone to be free from hunger. We pledge our political will and our common and national commitment to achieving food security for all and to an on-going effort to eradicate hunger in all countries, with an immediate view to reducing the number of undernourished people to half their present level no later than 2015. We consider it intolerable that more than 800 million people throughout the world, and particularly in developing countries, do not have enough food to meet their basic nutritional needs. This situation is unacceptable.[14]

Having joined this pledge, the U.S. government then published its own interpretation of it: "The attainment of any 'right to adequate food' or 'fundamental right to be free from hunger' is a goal or aspiration to be realized progressively that does not give rise to any international obligations."[15] The United States also challenged the FAO's claim that fulfilling the pledge would require all developed states combined to increase their ODA in agriculture by $6 billion annually (Alexandratos 1995): "As part of the *U.S. Action Plan on Food Security*, USAID [U.S. Agency for International Development] commissioned a separate study of the projected cost of meeting the World Food Summit target and a strategy for reaching this goal. The study, completed in mid 1998, focused on a potential framework for ODA investments and estimated that the target could be reached with additional

---

[13] UNDP 2000, 79. In this regard, the developed states fall far short of the "20:20 compact" made within the OECD, which prescribes that they and multilateral donors allocate at least 20 percent of their foreign aid, and developing states at least 20 percent of their national budgets, to meeting basic needs.

[14] Rome Declaration on World Food Security (<http://www.fao.org/wfs/policy/english/96–3eng.htm>).

[15] "Interpretive Statement" filed by the U.S. government in reference to the first paragraph of the Rome Declaration on World Food Security (<http://www.fas.usda.gov:80/icd/summit/interpre.html>).

global ODA of $2.6 billion annually, as compared to the FAO's estimate of $6 billion annually" (United States Department of Agriculture 1999, Appendix A). So the study proposes that the developed states should back their pledge by adding only $3.30 rather than $7.60 annually for each malnourished person. The hunger reduction plan adopted in Rome implicitly envisions well over 200 million deaths from hunger and preventable diseases over the 1997–2015 plan period. One might have thought that, even if the FAO's proposed annual increase of $6 billion were to reduce hunger faster than planned, this should be no cause for regret. Halving world hunger in nineteen years, after all, is glacial progress. And an extra $6 billion is not much to ask from the high-income countries, whose combined GNP in 1998 was $22,599 billion (World Bank 1999, 231).

The official position articulated by the United States and practiced by the developed countries can then be characterized by these three elements: We are able to reduce severe poverty and the hunger and diseases associated therewith at modest cost, we are willing to spend a tiny fraction of our national income toward such a reduction, but we are not legally or morally obligated to give any weight at all to this goal.

One may think that this position, though not explicitly conditioned on the belief that poverty reduction is best achieved through private investment and free markets, is nonetheless rendered more acceptable by the truth of this belief. Our denial of any obligation to reduce global poverty would be rendered more acceptable if the invisible hand of the new global economy were effectively doing the job on its own. But is it? The best evidence we have on this question derives from our actual experience with the freer, more global markets created after the end of the Cold War. During this period the developed states, which were led by the United States and which were dominant within the International Monetary Fund (IMF), the World Bank, and the World Trade Organization (WTO), had unprecedented power to shape the global economic order. So how did this "new economic architecture" affect global poverty? According to the World Bank, this period of globalization has brought healthy economic growth in aggregate – as well as a 25 percent *increase* in the number of people living below a constant 1985 U.S. dollar per day. The number of persons who are poor by this absolute measure "rose from 1.2 billion in 1987 to 1.5 billion today and, if recent trends persist, will reach 1.9 billion by 2015" (World Bank 1999, 25).[16]

In light of this evidence, it is then astonishing that the IMF accuses those who question the prevailing global economic order of harming the

---

[16] This growth in the number of poor is slightly faster than the growth of world population. The successor report, using the new poverty line, gives a dramatically different picture: People living on less than $1 a day numbered 1.1832 billion in 1987 and 1.1989 billion in 1998 (World Bank 2000, 23).

poor.[17] The protestors of Seattle and Washington are clearly right to demand that this order be rethought, as it is evident now that it alone will not eradicate poverty within anything like an acceptable time span. This failure is not surprising. The new global economic architecture is an extremely complex network of agreements and treaties about trade, investments, loans, patents, copyrights, trademarks, taxation, labor standards, environmental protection, use of seabed resources, and much else. As the details of this architecture were being negotiated, the interests of the affluent societies, which tend to be closely aligned on many issues, were bound to be dominant. These societies, containing about one-seventh of humankind, control most of the global product as well as access to the world's most lucrative markets and thus have a huge advantage over the rest in terms of bargaining power, information, and expertise. They were able successfully to push for open markets that are to their advantage and equally successfully to resist open markets that are not.[18]

To be sure, global markets are more open on the whole, and private investment is much more mobile than before. But such capital mobility has, on the whole, brought little progress to the world's poorest populations. This is due not only to the protectionism of the developed states (note 18). Even truly free markets would probably not bring rapid economic growth to areas where basic infrastructure is lacking and where the physical and mental development of prospective employees has been

[17] This accusation was made after the Seattle protests against the WTO and was endorsed by *The Economist* (December 11, 1999, 15), whose cover that week showed an Indian child in rags with the heading "The real losers of Seattle." See also "The Case for Globalisation" in *The Economist* (September 23 2000, 19–20 and 85–87). The next note provides additional factual background, as reported by *The Economist* itself.

[18] "Rich countries cut their tariffs by less in the Uruguay Round than poor ones did. Since then, they have found new ways to close their markets, notably by imposing anti-dumping duties on imports they deem 'unfairly cheap'. Rich countries are particularly protectionist in many of the sectors where developing countries are best able to compete, such as agriculture, textiles, and clothing. As a result, according to a new study by Thomas Hertel, of Purdue University, and Will Martin, of the World Bank, rich countries' average tariffs on manufacturing imports from poor countries are four times higher than those on imports from other rich countries. This imposes a big burden on poor countries. The United Nations Conference on Trade and Development (UNCTAD) estimates that they could export $700 billion more a year by 2005 if rich countries did more to open their markets. Poor countries are also hobbled by a lack of know-how. Many had little understanding of what they signed up to in the Uruguay Round. That ignorance is now costing them dear. Michael Finger of the World Bank and Philip Schuler of the University of Maryland estimate that implementing commitments to improve trade procedures and establish technical and intellectual-property standards can cost more than a year's development budget for the poorest countries. Moreover, in those areas where poor countries could benefit from world trade rules, they are often unable to do so. ... Of the WTO's 134 members, 29 do not even have missions at its headquarters in Geneva. Many more can barely afford to bring cases to the WTO" (*The Economist*, September 25, 1999, 89). The full texts of both studies are available on the Internet as, respectively, Working Paper 7 at <http://www.agecon.purdue.edu/gtap/wkpapr/index.htm> and Working Paper 2215 at <http://wbln0018.worldbank.org/research/workpapers.nsf/12e6920265e1e0d3852567e50050df1f/>.

irreparably impaired through disease, malnutrition, and illiteracy. In such areas a special effort, not purely market driven, is needed to jump-start development. It is only after people there have access to adequate food and shelter, vaccines, safe water, basic sanitation, basic health services, and primary education that these poorest areas will attract significant private investment, which may then be sufficient to sustain and continue the advance on its own. This is not an argument against globalization. But it does show that the developed states must remove their protectionist barriers and make a considerable non-market-driven effort to get the poorest quartile to the point where they, too, can benefit from globalization. Failing that, the new economic architecture will further increase global economic inequality and perpetuate or even aggravate the horrendous conditions among the poorest quartile.

The trend of ever increasing global economic inequality has been persisting for quite a long time, reaching far back into the colonial era. "The income gap between the fifth of the world's people living in the richest countries and the fifth in the poorest was 74 to 1 in 1997, up from 60 to 1 in 1990 and 30 to 1 in 1960." Earlier estimates are 11 to 1 for 1913, 7 to 1 for 1870, and 3 to 1 for 1820 (UNDP 1999, 3). In this regard, the post-Cold War period has merely continued a long-established trend. What is quite new with this period, however, is the capacity of the affluent states to effect massive and rapid reductions in severe poverty. The figure of 1.5 billion human beings in dire poverty may be daunting. But global inequality has now increased to such an extreme that this poorest quartile of humankind – with annual income of $100 per capita and thus collectively about $150 billion[19] – accounts for merely half a percent of the global product. Reforms that would double or even triple the income of this group would have no serious impact on high-income countries' GNP, which summed to $22,921 billion in 1999 ($25,730 per capita).[20] For the first time in human history it is quite feasible, economically, to wipe out hunger and preventable diseases worldwide without real inconvenience to anyone – all the more so because the high-income countries no longer face any serious military threat.

---

[19] These figures are derived from the average value of the (old) international poverty line, which above I have estimated at $145 per year (note 5 and surrounding text), and the fact that the poor, on average, live 31 percent below this poverty line (Ravallion and Chen 1997, 376).

[20] The thirty-four high-income countries represent 14.9 percent of world population and 78.4 percent of the sum of GNPs (World Bank 2000, 275). Consider also that "the world's 200 richest people more than doubled their net worth in the four years to 1998, to more than $1 trillion. The assets of the top three billionaires are more than the combined GNP of all least developed countries and their 600 million people" (UNDP 1999, 3). "The additional cost of achieving and maintaining universal access to basic education for all, basic health care for all, reproductive health care for all women, adequate food for all and safe water and sanitation for all is . . . less than 4% of the combined wealth of the 225 richest people in the world" (UNDP 1998, 30).

The moral upshot of all this seems obvious: We should provide a path out of poverty to that great majority of all poor people whom we can reach without the use of force. When we can save so many millions from hunger, disease, and premature death, wealthy states should not haggle over $3.4 billion, as the United States did in the aftermath of the World Food Summit. We should instead be willing to spend 1 percent of our GNP ($229 billion annually) specifically on poverty eradication, even 2 percent if we can do so effectively. We should spend this money so as to ensure that the poor, especially poor children, have secure access to food and shelter, vaccines, safe water, basic health services and sanitation, primary education, electricity, and road or rail links, and will thus be able to fend for themselves in the new global economy. If we can make so huge a difference to hundreds of millions at so little cost to ourselves, we must not refuse to make this effort.

While this call for greater solidarity is plausible in what it directs us to do, it is misleading in the grounds it suggests for this directive. The account appeals to a positive duty to protect persons from great harms and risks if one can do so at little cost.[21] I have no doubt that we have such a moral duty and that this duty requires us to make a serious effort toward poverty reduction. And yet it would be misleading to characterize our present and (quite predictable) future failure to make such an effort as a lack of beneficence. We are not bystanders who find ourselves confronted with foreign deprivations whose origins are wholly unconnected to ourselves. In fact, there are at least three morally significant connections between us and the global poor. First, their social starting positions and ours have emerged from a single historical process that was pervaded by massive grievous wrongs. The same historical injustices, including genocide, colonialism, and slavery, play a role in explaining both their poverty and our affluence. Second, they and we depend on a single natural resource base, from the benefits of which they are largely, and without compensation, excluded. The affluent countries and the elites of the developing world divide these resources on mutually agreeable terms without leaving "enough and as good" for the remaining majority of humankind. Third, they and we coexist within a single global economic order that has a strong tendency to perpetuate and even to aggravate global economic inequality.[22]

Given these connections, our failure to make a serious effort toward poverty reduction may constitute not merely a lack of beneficence, but our active impoverishing, starving, and killing of millions of innocent people by economic means. To be sure, we do not intend these harms, and we are thus not on a par with Stalin, who used economic policies and institutions specifically in order to impoverish and kill segments of the population he

[21] The problem of world hunger has often been addressed in these terms, for example, in Singer 1972 and in Unger 1996.
[22] For detailed explication of these three connections, see Pogge 1998.

deemed hostile to the Soviet regime. We may not even have foreseen these harms when we constructed the new global economic architecture beginning in the late 1980s. Now that we do know, our moral situation is more akin to that of Mao Tse-Tung in 1959. Mao did not foresee that his Great Leap Forward, begun in 1958, would acutely aggravate poverty in China. But when the catastrophic effects of these policies became evident in the great famine of 1959–62, he continued his policies and declined foreign help. Twenty to thirty million Chinese perished as a direct consequence of this moral failure. Continuing our current global economic structures and policies unmodified would manifest a similar moral failure. Perhaps we had reason to believe our own persistent pronouncements that the new global economic architecture would cease the reproduction of poverty. So perhaps we just made an innocent and blameless mistake. But it is *our* mistake nonetheless, and we must not allow it to kill yet further tens of millions in the developing world.

The call for greater beneficence in the face of world hunger is one that politicians, diplomats, international bankers, and economists are willing to entertain. Most of them will even agree with it, blaming our failure to do more on other politicians, diplomats, bankers, economists, or the voting public. The idea that our economic policies and the global economic institutions we impose make us causally and morally responsible for the perpetuation – even aggravation – of world hunger, by contrast, is an idea rarely taken seriously by established intellectuals and politicians in the developed world. But this subversive idea nonetheless plays an important role in that theorists of poverty and justice, consciously and unconsciously, expend much intellectual energy on making invisible this idea and the three connections that support it. Focusing on the third of these connections, I would like to indicate briefly some of the distortions arising from our interest in obscuring the role that the design of the global economic order plays in the perpetuation and aggravation of poverty.

A good example of such distortion in philosophical work is provided by John Rawls. When discussing the economic order of a single society, Rawls pays great attention to the fact that economic cooperation can be structured in many ways and that such structural alternatives have diverse distributional tendencies (cf. Rawls 1996, 265–67). In response to this fact, he not only insists that the shaping and reshaping of a national economic order should be controlled by all adult participants through a democratic political process. He also argues that justice requires citizens to aim for a national economic order that satisfies the difference principle, that is, that allows social and economic inequalities to arise only insofar as they tend to optimize the lowest socioeconomic position (Rawls 1999b, §§11, 12, 17).

What is true of a domestic economic order is clearly true of the international economic order as well: Alternative ways of organizing global economic cooperation have diverse distributional tendencies and differ, in particular, in how supportive or obstructive they are of economic development in the poorest countries and areas. In his recent treatment of international justice, Rawls seems briefly to acknowledge this point when he calls for correction of any "unjustified distributive effects" of cooperative organizations (Rawls 1999a, 43). But how is this vague demand to be specified? Rawls endorses "fair standards of trade to keep the market free and competitive" (Rawls 1999a, 43) – but, as he stresses himself (Rawls 1996, 267), free and competitive markets are quite compatible with huge and ever increasing inequality. What is needed is a principle that assesses alternative global economic orders in terms of their distributive effects, just as his difference principle assesses alternative ways of structuring a national economy. Yet in the international case Rawls specifically rejects any such principle that does not have "a target and a cutoff point" (Rawls 1999a, 115–19). He also rejects any international analogue to a democratic process which, at least in theory, allows a majority of citizens in a liberal society to restructure its economic order if it favors the rich too much.

Like the existing global economic order, that of Rawls's Society of Peoples is then shaped by free bargaining.[23] There is one crucial constraint, however, as Rawls insists on a universal minimum: "Peoples have a duty to assist other peoples living under unfavorable conditions that prevent their having a just or decent political and social regime" (Rawls 1999a, 37). This duty is unobjectionable and hugely important: If existing affluent societies honored it, malnutrition and preventable diseases would be much less common. Yet making this duty the only distributive constraint on global economic institutions is nonetheless implausible. If affluent and powerful societies impose a skewed global economic order that hampers the economic growth of poor societies and further weakens their bargaining power, such imposition is not made right by the fact that the former societies also keep the latter from falling below the minimum. Moreover, making this duty the only distributive constraint also misleads us to perceive the injustice of the status quo as insufficient assistance to the poorer societies, when it really consists in the imposition of a skewed global order that aggravates international inequalities and makes it exceedingly hard for the weaker and poorer populations to secure a proportional share of global economic growth. Rawls obscures, then, the important causal role that the global economic order plays in the reproduction of poverty and inequality, suggesting that each society bears sole responsibility for its own place in the economic rank-order: "The causes of the wealth of a people and the forms it takes lie in their political culture and in the religious, philosophical, and moral traditions that support the basic structure, as well as in the industriousness and cooperative talents of its members, all supported by their political virtues. . . . Crucial also is the

---

[23] His second and third laws state that "Peoples are to observe treaties and undertakings" and "Peoples are equal and are parties to the agreements that bind them" (Rawls 1999a, 37).

country's population policy" (Rawls 1999a, 108). Thus, he goes on, a society may be poor because of high population growth or low investment (Rawls 1999a, 117–18), and in any case, "if it is not satisfied, it can continue to increase savings, or, if this is not feasible, borrow from other members of the Society of Peoples" (Rawls 1999a, 114). In these ways, Rawls's account of international justice renders all but invisible the question of whether the global economic order we currently impose is harming the poor by creating a headwind against economic development in the poorest areas and is therefore unjust.

We find similar distortions in economic work. Our international bankers and economists tell us that our global economic order is fine and that protests against it (in Seattle and Washington) are actually harming the poor. The same bankers and economists also dutifully tell us about the horrendous conditions among the poor and about the lack of progress, lest anyone suspect them of not knowing or not caring enough.[24] So why does a global economic order designed with so much tender loving concern for the global poor not improve their condition? The official answer in unison: because their own governments in the developing countries are not pursuing optimal policies. Our bankers and economists differ on what the optimal policies are and hence on how their common claim should be elaborated. The more libertarian types on the right tell the story of the "Asian tigers" – Hong Kong, Taiwan, Singapore, and South Korea – as an example of how misery disappears under governments that allow free enterprise to flourish with a minimum in taxes and regulations. The more social-democratic types tell the story of Kerala, a state in India with a traditionally socialist government, as an example of how misery can be abolished even at low income levels if only governments make a serious effort to this end.[25] The stories vary, but the lesson is the same: With the right policies, any poor state can over time meet the basic needs of its people; therefore, nothing is wrong with the global economic order as it is.

These stories have the familiar ring of the Horatio Alger stories often appealed to in celebration of the unbridled American capitalism before the New Deal: In America, even a farm boy can become rich.[26] Left aside in such celebrations is the crucial question of why nearly all the relevant agents fail even though (supposedly) they can succeed. Once this question is asked, there are two obvious and complementary answers. First, what is possible for each may not be possible for all. Even if each farm boy could

---

[24] The World Bank recently interviewed sixty thousand poor people in the developing countries and published snippets of their responses, "Voices of the Poor," on its Web site. As we have seen (n. 4), the same World Bank also keeps the number of poor in check by quietly lowering the international poverty line.

[25] Amartya Sen has mentioned Kerala in many of his writings, and references to this state are now common in the literature (e.g., Rawls 1999a, 110).

[26] Horatio Alger (1832–99) was a highly successful U.S. writer of stories about the rise to prosperity of boys from poor backgrounds.

have become a millionaire in the world of Alger's stories, it was still quite impossible for more than a few to succeed. So we can indeed say that each farm boy who failed had himself to blame, for he could have succeeded. But we cannot blame the fact that over 99 percent failed on the farm boys themselves. In the system as it was, they could not have changed this fact, either individually or collectively. Similarly with unemployment: It does not follow from the fact that *each* person willing to work can find work that *all* such persons can. The situation is similar for poor countries as well. There was indeed a profitable niche in the world economy (better technology than other poor countries and lower labor costs than more affluent countries), which the Asian tigers exploited, but this niche would not have been profitable if many poor states had scrambled to occupy it all at once.

Second, there may be systemic reasons why many of the relevant agents do not make the necessary effort. Most farm boys may have lacked stamina and initiative because, having grown up in grinding poverty, they were suffering the lasting effects of childhood malnutrition and disease or of primitive schools that stifled ambition. With the governments of poor countries, the problem most often is not merely inability, but also unwillingness, to reduce domestic poverty. Yet this unwillingness, the corruption endemic to many of these governments, does not show that such poverty cannot be traced back to the existing global economic order. On the contrary, the prevalence of official corruption may itself be a consequence of our economic policies, of the global economic order we impose, and of the extreme international inequalities that have accumulated over two centuries. Let me develop this point a bit further.

A paradigm case of corruption is bribery. Bribes are a major factor in the awarding of public contracts in the developing countries, which suffer staggering losses as a result. These losses arise in part from the fact that bribes are "priced in": Bidders on contracts must raise their price in order to get paid enough to pay the bribes. Additional losses arise as bidders can afford to be noncompetitive, knowing that the success of their bid will depend on their bribes more than on the price they offer. The greatest losses probably arise from the fact that officials focused on bribes pay little attention to whether the goods and services they purchase in their country's behalf are of good quality or even needed at all. Much of what developing countries have imported over the years has been of no use to them – or even harmful, by promoting environmental degradation or violence (bribery is especially pervasive in the arms trade). May we then conclude that poverty in developing societies is the fault of their own tolerance of corruption and of their own leaders' venality?

This comfortable conclusion is upset by the fact that the developed states have permitted their companies not merely to pay bribes, but even to deduct these from their taxes. By providing financial inducements and moral support, these states have made a vital contribution to promoting and entrenching a culture of corruption in developing societies. Fortunately, this contribution is now being phased out. The first major step was the U.S. Foreign Corrupt Practices Act of 1977, enacted after the Lockheed Corporation was found to have paid a $2 million bribe not to a Third World potentate, but to Japanese Prime Minister Kakuei Tanaka. It took another twenty years until thirty-two affluent states, under OECD auspices and under public pressure generated by a new nongovernmental organization (Transparency International), signed a Convention on Combating Bribery of Foreign Officials in International Business Transactions, which requires them to criminalize the bribery of foreign officials.[27] It remains to be seen whether this convention will produce serious enforcement efforts and will thus reduce bribery and undermine the now deeply entrenched culture of corruption in many developing countries.

Surveying the ruling elites of many developing countries, one may well surmise that they would have done their best to enrich themselves, and done little for the eradication of poverty in their countries, even if they had not been bribed by foreigners. Many of these countries have not managed to become genuinely democratic, and their rulers can therefore hang on by force even if opposed by the vast majority of the population. Does this support the view that poverty in the developing societies is their own fault after all?

To see how this conclusion is problematic, consider a very central feature of the current global institutional order: Any group controlling a preponderance of the means of coercion within a country is internationally recognized as the legitimate government of this country's territory and people – regardless of how that group came to power, of how it exercises power, and of the extent to which it may be supported or opposed by the population it rules. That such a group exercising effective power receives international recognition means not merely that we engage it in negotiations. It means also that we accept this group's right to act for the people it rules, that we, most significantly, confer upon it the privileges freely to borrow in the country's name (international borrowing privilege) and freely to dispose of the country's natural resources (international resource privilege).

The international borrowing privilege includes the power to impose internationally valid legal obligations upon the country at large. Any successor government that refuses to honor debts incurred by a corrupt, brutal, undemocratic, unconstitutional, repressive, unpopular predecessor will be severely punished by the banks and governments of other countries; at minimum it will lose its own borrowing privilege by being

---

[27] The convention went into effect in February 1999, and at last count thirty-one states have ratified it (<http://www.oecd.org/daf/nocorruption/annex2.htm>; cf. <http://www.oecd.org/daf/nocorruption/links1.htm>). Among those still missing are Ireland, Italy, Luxembourg, the Netherlands, New Zealand, and Portugal.

excluded from the international financial markets. Such refusals are therefore quite rare, as governments, even when newly elected after a dramatic break with the past, are compelled to pay the debts of their ever so awful predecessors.

The international borrowing privilege has three important negative effects on human rights fulfillment in the developing countries. First, this privilege facilitates borrowing by destructive governments. Such governments can borrow more money and can do so more cheaply than they could do if they alone, rather than the entire country, were obliged to repay. In this way, the borrowing privilege helps such governments stay in power even against near-universal popular discontent and opposition. Second, the international borrowing privilege imposes upon democratic successor regimes the often huge debts of their corrupt predecessors. It thereby saps the capacity of such democratic governments to implement structural reforms and other political programs, thus rendering such governments less successful and less stable than they would otherwise be.[28] Third, the international borrowing privilege provides incentives toward coup attempts: Whoever succeeds in bringing a preponderance of the means of coercion under his control gets the borrowing privilege as an additional reward.

The international resource privilege enjoyed by a group in power is much more than our mere acquiescence in its effective control over the natural resources of the country in question. This privilege includes the power to effect legally valid transfers of ownership rights in such resources. Thus a corporation that has purchased resources from the Saudi or Suharto families, or from Mobuto or Sani Abacha, has thereby become entitled to be – and actually *is* – recognized anywhere in the world as the legitimate owner of these resources. This is a remarkable feature of our global institutional order. A group that overpowers the guards and takes control of a warehouse may be able to give some of the merchandise to others, accepting money in exchange. But the fence who pays them becomes merely the possessor, not the owner, of the loot. Contrast this with a group that overpowers an elected government and takes control of a country. Such a group, too, can give away some of the country's natural resources, accepting money in exchange. In this case, however, the purchaser acquires not merely possession, but all the rights and liberties of ownership, which are supposed to be – and actually *are* – protected and enforced by all other states' courts and police forces. The international resource privilege, then, is the power to confer globally valid ownership rights in the country's resources.

The international resource privilege has disastrous effects in many poor countries, whose resource sector often constitutes a large segment of the

---

[28] This effect is somewhat mitigated by authoritarian regimes being likewise held responsible for the debts of their democratic predecessors.

national economy. Whoever can take power in such a country by whatever means can maintain his rule, even against widespread popular opposition, by buying the arms and soldiers he needs with revenues from the export of natural resources (and funds borrowed abroad in the country's name). This fact in turn provides a strong incentive toward the undemocratic acquisition and unresponsive exercise of political power in these countries. The international resource privilege also gives foreigners strong incentives to corrupt the officials of such countries, who, no matter how badly they rule, continue to have resources to sell and money to spend. We see here how the local causal chain – persistent poverty caused by corrupt government caused by natural-resource wealth – can itself be traced back to the international resource privilege. Because of that privilege, resource-rich developing countries are more likely to experience coup attempts and civil wars and more likely also to be ruled by corrupt elites, so that – despite considerable natural wealth – poverty in these countries tends to decline only slowly, if at all.[29]

These brief remarks on bribery and on the international borrowing and resource privileges show at least in outline how the current global order we uphold shapes the national culture and policies of the poorer and weaker countries. It does so in four main ways: It crucially affects what sorts of persons exercise political power in these countries, what incentives these persons face, what options they have, and what impact the implementation of any of their options would have on their most-disadvantaged compatriots. In many ways, our global order is disadvantageous to the global poor by sustaining oppression and corruption, and hence poverty, in the developing world. It is hardly surprising that this order reflects the interests of the wealthy and powerful states. Their governments, dependent on our votes and taxes, work hard on shaping the rules for our benefit. To be sure, the global poor have their own governments. But almost all of them are too weak to exert real influence on the organization of the global economy. More important, these governments have little incentive to attend to the needs of their poor compatriots, as their continuation in power depends on

---

[29] Economists have known for some time of the negative correlation between developing countries' resource endowments and their rates of economic growth (the so-called Dutch Disease) – exemplified by the relatively low growth rates, over the past forty years, of resource-rich Nigeria, Kenya, Angola, Mozambique, Zaire, Venezuela, Brazil, Saudi Arabia, Burma, and the Philippines. The causal connections accounting for this correlation, however, are only now beginning to be fully understood. Cf. Ricky Lam and Leonard Wantchekon, "Dictatorships as a Political Dutch Disease," working paper (Yale University, January 19, 1999). This paper specifically supports the hypothesis that the causal connection between resource wealth and poor economic growth is mediated through reduced chances for democracy: "all petrostates or resource-dependent countries in Africa fail to initiate meaningful political reforms. . . . besides South Africa, transition to democracy has been successful only in resource-poor countries" (31); "a one percentage increase in the size of the natural resource sector generates a decrease by half a percentage point in the probability of survival of democratic regimes" (35).

the local elite and on foreign governments and corporations. Such rulers – able to sell the country's resources, to buy arms and soldiers to maintain their rule, and to amass personal fortunes – like the global order just the way it is. As do we: If ownership rights in natural resources could not be acquired from tyrannical rulers, for example, the resources we need to import would be scarcer and hence more expensive.

The conclusion is once again that the underfulfillment of human rights in the developing countries is not a homegrown problem, but one we greatly contribute to through the policies we pursue and the international order we impose. We have then not merely a positive responsibility with regard to global poverty, like Rawls's "duty of assistance," but a negative responsibility to stop imposing the existing global order[30] and to prevent and mitigate the harms it continually causes for the world's poorest populations. Because our responsibility is negative and because so much harm can be prevented at so little cost to ourselves, the reduction of severe global poverty should be our foremost moral priority.

Acknowledgments

This essay was written at the Princeton Institute for Advanced Study with a grant from the Research and Writing Initiative of the Program on Global Security and Sustainability of the John D. and Catherine T. MacArthur Foundation. I warmly thank both organizations for their generous support.

References

Alexandratos, Nikos, ed. (1995). *World Agriculture: Toward 2010, an FAO Study.* Chichester, England: J. Wiley & Sons.
Pogge, Thomas W. (1998). "A Global Resources Dividend." In *Ethics of Consumption: The Good Life, Justice, and Global Stewardship*, edited by David A. Crocker and Toby Linden. Lanham, MD: Rowman & Littlefield.
Ravallion, Martin, and Shaohua Chen. (1997). "What Can New Survey Data Tell Us about Recent Changes in Distribution and Poverty." *World Bank Economic Review,* 11, 357–82. Available at<www.worldbank.org/html/prddr/prdhome/peg/wps01/poverty. pdf>.
Rawls, John. (1996). *Political Liberalism.* New York: Columbia University Press. First published 1993.
———. (1999a). *The Law of Peoples.* Cambridge, MA: Harvard University Press.

[30] This is suggested by §28 of the Universal Declaration of Human Rights: "Everyone is entitled to a social and international order in which the rights and freedoms set forth in this Declaration can be fully realized."

————. (1999b). *A Theory of Justice*. Cambridge, MA: Harvard University Press. First edition published 1971.

Singer, Peter. (1972). "Famine, Affluence, and Morality." *Philosophy and Public Affairs*, 1, 229–43.

Unger, Peter. (1996). *Living High and Letting Die: Our Illusion of Innocence*. Oxford: Oxford University Press.

United Nations Development Programme (UNDP). (1996). *Human Development Report, 1996*. New York: Oxford University Press.

————. (1998). *Human Development Report, 1998*. New York: Oxford University Press.

————. (1999). *Human Development Report, 1999*. New York: Oxford University Press.

————. (2000). *Human Development Report, 2000*. New York: Oxford University Press.

United States Department of Agriculture (USDA). (1999). *U.S. Action Plan on Food Security*. Available at <http://www.fas.usda.gov:80/ icd/summit/usactplan.pdf>.

World Bank. (1999). *World Development Report, 1999/2000*. New York: Oxford University Press. Also available at <http://www.worldbank.org/ wdr/2000/fullreport.html>.

World Bank. (2000). *World Development Report, 2000/2001*. New York: Oxford University Press. Also available at <http://www.worldbank.org/ poverty/wdrpoverty/report/index.htm>.

World Health Organization (WHO). (1999). *The World Health Report, 1999*. Geneva: WHO Publications. Also available at <http:// www.who.int/whr/1999>.

3

MORALITY AND WORLD HUNGER

RÜDIGER BITTNER

The facts about world hunger are fairly well known; I do not need to present them here in any detail.[1] For the question I wish to raise I shall merely assume quite generally that the state of things with respect to world hunger is bad at present, and that it is getting worse overall. It is true, there have been local improvements, but globally the situation has deteriorated, both absolutely, in numbers of people affected, and relatively, in share of world income going to the bottom quarter of the world population, and both in the long run, over the last century, and in the short term, in the last decade.

I shall not inquire why this is so. I take it that the historical origins of the present economic and political situation, and the current economic and political interests both of the big powers and of the ruling elites in the poor countries suffice to explain the present state of affairs and its tendency to the worse. What I want to know, rather, is why morality has not managed to lead people to try to turn things around.

It has not. This is not to deny that far more people now than thirty years ago know of the extent of world hunger and far more people now feel themselves subject to a moral demand that they do their share to improve things. Still, in the general view of the moral landscape, it does not have an eminent position. World hunger is not an important matter, if importance is measured, not objectively, by how much and how many people are affected, but subjectively, by how much and how many of the unaffected care about it.

This itself is an astonishing phenomenon that needs explaining. You do not have to be a consequentialist in moral philosophy to think that doing what you are morally required to do, or showing a morally praiseworthy character in what you do, is especially urgent when failure to do so brings with it considerable human suffering. Yet the amount of human suffering that world hunger brings with it is not just considerable – it is vast. Hence, world hunger should be high on people's moral agenda. In fact it is not. Why?

---

[1] Thomas Pogge's article in this volume (2001) gives some relevant figures.

One answer would be to say that this is so because people are evil. They have a hardened heart, and so they are not sufficiently sensitive to what world hunger does to so many. That they get their moral priorities wrong is itself a sign of their viciousness. Having given this answer, the moralist can keep going and do moral business as usual, teaching people what is right and what is wrong, both to do and to think, even though it is an arduous task, seeing how bad they are at the start.

There is a second-order self-complacency about this answer, but I do not wish to be the second-order moralist objecting to it. More importantly, it may be an unwise answer to give. If morality does not succeed in giving world hunger the place on normal people's moral agenda it deserves, then it is unwise to exclude from consideration the possibility that this could be morality's own fault. We have been taught to admire the moralist holding up moral standards even if the heavens should fall. It may be cleverer, and more effective, to have a second look at the standards, and also at the way of holding them up, when the heavens are about to come down.

An answer along the same lines would be this: People are not so much evil as slow. What may rightly be called a global economy has not been in existence for all that long, and without it there is no reason to consider world hunger a moral issue for those having enough to eat. Without a global economy in existence, they may regret the widespread misfortune of other human beings, but they cannot see themselves involved in its production. Given, then, that the conditions that make world hunger a moral challenge are of fairly recent origin, it is small wonder that the news has not yet spread. Moralists, thus, should be patient, and in the meantime do their best in spreading the word. It took the general moral consciousness the better part of two hundred years to learn that political, economic, social, and legal privileges of men, as against women, are morally unacceptable. We may have to wait just as long for the moral significance of world hunger to become recognized.

This answer does not morally deprecate people, but it is at one with the first answer in holding that morality is not responsible for the insignificant place of world hunger in the contemporary moral landscape. People are responsible, though now because of a lack in perception on their part, not because of a moral failure. Moralists giving this answer may have reason to adjust their rhetoric, seeing how slow people are to perceive what actually should leap to their eyes, but they do not have reason to change their message. Yet again, such an answer would seem to be more comfortable than is warranted. The discrepancy between the magnitude of the moral fault, if moral fault indeed it is, that people bear in this regard and their moral insouciance is so jarring that it may well be doubted whether morality is just fine here, and time will put things straight. We may instead question whether there is not a systematic misfit between world hunger and its conception in moral terms. If there is, that could explain, and better than these two answers do, why world hunger is not the all-important moral issue for people that it could be expected to be.

Here is, in a word, what I suspect to be the reason for morality's failure to come to grips with world hunger: World hunger is a political problem.

And here is the immediate reaction to this suggestion: Yes, world hunger is a political problem, but why should that preclude, or make harder, its adequate treatment in moral terms? The burden of my argument is to explain why.

I have two explanations. The first is this: Doing what is right, because it is right, is paradigmatically intended to improve the situation of people who are in some way close to the agent. Political problems, by contrast, indiscriminately affect the near and the far.

As for me, I learned my basic moral lessons at my older sister's knees, who divided any incoming chocolate, and so on, evenly among the three of us children, thus ensuring that none of us would be very badly off, that is, go without any of the chocolate and without any respect. She did this, however, in view of, and for the sake of, this small group of people living together, and her doing it made the sense it did only within that setting. Justice is good for peace, it was said (Isaiah 32:17). This may not be true in general, since, with some people in some situations, justice may breed discord, not peace. Even so, it would seem that without peace either actually ensuing, or expected, or at least hoped for, the demands of justice make little sense. "Let justice be done, and should the heavens fall" is really a crazy saying: Justice is a thing for creatures who may enjoy peace in this world.

Peace is some joint life, not the mere absence of fighting. You do not live in peace with any human being anywhere with whom you are not in quarrel. You live in peace, if you do, with people living close to you. You live in peace with your neighbours, in that sense of the expression in which you were also told to love your neighbour (Lev. 19:18).

So here is the argument. An understanding of what we do in moral terms depends on those affected being close to us. Those who are affected by world hunger are not close to us. Hence, there is no viable moral understanding of world hunger. This is why world hunger has an inferior position on the contemporary moral map.

You will ask, How close is close? I do not have a criterion here. This is regrettable, but it may not harm the argument. If there is anything to the distinction between people close and those not close, the hungry will come out on the side of those not close, regardless of where the line is drawn.

It may be worth emphasizing, though, that the people close are not only the people near and dear. Your colleagues, for example, are close to you as well, your classmates are, and perhaps your neighbours, in the literal sense, or your clients. But any one of these may not be dear to you. People close to you are those who are part of your life. That has nothing to do with the intimacy of the near and dear.

You will object, Hasn't morality forever been trying to go beyond local sympathy, good will, and established ways of behaving? Think of one of the oldest documents of moral thought in our culture: "Thou shalt neither vex a stranger, nor oppress him; for ye were strangers in the land of Egypt" (Exodus 22:21; repeated 23:9). Strangers are being morally protected here, not neighbours.

It is true, strangers are being protected here, but strangers sojourning with us for some time. The prohibition says in fact: Don't vex or oppress those living among you whom it would be especially easy to vex or oppress, given their inferior legal standing. (The widows and orphans of Exodus 22:22 are in a similar situation.) What happens to the strangers in their own country, or indeed, on the journey home, is immaterial. The scope of the prohibition, then, is in fact only local. It tells us how to treat those who are neighbours for the time being.

You may insist: Isn't modern moral thought, at any rate, thoroughly cosmopolitan? Take Kant, its central figure: Didn't he teach that all human beings, not just our neighbours, ought to be treated as ends in themselves?

Certainly he did, but it is less clear on what grounds. This is not the place to go into the difficult question of how to prove the equivalence between Kant's standard formula of the supreme principle of morality and his formula of man as an end in himself.[2] It may suffice to note that the connection between the two is at least not obvious, since this already raises the suspicion that Kant's cosmopolitanism about the field of moral action is illicitly added to his cosmopolitanism about its principle. That is to say, Kant may have shown that moral agents act on principles that could receive the approval of all human beings, but he would not have shown that these principles require a certain kind of conduct towards all human beings. Moral agents would have the backing of all mankind, but they would not be facing all mankind in what they do.

Then you may object to the second premise of my little argument above: Given the present state of the world, the hungry in fact are close, by any reasonable standard of closeness. Their lot depends to a large extent on decisions made here, and they influence, if to a lesser extent, our economic situation in turn. It has all become one big system, effectively, and so nobody, wherever he or she lives, is anything other than close.

That is not what I mean by "close," though. No doubt people economically affect each other from one corner of the world to the other, yet they are not, therefore, all living together. They are living together in much smaller groups, in families, professions, firms. There is really no cosmopolis, no city of the world, if by a city we mean the place of a shared life. In fact, I should think that even cities, commonly so called, are not cities in this demanding sense. It may well be that with the radius of those whom

---

[2] Immanuel Kant (1903, 436). The most important attempt to show the equivalence of the formulae is Onora O'Neill's, in chapter 7 of her 1989.

we affect in what we do extending, the radius of our companions has shrunk. However this may be, it seems fairly clear that most people do not live their lives in the midst of humankind. With "closeness" being so narrowly understood, then, the second premise of the argument seems safe. The real issue is the first premise: that morality speaks to people only on how to deal with those with whom they are close.

Instead of further defending it, I shall turn to the second feature that makes world hunger a political rather than a moral problem – this "rather than" instead of "both . . . and" being precisely the contested point. Let us call "imputable" those states and events the merit or demerit, or the good or bad consequences, of which can be clearly credited to some specific agent or agents. Ordinarily, "to impute" carries a suggestion that the thing imputed is bad in some way, but let us use the word neutrally. And in philosophical contexts, the question of imputability is easily taken to be the question whether, in principle, anything can be imputed to anyone, and that question is not at issue here: I shall simply assume that the answer to this question is yes. Imputability here covers the smaller domain of those things which can readily, or perhaps unmistakably, be put down to some particular agents' account.

Here, then, is the second argument. Morality comes into its own with imputable states or events. Difficult political situations, and also the developments aggravating or mitigating them, are typically not imputable, and world hunger, in particular, is not. This is why morality has difficulty dealing with world hunger.

To defend the first premise, it is no accident that trial and judgment, God's or your own, have long been the predominant metaphors for moral assessment. Both criminal proceedings in court and moral judgment suppose that "you are the one," and if it turns out that you are not, they both fall to the ground. Now in the case of developments not imputable we do not, in view of the difficulty of finding the responsible agents, merely suspend moral judgment or divide the moral praise or blame into infinitesimal parts, one for each contributor. We tend to stop talking about morality entirely. As a harmless example, take grade inflation, which evidently is a development not imputable, in the sense indicated. I have often heard people express their regret over grade inflation; I think I have never heard anyone blame anyone for his or her share in bringing it about. You may say that this is precisely because grade inflation is harmless, so nobody bothers to set up a moral tribunal for it. But in fact it is no more of a bother to pass moral judgment than to express regret. That people do the one and not the other is a sign that they feel morality not to be on its proper ground with states or events that are not imputable.

As a less harmless example, take the case of a family whose members are locked into a grid of mutual hatred and contempt, of suffering and deprivation. Typically, such a state of affairs is not imputable. The individual mean remark or contemptuous smile is, but once you realize that these merely execute a fixed drama of mutual provocations and injuries, you will want to know who it was who set that up. And normally you cannot tell. True, you can say that they all did it together, but that does not make the effect imputable, as you cannot present the overall effect as the sum of individual contributions. The experience of such a family does not normally elicit our moral judgment. This is not because it would be itself morally dubious, and ineffective as well, to heap moral blame on those who are already miserable, for even in our hearts we will not pass moral judgment. It is because we do not see who did it. The situation now is awful, that is not in dispute; but as we do not know who is responsible for it, moral judgment, whether thought or spoken, sinks from our hands. To see that this is indeed the reason, imagine that you are convinced, rightly or not, that one family member more than all the others caused the present situation; then you may not refrain from moral judgment.

This is not to claim that a social development, like such a family going to ruins, is anything beyond the sum of what changed in the individuals concerned. The point here is not about what there is, but about what morality can handle; and it is not difficult to suppose that what consists of imputables may itself not be imputable and, therefore, may not lend itself to moral assessment.

Let us turn to the second premise, that political developments typically are not imputable: This statement needs to be understood as restricted to the modern age. There have been political structures centered to such an extent on one or a few ruling figures that changes in the political situation could clearly be attributed to some particular individual. Thus, it would be right to say, I suppose, that the end of the Roman republic was Caesar's doing. The time of such political structures, however, seems to be gone. Nothing of even moderate political significance is done in our day by just one or a few individual actors. Whatever effectively happens is the outcome of what a large number of people did, and in doing what they do these people may be pursuing the same or different, even opposite ends, or indeed ends unrelated to each other. Moreover, none of the actors involved overlooks their whole interplay. The outcome, therefore, is not clearly anybody's doing in particular. They did something together, that is true, but neither collectively nor individually were they masters over what emerged. That undermines the conditions for moral assessment.

It is a striking illustration of this point that discussions of the role of morals in politics often focus on doings of politicians that are not essentially political. The title of one of Thomas Nagel's essays is revealing: "Ruthlessness in Public Life" (1995). After all, to be ruthless you do not have to be active in politics. So the characteristically political import of people's actions does not show up in the moral discussion.

World hunger, in particular, is a clear case of a nonimputable state of affairs. We do not have a clear understanding of who brought it about, or who is bringing it about. Morally sensitive persons certainly suspect themselves to be contributing to it, but if they are not economists, and perhaps even then, they cannot tell with any confidence where they go right and where they go wrong. The effects of their everyday economic decisions on world hunger are obscure, and in any case ridiculously small. Charity is an option, that is true, but charity does not touch the sources of the evil. For that it would take political measures. Yet there is no path laid out in the political arenas in which these sensitive persons find themselves that they may be confident leads at least in the right direction. By the same token, they cannot judge with confidence the performance of others. Hence, nobody is clearly responsible. Moral assessment won't thrive on such ground.

So much for explaining morality's failure to come to grips with world hunger. If this explanation is sound in itself and accurate as a description of how people are reacting, then morality's failure is not accidental, and there is little hope that it may do better in the future. That is to say, we should give up waiting for morality to provide us with a reasonable attitude towards world hunger. It is not fit for the task. The natural question then is what is. On what lines do we find a reasonable attitude? As indicated earlier, my suggestion is that we should think of world hunger as a political problem. What does that mean?

It means that ending world hunger is a goal for the large political institutions in our world to pursue. There are other such goals: security within; social arrangements that respect freedom; prosperity; and others. People disagree on how to rank them. Those who put the end of world hunger fairly low on their list are not, therefore, either wrong or evil. They are just heading in a different direction. Against them I say: Ending world hunger is an important goal for political action. In saying this I do not rely on having the moral law on my side. Yet I shall not, therefore, be speechless when asked to support what I said. I have a lot to say on how splendid a thing it would be (or perhaps not even splendid: perhaps just a matter of putting things straight) to abolish world hunger. Admittedly, what I have to say will be argument, not proof, but this is hardly a drawback, given that we never have to offer more than argument in matters of any importance.

Worse perhaps, what I support by saying these things is in principle no different from a mere expression of taste. I dislike cigarette smoke, so I do not smoke, and do not invite people to smoke in my place. I do not want the suffering to continue that the current economic order inflicts, so I shall join political attempts to change that. The latter want is, by its content, far more weighty than the former, but it has no higher standing and no higher dignity.

This is not a relativist line of argument. A relativist in moral philosophy holds that moral judgments are not true or false, period, but true or false depending on context. The present argument, by contrast, is meant to show that the scope of moral judgment, that is, the range of things that moral judgment can be presumed to speak about, is smaller than generally assumed in moral philosophy; that moral judgment is tied to the conditions of closeness and imputability. As long as moral judgment keeps with scope, the present argument raises no suspicion that it should be valid relative to context only; and once it goes beyond that scope, it is, on the present argument, not merely valid relative to context only, but void entirely.

Still, isn't it relativism with respect to political goals to hold that giving the struggle against world hunger a high priority among them is not demonstrably right, and no better than an expression of taste? No, it is not, for while there is no proof for political priorities, there is argument, just as there is argument about matters of taste. (*De gustibus est disputandum.*) There are considerations that speak in favour of giving the abolition of world hunger a top place on the political agenda. Thus, those who do give it such a place are not merely doing something that is right for them. They are doing what, for reasons, they consider right. True, there are other considerations speaking against giving the abolition of world hunger a top place on the political agenda. Political discussion is the weighing of such considerations, and it has not so far reached a conclusion to which everybody, or nearly everybody, agrees. This does not prevent us from pursuing political aims for reasons.

The moral law will not settle our political disputes, not even in principle. Nothing better will support us in what we do in the political field than particular arguments about the merits or demerits of particular courses of action.

Acknowledgments

I am very grateful for the critical and thorough discussion a previous version of this chapter received at the conference in Bielefeld.

References

Kant, Immanuel. (1903). *Grundlegung zur Metaphysik der Sitten.* (First published 1785.) In *Gesammelte Schriften*, vol. 4, edited by Königlich Preussische Akademie der Wissenschaften, 385–463. Berlin.

Nagel, Thomas. (1995). "Ruthlessness in Public Life." In *Mortal Questions.* Cambridge: Cambridge University Press.

O'Neill, Onora. (1989). *Constructions of Reason.* Cambridge: Cambridge University Press.

Pogge, Thomas. (2001). "Priorities of Global Justice." *Metaphilosophy,* 32:1/2.

4

GLOBAL INEQUALITY AND INTERNATIONAL INSTITUTIONS

ANDREW HURRELL

This chapter considers the links between international institutions and global inequality. International institutions, including in particular international economic institutions, are currently under attack from both left and right. For the left and for many new social movements, such institutions are handmaidens to the destructive and inequitable forces of global capitalism. For the right, they are threats to the efficient working of global market economy and to the cohesion and autonomy of nation-states. I want to steer as clear as possible away from arguments as to what the economic roles of institutions in the management of global capitalism should be – as, for example, in recent debates on the reform of the international monetary system or of the World Trade Organization (WTO) after Seattle. Instead I wish to consider how international institutions might be morally important; how international institutions have changed; and what those changes imply for global economic justice. Institutions form a central element in what I term the normative structure of international society. My understanding of normative structure focuses on international legal rules and institutional practices, on international political norms (for example, shared understandings of great power management, or concepts of humanitarian intervention, self-determination, or sustainable development that have both a legal and political life), and on the dominant ideologies and social practices that animate them.

My argument is that the normative structure of international society has evolved in ways that help to undercut the arguments of those who take a restrictionist position towards global economic justice. There is now a denser and more integrated network of shared institutions and practices within which social expectations of global justice and injustice have become more securely established. But, at the same time, our major international social institutions continue to constitute a deformed political order, above all because of the extreme disparities of power that exist within both international and world society. This combination of density and deformity shapes how we should think about international justice in general and has important implications for the scope, character, and modalities of global economic justice. Having laid out a view of normative development and where it leads, the second part of the chapter will look briefly at some of the reasons why international distributive justice remains so marginal to current international political practice.

The Normative Structure of International Institutions

Our first question is, How and why do international institutions matter morally? We can begin with a very common intuition: it is impossible to deduce general principles of global justice that could be applied to the whole world because of the absence of an international community or society within which they could be situated, and to which they could be applied. The weakness of international institutions and the character of the international normative order are taken by many as crucial indicators of this absence.

Of course those who seek to refute the restrictionist or rejectionist views of global justice and the scope of duties beyond borders do not look only at institutions. Instead they consider the broad range of changes that have occurred within each of the three arenas of social order: civil society, the state, and the market economy. Those changes are most commonly gathered together under the heading of "globalization." For all the problems of definition, globalization involves the dramatic increase in the density and depth of economic, ecological, and societal interdependence, with "density" referring to the increased number, range, and scope of cross-border transactions; and "depth" referring to the degree to which that interdependence affects, and is affected by, the ways in which societies are organized domestically.

Taken together these changes have shifted the way in which many political theorists consider questions of global justice. In the first place, they have necessarily altered the scope of justice. On this view, for example, it is no longer possible to accept Martin Wight's classic distinction between domestic society as that arena within which understandings of the good life might be debated, developed, and potentially realized, whilst international relations are condemned to remain forever an arena of "mere survival" (Wight 1966). To take only the most obvious example, "mere survival" in relation to the protection of the global environment depends fundamentally on how societies are organized domestically and on how their various conceptions of what the good life entails (their comprehensive doctrines in Rawlsian terms) can be brought together and reconciled.

Second, integration and globalization have eroded and undermined the boundedness of political communities whose particular cultures, traditions, and ways of living are given so much weight by communitarians. Third, these changes have given a new reality to the sense of sharing a single world and to the nature of plurality, connection, and finitude (O'Neill 1996, chapter 4). In an integrated world, after all, what possible sense can one make of Rawls's concentration on bounded political communities whose basic structure is defined in terms of "self-sufficient schemes of cooperation *for all the essential purposes of human life*" (Rawls 1993a, 301, emphasis added)? For moral cosmopolitans the circumstances of justice and the nature of social cooperation have been altered so fundamentally that we are entitled to transpose egalitarian concepts of distributive justice that apply within the state onto the international or transnational level (Pogge 1989; Beitz 1999b).

Before I turn to institutions, let me say a few words about markets and civil society. The increasing integration of markets (not just cross-border transactions but also integrated transnational production structures) seems intuitively to have important normative implications and to buttress claims for moral cosmopolitanism. But there are real problems. In part, these have to do with empirical work showing the limits of economic globalization and the extent to which it is neither self-evidently new nor any more far-reaching than in the past. But, more importantly, we are faced with the old difficulty of relating empirical accounts of an increasingly unified world to normative accounts of the emergence of a world community (Brown 1995). However dense and intense economic exchange may be, it does not translate easily or automatically into a shared awareness of a common identity, a shared community, or a common ethos. This is especially true given the massive inequalities within contemporary global capitalism.

There is also a real danger in tying notions of moral community too closely to networks of economic interaction, particularly when so many of the world's most vulnerable people are precisely those who are excluded or marginalized from integration processes that are misleadingly described as "global." Much of the rhetoric of an economically globalizing and unifying world, then, fails to distinguish among three senses of the idea of unity: unity as interdependence and interconnection; unity as uniformity in the character of the states and societies that make up the global system; and unity as consciousness of a shared humanity or commitment to some shared set of purposes.

Transnational civil society refers to those self-organized intermediary groups that are relatively independent of both public authorities and private economic actors; that are capable of taking collective action in pursuit of their interests or values; and that act across state borders. The roles of such groups within international society have increased very significantly: first, in the formal process of norm creation, standard-setting, and norm development; second, in the broader social process by which new norms emerge and find their way onto the international agenda; third, in the detailed functioning of many international institutions and in the processes of implementation and compliance; and finally, in direct participation in many governance activities (disbursing an increasing proportion of official aid, engaging in large-scale humanitarian relief; leading efforts at promoting democracy or post-conflict social and political reconstruction). In all of these areas the analytical focus has been on transnational networks – for example, knowledge-based networks of economists, lawyers, or scientists; or transnational advocacy networks which act as channels for flows of money and material resources but, more critically, of information, ideas, and values.

But, as with markets, there are very real problems and limits, and there is a need to counter a certain romanticization of the potentialities of transnational civil society (but not, as is the current danger, to go too far in the other direction). Civil society is, after all, an arena of politics like any other in which the good and thoroughly awful coexist, in which the pervasive claims made by nongovernmental organizations (NGOs) to authenticity and representativeness need to be tested and challenged, and in which outcomes may be just as subject to direct manipulation by powerful actors as in the world of interstate politics. Moreover, however much normative change may result from the efforts and activities of transnational actors, it is only through political institutionalization that new norms and rules can be sustainably and equitably implemented.

We know all too little about social order, but what we do know suggests that all three arenas matter and that much hinges on the often delicate balance amongst them. Moreover, although it is useful to talk analytically of three arenas, it is the linkages that are most interesting and most important – for example, the way in which civil society feeds positively into state-based order through the provision of legitimacy, and into market-based order as the repository of the trust and other forms of social capital without which markets will not function. State action may by shaped by NGO lobbying, but it is often state action that is crucial both in fostering the emergence of civil society and in providing the institutional framework that enables it to flourish. And very critically state power is increasingly determined by the ability of governments to work successfully within civil society and to exploit transnational and transgovernmental coalitions for their own purposes.

So I do not want to ignore or downplay the roles of global markets and transnational civil society, nor the importance of insisting on the moral responsibility of those acting within these arenas (O'Neill 2001). But there are real difficulties involved in relating those roles too neatly or too unproblematically to the emergence of a moral community or to moral cosmopolitanism. In addition, there are good reasons for according normative priority to political institutions. As many have noted, justice requires agents with the capacity and potential to promote change and reform. For all the changes in the role of the state, it is extremely difficult to understand how global capitalism could be managed in the interests of either greater stability or greater equity except through the reform or reconstruction of international institutions and revitalized schemes of interstate cooperation. Modern markets are, after all, political constructions despite Hayekian or Nozickian idealizations. I also believe (but can do no more than assert the claim here) that popular understandings of globalization have vastly exaggerated the alleged demise of the nation-state and its degree of powerlessness.

Before proceeding further, a few definitional points are in order. Distributive justice must, as Beitz argues, cover not merely direct financial transfers, but the ways in which major social institutions work to distribute all kinds of material resources, including income, education, and health care (Beitz 1999a, 271). International institutions are made up of two elements: first, clusters of connected norms, principles, and rules (constitutive, transactional, and societal); and, second, clusters of norms organized into stable and ongoing social practices. Those practices may well be connected with a formal international organization but do not need to be. So eliminating the World Bank or the WTO is a shift from one set of institutional structures to another, not the end of institutions. The very densely integrated international economy of the late 19th century was institutionalized, but in a very different form from its late-20th-century counterpart.

More importantly, international institutions are not simply things that preexisting states construct for their own purposes, instrumental or moral – which is the way in which many statist and communitarian theorists seem to understand things. On the contrary, it is the institutional structure of international society that constitutes the actors and that *necessarily* mediates the relationship between universalizing and particularizing practices. State sovereignty is, and always was, a shared social quality. Absolute independence and supreme authority have to be limited for the same quality to inhere in other states and for international law to impose any kinds of restrictions on states. Or as Robert Walker puts it: "Sovereignty is a claim to particularity that can be meaningful *only in relation* to something more general" (Walker 1999, 154–55). Rawls seems to recognize this, at least implicitly, in his determination to begin with peoples rather than states (Rawls 1999, 23–30). Unfortunately, the multiple ambiguities over who is to count as a people and how individuals are to be related to peoples can only be resolved (or at least only peacefully and sustainably resolved) through the construction of shared international rules. The point, then, is that those who stress the importance of bounded political communities are in practice already far more committed to the idea of an international community than they seem to assume.

As mentioned earlier, many of those who either deny the possibility of international distributive justice or see it only in highly constrained forms place great emphasis on the absence or weakness of international institutions or other cooperative arrangements.

> Now although in the contemporary world there are clearly forms of interaction and cooperation occurring at the global level – the international economy provides the most obvious example, but there are also many forms of political cooperation, ranging from defence treaties through to environmental protection agreements – these are not sufficient to constitute a global community. They do not by themselves create either a shared sense of identity or a common ethos. *And above all there is no common institutional structure that would justify us*

in describing unequal outcomes as forms of unequal treatment. (Miller 1999a, 190, emphasis added)

As it stands, this argument is problematic for two reasons. In the first place it says nothing about the criteria that would help us decide when we had reached a point of institutional change when something morally significant was happening. What might "sufficient to constitute a global community" mean? But, secondly, institutions cannot be understood as simple reflections of some preexisting and static community. Institutions reflect, but also actively shape, communities. Thus state institutions have been tremendously important in the creation and development of national communities. Indeed the promotion of some degree of distributive justice has often been an important element in state strategies of nation-building, often for crudely instrumental purposes. Think, for example, of the extent to which concern with economic justice and social citizenship was, at least in part, motivated by the need to persuade citizens to sacrifice their lives in an age of total war.

So how can we arrive at a more dynamic view of the link between institutions and morally relevant communities? Curiously perhaps, elements of an answer can be found in Rawls. Now, on one hand, what is most striking about *The Law of Peoples* is its static, backward-looking character. The image of the international system that Rawls presents is strikingly old-fashioned and profoundly at odds with even modest claims about international change and evolution. But, on the other hand, Rawls's own work highlights the potential for a two-way and self-reinforcing link between the institutions of the basic structure and the political culture of the people governed within those institutions. Thus society's "main political, social and economic institutions and how they fit together into one unified system of social co-operation" determine the basic structure and govern "the initial focus" of how to think about matters of justice (Rawls 1993a, 11–12).

But the emphasis here should be on "initial" since Rawls also recognizes the possibility of self-reinforcing change. "In addition, the institutions of the basic structure have deep and long-term social effects and in fundamental ways shape citizens' character and aims, the kinds of persons they are and aspire to be" (Rawls 1993a, 68). When writing about domestic society there is a strong sense that institutions play a central role in moving from self-interested cooperation towards a full overlapping consensus. They have important socializing influences on citizens, and Rawls presents a psychological account of how people come to accept and internalize principles of justice. Equally, when looking at international life, change, evolution, and learning are all recognized. "The idea of a reasonably just society of well-ordered peoples will not have an important place in a theory of international politics until such peoples exist and have learned to coordinate their actions in wider forms of political, economic and social cooperation" (Rawls 1999, 19). Or again: "Thus, when the Law of Peoples is honoured by people over time, with the evident intention to comply, and these institutions are mutually recognized, these peoples tend to develop a mutual trust and confidence in one another. Moreover, peoples see those norms as advantageous for themselves and for those they care for, and therefore, as time goes on they tend to accept that law as an ideal of conduct" (Rawls 1999, 44). And finally, "What encourages the statesman's work is that relations of affinity are not a fixed thing, but may continually grow stronger over time as peoples come to work together in cooperative institutions they have developed. . . . The relatively narrow circle of mutually caring peoples in the world may expand over time and must never be viewed as fixed" (Rawls 1999, 112–13).

Given that such a prominent restrictionist as Rawls accepts the possibility of morally relevant institutional change and evolution, I want to spend a little time trying to give some sense to the immense changes that have taken place in the institutions of international society, but also to stress the combination of *density* and *deformity* that complicates the sorts of conclusions that we might be able to draw.

We can point to a steady move towards a denser and more integrated network of shared institutions and practices. As is well known, the international law and principles of international society that developed within the classical European state system were largely concerned with elaborating limited rules of coexistence. This pluralist conception of international law was built around the goal of coexistence and reflected an ethic of difference. It was to be constructed around the mutual recognition of sovereignty and aimed at the creation of certain minimalist rules, understandings, and institutions designed to limit the inevitable conflict that was to be expected within such a fragmented political system. In Rawls's terms, it was more a modus vivendi than a meaningful legal or moral community.

This pluralist image has always had its critics and has come under tremendous challenge in the course of this century. Three dimensions of change are especially important. The first has to do with the content of norms. In contrast to mere coexistence, the norms of this more solidarist law involve more extensive schemes of cooperation to safeguard peace and security (for example, prohibiting aggression or broadening understandings of what constitutes threats to peace and security); to solve common problems (such as tackling environmental challenges or managing the global economy in the interests of greater stability or equity); and to sustain common values (such as the promotion of self-determination, human rights, or political democracy). So the rules of the economic system have long since ceased to be confined to issues of "fair trade." On the contrary, the thirty thousand pages of the WTO treaties affect very deeply almost every aspect of how states organize their domestic economies.

A second dimension has to do with the justification and evaluation of norms. Alongside the old idea that actors create and uphold law because it provides them with functional benefits, the post-1945 period has seen the emergence of a range of internationally agreed core principles – respect for fundamental human rights, prohibition of aggression, self-determination – that may underpin some notion of a world common good and some broader basis for evaluating specific rules. Thus the density, scope, and complexity of the agreements, norms, and rules in which states and societies are already enmeshed provide some basis for positing a community interest or an agreed set of purposes and values against which new substantive norms may be judged – the idea of an objective community interest or of the common interest of global society. This may be viewed in terms of the surreptitious return of natural law ideas or of a philosophically anchorless, but nevertheless reasonably solid pragmatic consensus. And the third dimension has to do with moves towards the more effective implementation of these norms and the variety of attempts to move beyond the traditionally very "soft" compliance mechanisms and to give more effective teeth to the norms of this more ambitious society.

As this increasingly solidarist legal order has developed, so a crucial ambiguity begins to open up around the idea of states as the principal agents of world order. Within the pluralist world, states could be understood as "agents" simply in the sense of those acting or exerting power and of doing so for themselves: "The law of nations is the law of sovereigns," as Vattel famously put it. But the expanding normative agenda of solidarism has opened up a second and different meaning of agency – the idea of an agent as someone who acts for, or on behalf of, another. Within the solidarist order states are no longer to act for themselves as sovereigns; but rather, first, as agents for the individuals, groups, and national communities that they are supposed to represent; and second, as agents or interpreters of some notion of an international public good and some set of core norms against which state behaviour should be judged and evaluated.

Moreover, change has not only involved interstate institutions, but has also seen the emergence of transnational governance structures. One argument here points simply to the increasingly active role of firms and NGOs in the process of norm creation – either as lobbyists within individual states or as participants directly within international regimes and institutions. A second argument concentrates on the role of nonstate actors as the generators of norms that are then taken up and assimilated into international legal structures. The third, and most radical position, highlights the emergence of private authority structures that exist largely autonomous from the framework of both municipal and international law: private systems of arbitration and dispute settlement, privatized rule production resulting from technical standardization, internal regulations within transnational firms, and private regimes governing particular sectors of the global economy.

So clearly international institutions, once created, can and do develop over time. The ever expanding normative ambition of international society has been driven by various factors. First, by prudential imperatives and the degree to which increased interdependence has increased the demand for international cooperation. Second, by changes in the organization of domestic society, and in the powerful transnational ideological forces that have shaped those changes. Thus the legitimacy of governments (democratic and authoritarian) has come to depend on their capacity to meet a vastly increased range of needs, claims, and demands. Third, by the steady growth of demands that the norms of international society should express, not just pragmatic or material interests, but also common moral purposes. Often this stems from the drive to universalize that is inherent in most of the world's most developed ethical systems, religious or secular. Fourth, by the actions of powerful states promoting their own values and interests. And finally, by the ability of apparently weaker actors to use the institutional platforms and to exploit already established patterns of legal argument to promote new and often far-reaching rules and institutions (as with the International Criminal Court).

Once created, institutions act as platforms for on going normative debate, for the mobilization of concern, and for debating and revising ideas about how international society should be organized. However much social scientists (and technocratic practitioners) insist on analysing international institutions solely in terms of the provision of international public goods, normative issues cannot be kept out of the picture. In addition, there is an inherent tendency for all normative systems (especially reasonably well institutionalized judicial systems) to expand and develop, and to enmesh actors within certain patterns of discourse, reasoning, and argumentation. And finally, we have good reason for believing that international institutions have acted as powerful agents for the diffusion and socialization of norms.

It is, then, far from obvious that international institutions cannot move different states and societies towards "shared understandings of the meaning of social goods," to use Michael Walzer's phrase (Walzer 1983). Indeed there is no reason in principle why internalist or conventionalist accounts of justice need to be confined within state borders and used to buttress communitarian positions. Shared and institutionally embedded understandings as to what constitutes justice and injustice are no longer confined within national communities. In examining the changing structure of international society we surely are dealing with "an identifiable set of institutions whose impact on the life chances of different individuals can be traced" (Miller 1999b, 5); or, in Rawls's terms, with political, social, and economic arrangements that "define men's rights and duties and influence their life prospects, what they can expect to be and how well they can hope to do" (Rawls 1971, 7). After all, the *acquis communitaire* of the European Union now consists of some eighty-six thousand pages of standardized legislation.

This international institutional order does involve "publicly recognized rules that all acknowledge" (through the doctrine of consent and the still strong idea of consensualism in international law) and does provide a shared basis for the public justification of actions. International law does constitute a unified normative order (Dupuy 1999); and it is, as we have seen, subject to change and reform, at least part of which has served the interests of justice.

And yet the elements of *deformity* are equally evident. We are not dealing with a "now vanished Westphalian world" (to paraphrase Allan Buchanan), but rather with a world in which solidarist and cosmopolitan models of governance coexist, usually rather unhappily, with many aspects of the old Westphalian order (Buchanan 2001). First, there is deformity in terms of the distribution of advantages and disadvantages: in the way, for example, security is defined and the choices taken by institutions and states as to whose security is to be protected; or, very obviously, in the massive inequalities of the global economic order. Second, there is deformity in terms of who sets the rules of international society. Institutions are not, as some liberals would have us believe, neutral arenas for the solution of common problems, but rather sites of power, even of dominance. The vast majority of weaker actors are increasingly "rule takers" over a whole range of issues that affect all aspects of social, economic, and political life. Third, there is deformity in terms of the very different capacity of states and societies to adapt to the demands of a global economy, combined with the extent to which the economic choices of developing countries are, if not dictated, then certainly shaped by the institutions dominated by the strong and often backed by coercion in the form of an expanding range of conditionalities. And finally, deformity is evident in the limited capacity of international law and institutions to constrain effectively the unilateral and often illegal acts of the strong. In this sense we are not moving beyond sovereignty, but rather returning to an earlier world of differentiated and more conditional sovereignties.

None of this is to suggest that the increased aspirations of international society are not part of the fabric of contemporary international relations. But it is to say that this society remains deeply contaminated by power and that the political theorist can only ignore the persistence of this structural contamination at the cost of idealization; that where solidarist cooperation is weak or breaks down, the older imperatives of pluralist order continue to flourish; and that even when genuinely consensual, the promotion of solidarist values both depends on, and reinforces, the power and privileges of the dominant state or states.

The problem is not simply that institutions reflect unequal power or that globalization is related to increases in many different forms of inequality. It is also that many of the most important institutions depend for their effectiveness on inequality and hierarchy. This means that the problem cannot be solved by "democratizing" international institutions. Nor is it a problem that can be dealt with by dispersing power. The fundamental problem with models of dispersed sovereignty is that, whilst they correctly acknowledge the dangers of centralized power, they fail to acknowledge the necessity of such power for social order and the promotion of common moral purposes. This is most obviously true in the field of security. But it also applies to economic order and, by extension, to economic justice. Think, for example, of the need for effective states with sufficient legitimate power and authority to tax transnational corporations; or to enforce equitable burden sharing in the management of financial crises.

As David Miller has argued, there are good reasons to separate out issues of procedural fairness from questions of distributive justice (Miller 1999b, chapter 5). But it is also clear that there are important points of intersection. Perhaps the most important concerns what might be called the political prerequisites for a meaningful justice community. There will always be much debate as to what exactly should be included under this heading. But at a minimum we might list: some acceptance of equality of status, of respect, and of consideration; some commitment to reciprocity and to the public justification of one's actions; some capacity for autonomous decision making on the basis of reasonable information; a degree of uncoerced willingness to participate; a situation in which the most disadvantaged perceive themselves as having some stake in the system; and some institutional processes by which the weak and disadvantaged are able to make their voice heard and to express claims about unjust treatment. As Judith Shklar puts it: "Procedural justice is not merely a formal ritual, as is so often charged. It is a system that in principle gives everyone some access to the agencies of rectification and, more significantly, the possibility of expressing a sense of injustice to some effect, at least occasionally" (Shklar 1990, 124).

There has been much discussion of how procedural fairness in international life might be improved (see, for example, Held 1995). There is also a fruitful and fascinating literature on how the conditions of political process can themselves help to provide the basis for moral legitimation (for example, Linklater 1998). But in international life it is on the minimum preconditions that we should focus: philosophically, on what might, in abstract terms, constitute that minimum; and empirically, on the degree to which the deformities of the international political order push us close to (but in my own view not below) that minimum.

In one of the most important passages in *The Law of Peoples*, Rawls recognizes that one of the three reasons for being concerned with inequality "concerns the important role of fairness in the political processes of the basic structure of the Society of Peoples" (Rawls 1999, 114). Domestically, says Rawls, this concern covers both the fairness of formal political processes and the background social conditions that shape an individual's chance of attaining favoured social positions. But even though inequality has always been so much more extreme internationally, Rawls appears unwilling to pursue this same logic very far. He does accept that "cooperative institutions that have unjustified distributional effects" would need to be corrected (Rawls 1999, 115). So, although opening the door to a crucial issue, his treatment grossly underplays just how determining unequal power is in world politics – and would remain within his Society of Peoples under the terms on which it is to be constituted.[1]

The idea of an international society begins with the rejection of the image of the world as a crude Hobbesian struggle in which morality plays no part (Bull 1985; Beitz 1999b). The realist image is indeed wrong. And yet the deformities of the international political order cannot easily be swept aside. So what does all this imply for distributive justice? Let me make three points.

The first has to do with the *scope* of claims for distributive justice. There is obviously a great temptation to read this combination of density and deformity as requiring rich states to engage in very significant reformist or redistributionist schemes. The density of international institutional practices has altered the circumstances of justice so fundamentally that distributive justice cannot be kept within the boundaries of ever more open and penetrated states. And it is the very deformity of those practices that provides clear guidelines as to what needs to be changed – both in terms of substantive economic outcomes and of the fairness of the processes by which the rules governing the global economy are promulgated and implemented. Having stated clearly what justice requires, the redistributionist cosmopolitan can then accept the severity of the political obstacles and the likelihood of, at best, incremental progress.

However, to argue in this way is to misconstrue the political and moral obstacles that stand in the way of greater global justice. There is indeed good reason for believing that the density of international society does make a real difference to our responsibilities to the most vulnerable and most deprived of distant strangers. Thus we have seen the emergence of an international and transnational culture of human rights that involves a widely shared common language, an inclusive moral vocabulary, and an authoritative and well-developed normative structure from which very few groups are prepared to try and exempt themselves. This shared discourse implies a general acceptance of certain general principles and processes, and of a particular kind of rationality and argumentation. It limits the range of permissible justifications and motivations; it empowers particular

---

[1] Unequal power has important implications for others who take a restrictionist stance on international distributive justice. Thus, for example, when Walzer discusses the injustice of current international distributions, he writes: "But if we tell a different story – of imperial wars; conquests; occupations, and interventions; the political control of trade, and so on – then we are likely at the end not only to be morally troubled but concerned specifically about the *injustice* of the resulting inequalities. We will be concerned because of our own belief, now widely shared, that political power in international society should be distributed in accordance with the principle of collective freedom and self-determination" (Walzer 1995, 292). Whilst this move is in the right direction, the difficulty is that self-determination within individual societies does not provide a secure basis for controlling and legitimating political power within international society as a whole.

groups and particular institutions; and it helps create incentives for social-ization and internalization. It is, of course, shaped by its historical origins within a particular culture; but it is open, dynamic, and resistant to perma-nent capture by a particular interest or power-political grouping. However varied the philosophical, political, or cultural backgrounds from which it is approached, the emergence and spread of this transnational moral and legal discourse represents a major historical development.

It is therefore possible to present a case for tackling global economic inequalities in terms of the values and discourse of an already existing international political and moral culture, above all as expressed within the context of economic and social human rights. The normative structure contains widely (but not universally) recognized social expectations against which the suffering engendered by the current distribution of economic goods represents a staggering injustice.

But whilst the idea of a global moral community is not entirely illusory, the elements of deformity provide good grounds for arguing that it is certainly fragile and cannot bear too much weight. The elements of defor-mity highlight the weaknesses of the political order on which the possibil-ity of implementing the reforms required by justice will necessarily depend. We know that Sweden exists. But we have no experience of social democratic liberalism beyond the state. Indeed we have many good theo-ries that tell us just how difficult any such enterprise is likely to be. In addi-tion, the persistence of deformity suggests that we need to be constantly sceptical of the universalist "we" who talks loftily about the principles of global justice. Given the deformity of the international political order, won't this "we" inevitably become the most powerful state or group of states? It also suggests that we need to take very seriously the limits to people's empirical sense of their global responsibilities and the ways in which these need to be balanced with local identities and particularist affections. After all, what meaning can be attached to even the purist and most serene universalist voice (whether of the Kantian liberal or of the reli-gious believer) echoing down from the mountain if those to whom it is addressed do not believe themselves to be part of even the thinnest and most fragile shared community?

How can we ensure a political order in which the reasonableness of the best moral arguments are accepted as legitimate? The most persuasive answer is to nurture (but not uncritically accept) the normative consensus that has come to develop within international society; to build arguments and proposals for greater distributive justice out of the values and modes of reasoning that have already begun to take root; and to pay very close attention to the balance between substantive principles of global distribu-tive justice on the one hand, and the principles of fair institutional process on the other. Of course political theory is in the business of stating clearly what justice requires, and of pushing out the normative boat at least to the margins of what conventional opinion takes to be plausible. And yet, especially in the international realm with its huge disparities of power and the pervasiveness of deep value pluralism, political theory also needs to uncover, interpret, and critically develop understandings of morality that exist within international institutional and transnational contexts.

A second implication concerns the *character* of distributive justice and the tensions that exist between two possible alternatives. If the resources available or the scope for other forms of assistance is limited by political reality, or by the degree of strenuousness that can be legitimately demanded from rich societies (a concept that I can understand practically but not morally), then our elementary moral intuition would suggest that efforts should be concentrated on the most deprived and most vulnerable. Poverty and deprivation within developing societies should trump any concern with global inequality among states.

And yet there is a real sense in which Rawls is correct to stress the importance of assisting burdened societies – "peoples living under unfavourable conditions that prevent their having a just or decent political or social regime" (Rawls 1999, 37). Rawls, of course, wishes to hedge the duty of assistance (hence his view that the aim should be not development per se, but changes in the political culture of the assisted people to foster well-orderedness, and his claim that well-orderedness does not equate with wealth). But he does bring into focus the need to think in terms of societies as well as individuals. Why does this matter? First, because poverty reduction and the relief of individual suffering are not enough and cannot displace the need for economic growth and development. Together with political development this is something that is most likely to be achieved within functioning and stable societies. Second, because only through successful development and through effective social and political regimes are we likely to achieve the conditions of fairer international bargaining over the ground rules and outcomes of the global economy. Greater interstate justice is instrumentally necessary to achieve the sorts of outcomes desired by the moral cosmopolitan.

My third point concerns the *modalities* by which global economic justice might be pursued and the critical, but difficult, issues of responsibility and conditionality. Existing debates devote much time to the assignation of responsibility for the massive inequalities that exist and the rising levels of poverty globally. According to those who seek to deny or restrict claims for distributive justice, successful economic development reflects national choices and domestic political culture ("the causes of the wealth of a people and the form it takes lie in their political culture and in the religious, philosophical, and moral traditions" [Rawls 1999, 108]). Thus Rawls cites Landes to show that resources and endowments are not crucial to successful economic development. Both Miller and Rawls cite Sen to demonstrate that extreme disasters such as famines can be averted by even poor societies. Such positions recall the hugely influential neoliberal critics of import substitution, economic statism, and dependency theory of the early 1980s, and the work of Robert Bates and Anne Krueger on rent-seeking élites. The basic message is that the problems of inequality and underdevelopment lie within domestic societies rather than with the international system.

This view clearly underplays the vulnerability of developing societies to global markets, a situation which economic liberalization, whatever its benefits, has inevitably increased. It neglects the degree to which the emergence over time of the "unfavourable conditions" that afflict poor societies has as much to do with external and global factors as with internal ones; and it ignores the extent to which national economic policy is shaped by international economic institutions and powerful states. How can a developing country be held responsible when the content of its economic policy is shaped by external pressures and by policy injunctions enforced by far-reaching conditionalities? Without moving back to first generation dependency theorists who unconvincingly placed all responsibility on the external (the development of underdevelopment), there is enough evidence of the importance of external influences and of the impact of the global system to suggest that the idea of coresponsibility should act as the overall guiding principle.

But even if we accept the broad notion of shared responsibility, there will always be judgements to be made regarding the responsibility of particular governments at particular times. It is neither politically realistic nor morally acceptable that responsibility should play no role at all in our judgements about who is to be the subject of reform and redistribution and of what kind. The difficulty lies in how responsibility is to be assigned and by whom. I doubt that general principles will take us very far. Even assuming high levels of technical competence and an absence of special interests, I suspect that judgements of how far a government or society has contributed to its own problems will always vary from issue to issue, country to country, and period to period. The only way out is therefore to place a good deal of weight on working towards fairer institutions and on reforming the process by which such judgements can be agreed and acted upon.

The other, and related, issue concerns the conditionality of assistance and of other actions designed to promote development (such as membership of regional or international bodies). The 1980s and 1990s witnessed an explosion of externally imposed conditionalities on trade, aid, and investment, covering everything from the nature of economic policy (both micro and macro), to levels of arms spending, to the promotion of sustainable development, to the promotion of human rights and democratic governance. These conditionalities have been subject to a host of shifting objectives, economic policy ideas, and often crude political interests that have had very little to do with the interests of the poorest or most vulnerable. Indeed it is worth noting that aid flows in the 1990s were just as volatile as capital flows.

Quite apart from the question as to whether conditionality is actually effective, serious problems arise. First, the proliferation of conditionality undercuts the meaningfulness of political community and runs directly counter to such favoured liberal goals as the democratic accountability of governments to their citizens. How can international and transnational involvement in domestic politics avoid shifting political power within the state? How can citizens hold their governments accountable for policies chosen in Brussels, Paris, or Washington? Perhaps more fundamentally, how can societies learn the practice of democratic politics without the freedom to make bad choices? Second, as conditionality cuts ever deeper into the ways in which societies organize themselves, so the issue of legitimate difference becomes more serious. It might be quite easy to say that economic aid can legitimately be tied to upholding internationally agreed core human rights. It is much less obvious that it should be tied, say, to some particular set of domestic economic policies deemed by an external NGO, government, or aid agency to be especially worthy. The legal and moral problems surrounding intervention focus on its coercive character. Conditionality, by contrast, is "softer" and therefore apparently less morally troubling. But, certainly in its recent forms, it is arguably more far-reaching in its attempted influence over the long-term character of how other societies develop.

The redistributionist cosmopolitan is inherently less worried about external interference and less deferential to claims that domestic ways of doing things need to be respected as a matter of principle. (Rawls, by contrast, seems to rule out anything more than helpful advice.) But if serious efforts to reduce global poverty do come about, then the potential power of external actors will grow, and the dangers for democratic politics and political autonomy and for legitimate difference will come into starker relief. No doubt, developing a set of balancing principles and guidelines will be important. But so too will be increasing the element of fairness in the operation of the institutions that manage poverty reduction. At the moment the practice of conditionality rests on the choices and power of a small group of powerful states and is applied in a wholly selective manner. Coercive developmental paternalism continues to be the order of the day (even though the moral case has never been clearly or convincingly enunciated). This must place strain on the normative coherence of the international legal order and on the legitimacy and effectiveness of international institutions. In this, and other areas, it is not at all clear that moral cosmopolitanism can be easily delinked from political cosmopolitanism, from the politics of institutional reform, and from the distribution of political power.

The Gap between Theory and Practice

Our second question is, How should we think about the very obvious gap that exists between the arguments of even the most restrictionist political theorists writing on global economic justice and current political practice? In any discussion of global economic inequality, it is undoubtedly important to distinguish between a limited duty of assistance, the need for greater economic justice that follows from taking human rights seriously (especially economic and social rights), and a duty based on some clear principle of egalitarian justice. But, equally striking, is the enormous gap that exists between what even the most restrictionist political theorists argue to be required by justice and the way in which the global economy is currently organized. From this perspective, what is notable about *The Law of Peoples* is not its limits, but rather just how far Rawls has moved since his earlier 1993 Amnesty Lecture (Rawls 1993b). If we were to take his injunctions of assistance seriously, this could be interpreted as requiring high levels of redistribution and significant elements of reform. It would certainly require measures that are way ahead of what we currently see or are likely to see. The same may be said about the need to deal with severe material deprivation or with situations of exploitation, as emphasized by David Miller (1999a).

It is difficult to write on global inequality without at least trying to confront the yawning gap that exists between theory and practice, and without thinking, even briefly, about some of the factors that may explain it. Saffran puts the challenge to moral cosmopolitans well: "Since our moral theories lead to implications so contrary to any likely behaviour, they clearly omit important considerations and we should be sceptical about their cogency" (Saffran 1989, 319).

The picture is clearly not a happy one. First, take development aid. It may be possible to argue, as David Lumsdaine suggests, that the striking fact about the post-1945 foreign aid regime is not that political and instrumental factors impinged at all, but that such a high percentage was not motivated directly by power or interest. "As much of a third of aid mainly served donors' commercial, colonial, or strategic goals. However, most foreign aid was based on donors' humanitarianism and their perceptions of the world as an interdependent community" (Lumsdaine 1993, 4). But this provides rather small comfort given both the steep fall in overall aid levels since the end of the Cold War and the belief, most notable in the United States, that aid has to be justified in terms of hard national interests if it is to be saleable politically (see Kapstein 1999).

Second, take regional arrangements. Even if global concern is limited, we might expect greater potential for moral change at the regional level because of high levels of integration, shared historical background, and stronger and more effective institutionalization. And yet the experience of "distribution beyond borders" even within regions is hardly encouraging. The European Union (EU) is the only regional arrangement with any mechanisms for redistribution (in the form of regional and structural funds). And yet these mechanisms were driven by instrumental and pragmatic factors (above all the bargains that preceded earlier waves of enlargement). And they are now being eroded by newer instrumental concerns (above all, the pressures resulting from the current wave of enlargement).[2]

No other regional arrangement has even contemplated resource transfers to deal with deprivation or inequality or even to compensate for the losses entailed by integration. The North American Free Trade Agreement (NAFTA) provides a particularly telling example. If arguments about ever denser integration leading to shifting understandings of moral community were to have force, then the U.S.-Mexico relationship should be a likely candidate. It is a relationship characterized by extremely high levels of economic and societal interdependence; by high levels of deprivation in Mexico, a good deal of which can be implicated in problems likely to have negative spillover effects on the United States; and by a rich and privileged partner well able to afford assistance. And yet the absence of any debate is telling.

Third, take the normative debate surrounding international economic institutions. Here the situation is arguably a good deal worse than in the 1970s. When we look back at the North/South debates of the 1970s, it is striking to note the salience of global inequality amongst states as an issue of debate and the political space that was given to arguments that the metarules of the international economic order needed to be reformed in the interests of interstate justice. As we move into the 1980s, that (always limited) political space diminished significantly. In the case of trade, although it would be wrong to suggest that developing countries received no benefits from the Uruguay Round, the principle of special trading status for developing countries and privileged market access had been pushed off the General Agreement on Tariffs and Trade (GATT) agenda by the mid-1980s. Although the World Bank had come to focus on poverty with the arrival of Robert McNamara in 1968, the situation changed significantly in the early 1980s. To quote Nicholas Stern, "Its attention to equity issues from 1982 to the end of the decade appears to have been somewhat token, at least relative to its record in the 1970s" (Stern 1997, 544).[3]

The dominant economic story of the 1980s was a blanket denial on the part of the international financial institutions (IFIs) and of Northern governments that the international system was in any way responsible for

---

[2] It may be the case that some of the concern with economic injustice and inequality is being addressed within the EU through an expanded range of social and economic rights, thereby creating external pressure on states to be more concerned with inequality and deprivation within their boundaries. And yet the efficacy of this tactic is unproven and its viability likely to be confined to rich states.

[3] Recognising the return of poverty concerns in the early 1990s, Stern states: "Nevertheless, six or seven years in the later 1970s and four or five years at the end of the 1980s and early 1990s is not a high proportion of the Bank's fifty years" (1997, 550). It is worth remembering that the Bank's Articles of Agreement contain no reference to poverty or to related notions such as social welfare or equity (and maybe also that the index of this two-volume history does not contain an entry for inequality).

underdevelopment, and a firm insistence that market-liberalism provided the answer to both economic development and poverty. Even as concern with the "human dimensions" of economic development began to reemerge in the mid-1990s, the broader dimensions of global inequality remained off limits. Instead there was a renewed focus on poverty and on limited and targeted measures to assist the most deprived: "economic growth is the most significant single factor that contributes to poverty reduction" although "some poor and vulnerable groups can be adversely affected in the short-run" (IMF 2000, para. 17–18).

Finally, it is striking that rich states have resisted any kind of formal obligation to tackle global economic injustices and have entered formal reservations whenever international declarations might be understood as moving in that direction.[4] This suggests, incidently, that words are not all that cheap and that states do take legal, and even moral, obligations seriously. It therefore attests to the existence of an international community, but in a way that does not help us establish the reality of concern for distributional justice. Rich states have also successfully defended international institutions that are based both formally (as in the voting structures of the Bank and Fund) and informally (as in the closed club character of the Group of 7, the Bank of International Settlements [BIS], or the Financial Stability Forum) on exclusion and unequal power. Even after the crises of the 1990s, "[D]iscussion of [financial] reform will thus proceed in a forum dominated by the leading industrialized countries, in spite of the fact that globalization has geographically expanded the regions affected by capital flows, as well as the nature and depth of the issues and reforms that any international institution has to deal with" (Woods 2000, 209).

The contrast with environmental issues is an instructive one. In this case there has been a rather striking acceptance by Northern countries of both aspirational declarations on the part of the strong, and also of legal obligations (Franck 1995, chapters 11 and 12). These obligations do involve principles of equity and a degree of commitment to distributive justice – as

---

[4] See, for example, the U.S. reservations entered to the Declaration and Programme of Action of the 1995 Copenhagen Summit. On the U.S. view, these are "not legally binding and . . . consist of recommendations concerning how States can and should promote social development" (United Nations 1995, chap. 5, para. 17). It is also important to remember that the United States has never ratified the International Covenant on Economic, Social, and Cultural Rights and that, as Forsythe puts it, "[W]hen the USA talks about its support for the Universal Declaration of Human Rights, it simply omits any reference to those articles endorsing fundamental rights to adequate standards of food, clothing, shelter, health care and social security" (Forsythe 2000, 145). More recently, Canada and the EU proposed a draft declaration to the 2000 Geneva World Summit for Social Development which speaks of "our determination and duty to eradicate poverty"; but this duty is only loosely specified ("we will strive to fulfill the yet to be attained internationally agreed target of 0.7% of GNP of developed countries for overall ODA as soon as possible"), and even they rejected the G77 draft, which argued for "equitable distribution of wealth within and among nations" (United Nations 2000, Part 1, para. 5–6).

with the acceptance by the North of responsibility for past environmental harms; the idea of differentiated responsibilities in moving towards more sustainable futures; and the acceptance of resource and technology transfers (as within the ozone, climate change, and biodiversity regimes). The industrialized states have even made concessions in terms of the decision-making processes that allow for more balanced representation between North and South (as on the Global Environmental Facility). Without wishing to make too much of these gains, it seems clear that considerations of justice have had a degree of greater play here.

The contrast between global environmental regimes and those that govern the core features of the global economy seems all too clearly explicable in terms of the balance of power and of political interest. Crudely speaking, the global environment is an area where the poor matter to the rich and where concessions have had to be made in the interest of creating new cooperative regimes. In addition, the environment was an issue area in which Northern civil society groups mobilized successfully and incorporated some justice concerns because of their broader interest in sustainability. This contrast reinforces the claim that a meaningful justice community requires some degree of equality of power.

Apart from power and from an inability to force global economic injustice onto the political agenda, what else might be important? First we might highlight continued scepticism over aid. There have certainly been important claims that we now know far more about how to make aid work. But there are equally good grounds for doubt. The corruption and abuse of the EU aid system is one obvious example. But before isolationists bemoan yet again the failings of international bodies, it is important to highlight the multiple weaknesses and failings of US (and other bilateral) assistance programmes to Russia and to the transition economies. (For a strong indictment see Wedel 1998.)

Second, there is the continuing weakness of the classic "global common interest" arguments for more attention to redistribution. It may be true that the 20 percent of the world's population living in countries belonging to the Organization for Economic Cooperation and Development (OECD) cannot insulate itself from the instability and insecurity to which injustice and deprivation give rise. It may also be true that the North cannot do without the political support of major developing countries if collective and cooperative solutions are to be found to global problems. And yet, the difficulties of matching broad and long-term shared interests with short-term political imperatives, and with particular constellations of political and social interests, remain as formidable as they were during the debates on North/South relations in the 1970s. Moreover, if the negative features of global interdependence do not bite sharply and directly, then it is perhaps not surprising that the citizens of the developed world are unwilling to give up "the peace and quiet that injustice can and does offer," to quote Shklar once more (Shklar 1990, 45).

Finally, it is important to be clear about reasons that do not apply. The failure to address economic injustice both domestically and globally has nothing (or only very little) to do with the allegedly inherent tendencies of globalization to undermine the nation-state or to make welfare states unviable. The size and economic role of the state has remained remarkably constant despite globalization and neoliberalism. There is also considerable variation in patterns of social and economic inequality across the OECD world despite the degree to which all have been subject to the challenges of globalization and technological change. This suggests that patterns of inequality have much to do with changing domestic social norms (Atkinson 1999) and with the inability of politicians (and political theorists) to convince electorates that inequality can or should be tackled. The failure of efforts to deal with global inequality reflects the clear political choices and the clear preferences of powerful political actors.

What hope of progress? First, as I have argued above, international institutions are important platforms for moral debate. Those who lead international institutions resolutely try to defend the idea of institutions as technocratic providers of international public goods or of neutral technical knowledge. But it has been consistently impossible to maintain this position. It is significant, and at least a small sign of progress, that arguments about effectiveness and efficiency have to be made in the language of morality. Thus both the Fund and the World Bank have over the past two years sought to emphasize their contributions to the poor and, in the case of the Bank, this has involved a new Poverty Reduction Strategy with its Comprehensive Development Framework.

Second, there are the intrinsic limits to hierarchical institutions, especially in an age of globalization. Increased recognition of these limits may necessitate greater participation by the developing world (and greater pluralism more generally) and this may, in turn, help to open up the possibility of bargain or institutional reforms in which issues of global inequality can be put on the table. If rich states and international institutions are to develop effective policies on economic development, environmental protection, human rights, the resolution of refugee crises, or the fight against drugs, then they need to engage with a wide range of states and to interact, not just with central governments, but with a much wider range of domestic political, economic, and social actors. If you want to solve problems in a globalized world, you cannot simply persuade or bully governments into signing treaties. Equally, if international institutions are to be effective, they must also be legitimate. Legitimacy, in turn, depends partly on the degree of participation by weaker actors in the process by which decisions are made; partly on the institution's degree of autonomy to act according to agreed legal procedures and/or technical standards; and partly on being seen to possess at least a degree of autonomy from the most powerful states.

Acknowledgments
I would like to thank Vicki Nash and Jikon Lai for their work as research assistants, Ngaire Woods for many fruitful conversations on the themes of this chapter, and the participants in the Bielefeld Workshop for their comments on an earlier version.

References

Atkinson, Anthony. (1999). "Is Rising Inequality Inevitable? A Critique of the Transatlantic Consensus." Wider Annual Lecture. Helsinki: UNU/WIDER.

Beitz, Charles R. (1999a). "International Liberalism and Distributive Justice: A Survey of Recent Thought." *World Politics,* 51, 269–96.

———. (1999b). *Political Theory and International Relations.* 2nd ed. Princeton: Princeton University Press. First edition published 1979.

Brown, Chris. (1995). "International Political Theory and the Idea of World Community." In *International Relations Theory Today*, edited by Ken Booth and Steve Smith, 90–109. Cambridge: Polity Press.

Buchanan, Allan. (2001). "Rawls's Law of Peoples: Rules for a Vanished Westphalian World." *Ethics*, 110, 697–721.

Bull, Hedley. (1985). *The Anarchical Society: A Study of Order in World Politics.* 2nd ed. Basingstoke: Macmillan.

Dupuy, Pierre-Marie. (1999). "The Danger of Fragmentation or Unification of the International Legal System and the International Court of Justice." *Journal of International Law and Politics*, 31:4, 791–807.

Forsythe, David P. (2000). *Human Rights in International Relations.* Cambridge: Cambridge University Press.

Franck, Thomas M. (1995). *Fairness in International Law and Institutions.* Oxford: Clarendon Press.

Held, David. (1995). *Democracy and the Global Order: From the Modern State to Cosmopolitan Governance.* Cambridge: Polity Press.

International Monetary Fund (IMF). (2000). *Social Policy Issues in IMF Supported Programs: Follow-up on the 1995 World Summit for Social Development.* Washington, D.C.

Kapstein, Ethan B. (1999). "Reviving Aid: Or Does Charity Begin at Home?" *World Policy Journal,* fall, 35–44.

Linklater, Andrew. (1998). *The Transformation of Political Community: Ethical Foundations of the Post-Westphalian Era.* Cambridge: Polity Press.

Lumsdaine, David H. (1993). *Moral Vision in International Politics: The Foreign Aid Regime, 1949–1989.* Princeton: Princeton University Press.

Miller, David. (1999a). "Justice and Global Inequality." In *Inequality, Globalization and World Politics,* edited by Andrew Hurrell and Ngaire Woods, 187–210. Oxford: Oxford University Press.

Miller, David. (1999b). *Principles of Social Justice*. Cambridge: Harvard University Press.

O'Neill, Onora. (1996). *Towards Justice and Virtue: A Constructive Account of Practical Reasoning*. Cambridge: Cambridge University Press.

―――. (2001). "Agents of Justice." *Metaphilosophy*, 32:1/2.

Pogge, Thomas W. (1989). *Realizing Rawls*. Ithaca: Cornell University Press.

Rawls, John. (1971). *A Theory of Justice*. Cambridge: Harvard University Press.

―――. (1993a). *Political Liberalism*. New York: Columbia University Press.

―――. (1993b). "The Law of Peoples." In *On Human Rights*, edited by Stephen Shute and Susan Hurley, 41–82. New York: Basic Books.

―――. (1999). *The Law of Peoples*. Cambridge: Harvard University Press.

Saffran, Bernard. (1989). "Markets and Justice." In *Markets and Justice*, edited by John W. Chapman and J. Roland Pennock, 303–27. *Nomos* 31. New York: New York University Press.

Shklar, Judith N. (1990). *The Faces of Injustice*. New Haven: Yale University Press.

Stern, Nicholas, with Francisco Ferreira. (1997). "The World Bank as 'Intellectual Actor.'" In *The World Bank: Its First Half Century*, vol. 2: *Perspectives*, edited by Devesh Kapur, John P. Lewis, and Richard Webb, 523–609. Washington, D.C.

United Nations. (1995). *Report of the World Summit for Social Development (Copenhagen, 6–12 March 1995)*. Preliminary version of the report dated 19 April 1995. A/CONF.166/9. Available at <http://www.un.org/esa/socdev/wssd/documents/index.html>.

―――. (2000). *Review and Appraisal of the Implementation of the Outcome of the World Summit for Social Development*. Dated 14 April 2000. A/AC.253/L.5/Rev.2.

Walker, Robert J. (1999). "The Hierarchicalization of Political Community." *Review of International Studies*, 25, 151–56.

Walzer, Michael. (1983). *Spheres of Justice*. New York: Basic Books.

―――. (1995). "Response." In *Pluralism, Justice, and Equality*, edited by David Miller and Michael Walzer, 281–97. Oxford: Oxford University Press.

Wedel, Janine R. (1998). *Collision and Collusion: The Strange Case of Western Aid to Eastern Europe, 1989–1998*. Basingstoke: Macmillan.

Wight, Martin. (1966). "Why There Is No International Theory." In *Diplomatic Investigations: Essays in the Theory of International Politics*, edited by Herbert Butterfield and Martin Wight, 17–34. London: Allen and Unwin.

Woods, Ngaire. (2000). "Globalization and International Institutions." In *The Political Economy of Globalization*, edited by Ngaire Woods, 202–23. Basingstoke: Macmillan.

5

GLOBAL DISTRIBUTIVE JUSTICE

WILFRIED HINSCH

Global justice is an intricate subject. At this point, it is by no means clear to me that it allows for straightforward solutions. In any case, I shall not make definite proposals regarding the specific content of principles of global justice. Rather, I will confine myself to some general considerations about the construction of a liberal conception of global distributive justice. More specifically, I will focus on the intersocietal distribution of income and wealth. The Difference Principle will be used to illustrate what a reasonable egalitarian conception of justice in this realm might look like.

I. Moral Federalism

There are two opposed views as to the appropriate domain of principles of distributive justice. On the first view, distributive justice is an exclusively domestic idea, regulating social and economic inequalities within states or societies.[1] Global justice is realized as a conjunction of internally just states that cooperate on the basis of a conception of international justice which includes principles of nonaggression or fidelity to contract and perhaps also a duty of mutual aid, but no principles of distributive justice. John Rawls develops a view of this kind in his *The Law of Peoples* (1999a, henceforth LP).

On the second view, principles of distributive justice apply irrespective of national borders directly and primarily to the global community of world citizens at large, the aim being that each citizen receives his or her due share of global wealth as determined by a global conception of justice. It is admitted, though, that as a matter of practical politics regional or national governments may be instrumental in bringing about a distributively just international order. I take Charles Beitz (1979), Thomas Pogge

---

[1] I shall use "state," "state-like organized people," and "society" interchangeably to refer to a politically independent state with a government of its own. "Society" with a capital letter refers to the global community of state-like organized peoples and its common institutions and principles.

(1989), and Brian Barry (1999), among others, to hold cosmopolitan views of this kind.

Distributive statism and distributive cosmopolitanism implicitly share one basic assumption. It is the idea that at the elementary level of identifying first principles of distributive justice, there can be only one basic domain of application, which, then, is taken to be either the state or the world community. Thus, there seems to be an alternative to both views: a model with a two-tier structure that comprises principles of both domestic and global – or rather intersocietal – distributive justice. In such a model the principles regulating the domestic and the global distribution of wealth, respectively, need not be the same. Moreover, a two-tier structure might allow for a plurality of partly diverging domestic conceptions of justice (not all of which need to be liberal conceptions), provided only that there is a single and unified set of principles regulating intersocietal cooperation. We may dub this idea of global justice *moral federalism*: a plurality of widely independent states internally organized by at least partly diverging conceptions of justice (some of which may be liberal, some of which may not) cooperating on the basis of a common conception of global justice.

I do not want to elaborate on moral federalism in this chapter. My aim is to defend a version of intersocietal egalitarianism against objections Rawls has put forth in LP. Nevertheless, I should like to say a little more about the idea because it provides the background of my argument.

Perhaps the three most important reasons for *political federalism* – for having a plurality of more or less independent states rather than a global world state – are (1) the need to protect against the threat of a tyrannical world government, (2) the exigencies of an efficient provision of local public goods, and (3) the commonsense insight that a piece of land or, indeed, any good or resource, is better taken care of if it is assigned as property (with exclusive or almost exclusive control of its use) to a person or a group of persons rather than to the entirety of mankind. These are, indeed, strong if not overriding reasons for a federal structure of the international order in which state-like organized peoples have sufficient resources and sufficient political independence to be a safeguard of the liberty, security, and well-being of their citizens. Note, however, that these reasons are fully compatible with distributive cosmopolitanism. At least in principle, one can easily imagine an international order of more or less independent states united by contracts and mutual agreements, regulated by principles of global distributive justice that apply directly to the global community of world citizens rather than to states or state-like organized peoples. Political federalism and moral federalism are not the same, and compelling reasons for the first are not by themselves also compelling reasons for the second (cf. Barry 1999).

From a liberal point of view, the main reason for moral federalism is the idea of individual autonomy taken together with the fact of reasonable pluralism. Liberal conceptions of justice assert a fundamental interest of persons to live in accordance with principles that are acceptable in the light of their most deeply held normative commitments. We may call this *positive autonomy*: being able to live as one wants to live (leaving aside for the moment the necessary qualifications as to the rationality and reasonableness of one's ambitions and commitments). Corresponding to the fundamental interest in positive autonomy, liberal theories also assert a prima facie claim of persons not to have norms imposed on them which, upon due reflection, turn out to be unacceptable in the light of their normative conceptions of what is right and what is good. We may call this *negative autonomy*: not to be forced to live in ways contrary to one's more important ambitions and moral or religious commitments (leaving qualifications aside again). Positive autonomy and negative autonomy are not two different things but rather two sides of the same idea of autonomy, which yields the contractualist requirement of (at least hypothetical) reasoned consent for principles of justice (and, indeed, all morally binding norms).

Now, to acknowledge the fact of reasonable pluralism means to recognize that a plurality of diverging conceptions of the good and the right – religious and nonreligious, liberal and nonliberal – may all meet elementary minimum requirements of rationality, practicability, and impartiality. In the contractualist process of identifying first principles of justice for a pluralistic society (be it a domestic society or the global Society of Peoples), these conceptions have to be taken seriously: first, as a source of ideas and principles that eventually may find general approval and, second, as a possible basis for reasonable objections against proposed principles of justice. If a proposed principle proves to be unacceptable in the light of one or more of these sufficiently reasonable conceptions, the principle has to be rejected as a morally binding norm of universal application – or at any rate, this is what we say in ideal theory. This is a consequence of the liberal idea of negative autonomy.

The liberal idea of autonomy and the contractualist requirement of reasoned consent introduce an asymmetry in the process of identifying principles of justice, which comes out starkly in the face of reasonable pluralism. In order to be adopted as a valid principle in a social context (global or domestic) characterized by a profound cultural, religious, and moral pluralism, a principle needs the support of all reasonable conceptions of the good and the right that are involved. In order for a principle to be rejected, on the other hand, one reasonable objection of sufficient weight on the basis of a single moral or religious conception may suffice. Again, this is a consequence of the idea of negative autonomy.

As a rule of thumb, we may say that the more diverse and heterogeneous are the moral and religious doctrines with their own conceptions of the good and the right that a society encompasses, the more difficult will it be to identify principles that are at the same time collectively acceptable and sufficiently specific to have practical meaning. This is not to deny that even in the case of a group as diverse and heterogeneous as the global community of peoples, there are principles of individual liberty, well-being, and tolerance that cannot be reasonably rejected. We assume that moral or religious doctrines have to meet elementary requirements of rationality and impartiality, and, moreover, that they have to acknowledge the fact of reasonable pluralism, in order to provide an appropriate basis for the assessment of principles of justice. Hence, there seems to be at least some common ground given by the constraints of what can be regarded as reasonable criticism and rejection of a proposed principle. Autonomy and reasonable pluralism taken together are by no means incompatible with the assertion of universal basic human rights. They may, however, be incompatible with the idea, cherished by many liberals, that all reasonable conceptions of *domestic* justice have to be comprehensively liberal in the sense of securing the same set of basic rights and liberties that are protected by the constitutions of Western constitutional democracies.

Leaving this aside for the moment, it seems clear that given the globally prevailing cultural, religious, and moral pluralism, principles of international justice have to be fairly sparse and minimalist to be globally consistent with negative autonomy. There is a trade-off, then, between securing the values of negative autonomy and realizing the values of positive autonomy at the same time. The more people with reasonable but incompatible conceptions of the good and the right that are involved, the less able each group of like-minded persons will be to have political and social institutions regulated by principles that fully express their peculiar normative commitments. Vice versa, the more any particular group will be able to express itself in the institutions of a society, the less other groups with contrary commitments will find their negative autonomy adequately protected.

Liberal theorists tend to focus on the value of negative autonomy in solving political conflicts arising from this trade-off, and they do so for good reasons. Most of the time, not being able to constrain others in ways congenial to one's own moral outlook is a lesser evil than being constrained by others in unwanted ways. Still, the value of negative autonomy derives from the value of positive autonomy – why else should we care about not imposing norms on individuals that are contrary to their well-considered normative commitments? – and liberals should care about it. And one way of doing this is to embrace the idea of moral federalism.

In a situation of profound moral and religious pluralism, the universal realization of the values of positive and of negative autonomy becomes a problem of local public good provision. We do not need to entertain communitarian fantasies of culturally and normatively perfectly homogeneous political societies in order to realize that in political units smaller than the global community it will be easier to find a reasoned consensus on more specific principles of justice[2] (and also on other principles) than

---

[2] The phrase "more specific principles" in this context is taken comparatively to refer to principles that impose more constraints on individual freedom of choice than others.

on a global scale. This will be even more likely if we take these units to be historically evolved state-like organized peoples with a political history and common local traditions shared by all, or almost all, of their members. As a consequence, a system of state-like organized peoples internally regulated by domestic conceptions of justice of their own would be able to realize locally a degree of positive autonomy (without infringing on the negative autonomy of other peoples) that no system with only global principles of justice could possibly achieve. From a liberal point of view, this seems to be a strong reason for embracing moral federalism as a model of global justice.[3] Now, let us turn to the more specific problems of distributive justice concerning the appropriate distribution of global wealth.

II. The Pull toward Global Distributive Equality

In the broad Rawlsian sense, income and wealth are all-purpose means that have instrumental value for individuals irrespective of their more comprehensive conceptions of life in all sorts of social environments. Wherever we look, the distribution of income within societies and the distribution of wealth among societies seem to be sources of public controversy and political conflict. This suggests that the reasoning in favor of moral federalism and tolerance toward views that are not comprehensively liberal – a reasoning outlined in the last section – may not apply with equal force and generality in the field of distributive justice. To be sure, we can hardly expect nonliberal societies to endorse egalitarian liberal principles (e.g., the Difference Principle) as guidelines of domestic social justice. The justifications given for egalitarian principles typically hinge upon the assumption that all members of society have as equal citizens prima facie equal claims to share the fruits of social cooperation. Needless to say, this assumption seems unacceptable from many nonliberal points of view. Given reasonable pluralism and the principle of autonomy, a liberal conception of global justice has to allow for a plurality of mutually incompatible principles of domestic social justice.

Things look different, however, when we turn to distributive justice not within societies, but among societies conceived of as participants in a system with an international division of labor. Intersocietal cooperation on the basis of mutually acceptable rules is cooperation among state-like

---

[3] Keep in mind that the pluralism of domestic conceptions of justice is to be conceived of as a constrained pluralism. It is assumed that all conceptions involved satisfy certain general criteria of domestic justice (e.g., a guarantee of basic human rights) and that they are not incompatible with principles of global justice that regulate intersocietal cooperation. Of course, the general requirements of justice applying to all domestic societies can be worked out along different lines. Rawls's conception of decency (LP 64ff.) may be interpreted in this way even though Rawls himself clearly distinguishes between decency and justice. He also would not admit that a decent but nonliberal society could be fully just (LP 83f.).

organized peoples that invariably claim to be recognized as equals. In the light of each people's vital interests in its independence, security, and territorial integrity, and given the importance to a people and its citizens of being respected by other peoples on a basis of fair equality, it would simply be unreasonable to expect the representatives of any people to accept voluntarily a less-than-equal status in a league of nations. On the basis of their shared comprehensive doctrines, perhaps, the members of nonliberal societies may hold different views as regards the nature of domestic social cooperation. In particular, they may see it for religious or other reasons as, at least in some respect, a form of cooperation among unequals. Thus, they may accord a less-than-equal status to women in the sphere of political decision making, as is the case in many Islamic countries. Yet in the absence of any globally shared nonegalitarian comprehensive doctrine like Islam, no people can reasonably expect other peoples who are willing to cooperate fairly to accept anything but an equal status in the envisaged scheme of intersocietal cooperation. Therefore, when the terms of global cooperation are specified, the interests and claims of the peoples involved have to be given equal weight and consideration whenever their capacity for self-determined political decision making, their security and territorial integrity, and, more generally, the fundamental well-being of their citizens are affected.[4]

Given this much, it may, indeed, seem hard not to end up with a conception of global distributive justice that is, at least in spirit, egalitarian. A little imagination suffices to see how a familiar set of liberal arguments supporting egalitarian principles would come to do its work once the basic assumption has been established that the actors in a global community of political societies – that is, state-like organized peoples – stand in a relation of basic equality and have equal claims and rights. Given economic cooperation among societies sufficiently dense to raise questions of distributive justice, all peoples involved, in virtue of their equal standing as participants in a system of international production and exchange, prima facie have equal claims to share the fruits of their joint cooperative efforts. This establishes a presumption in favor of equality: in the absence of special reasons to accept an unequal distribution, global wealth has to be distributed equally among all peoples involved in the scheme of international cooperation.[5]

---

[4] In *The Law of Peoples* Rawls stresses the importance to a people of being recognized by other peoples as an equal partner in international cooperation (34f., 37, 40f., 60ff., 69f., 122).

[5] This is not to say that all liberal theories proceed on the basis of this presumption or that all liberal theorists, implicitly or explicitly, endorse it. Thomas Scanlon (1996), for one, is clearly skeptical about a merely formal notion of equal consideration: "taken by itself it is too abstract to exercise much force in the direction of substantive equality" (1). Moreover, in his view the claim that participants in a cooperative scheme have equal claims to the fruits of cooperation is too controversial to take it "as *the starting point* of a particular conception of justice" (9). Still, he acknowledges that the presumption plays a major role in egalitarian theories and analyzes with some care its place in Rawls's conception of justice as fairness (cf. 7–9).

Inequalities of social wealth, then, turn out to be in need of justification – globally not less than domestically – which must be given in terms of reasons that all parties can be reasonably expected to accept. Paradigmatically, they are either desert-type reasons of superior productivity or prudential reasons of mutual advantage, but we also have, as we shall see later, to take into account differential claims of need. In any case, we must avoid allowing factors that are arbitrary from a moral point of view to influence the distribution of wealth among societies. Since a good many of the existing inequalities of wealth among societies are neither mutually advantageous nor the result of meritorious superior productivity, the presumption in favor of equality will lead us to an egalitarian redistribution of much existing global wealth. We could even strengthen this line of argument by taking up Rawls's radical critique of desert-based claims for more than an equal share of income or wealth, found in his *A Theory of Justice* (Rawls 1999b [henceforth TJ], 88f., 273–277). If there are no valid claims of desert to be taken into account (leaving differential claims of need aside for the moment), only mutual advantage seems capable of justifying economic inequalities. And this, in turn, will lead us straightaway to the Difference Principle (cf. Hinsch forthcoming, Chap. 9).

Of course, the preceding paragraph does not show that an adequate conception of intersocietal distributive justice has to be an egalitarian conception. Indeed, it is not meant to provide a sustained argument. Rather, it sketches a line of reasoning that could be worked out in various ways, for instance (if you still believe in decision-theoretical models), in setting up a global "original position" with representatives of peoples as symmetrically situated parties to a global social contract. Still, I hope that the preceding paragraph helped to explain why liberals should find it difficult to get around an egalitarian conception of global distributive justice.

I take it, then, that a just global order will be a Society of Peoples organized in different state-like political societies. Internally these societies will be regulated by different principles of domestic political and social justice, some of which are egalitarian and some of which are nonegalitarian. Externally, however, there would be a place for a global application of the Difference Principle. As a condition of international background justice, it could regulate the global distribution of wealth among societies. In this case a just global distribution of wealth would maximize the wealth of the economically least privileged society in the global Society.[6]

---

[6] There is the question of how to identify the least-privileged people, which I shall not pursue. It could be done in various ways, for example, by means of an index of aggregate or average social wealth or by comparing the various indices of the wealth of the least-privileged groups in all domestic societies involved. The latter seems to be more in line with the Rawlsian spirit of the Difference Principle – that is, to judge collective economic achievements always from the point of view of the least privileged. We have to keep in mind, however, that not all societies will accept the Difference Principle as a standard of domestic justice, and that they may also reject a focus on the economic prospects of least-privileged groups in making international comparisons of wealth.

Constructed in this way, a global difference principle would operate analogously to a domestic principle of background justice. In the case of domestic justice, the Difference Principle regulates the distribution of social wealth by political institutions, but it does not extend to all distributive decisions of particular groups, communities, and organizations (churches, universities, families) within the political society (cf. Rawls 1978, sect. 2, 48–50).

III. Distributive Justice or Mutual Aid

Rawls famously denies that the Difference Principle, which he endorses as a principle of domestic liberal justice, should be applied on a global scale. In *The Law of Peoples* he replaces it by a nonegalitarian principle of mutual aid. In his view, well-ordered societies have a duty to assist burdened societies in their attempt to become well ordered, but he denies that they are also required to transfer wealth to less advantaged societies in order to satisfy egalitarian principles of distributive justice, the demands of which go beyond what is necessary to a global society of internally well ordered societies (LP 106).

A burdened society is a society that is not effectively regulated by a public conception of justice (be it liberal or nonliberal), because of a lack of resources (traditions, institutions, human capital, technology) that could in some way or other be compensated by the efforts of more resourceful and already well ordered societies. That there is such a duty of assistance, though certainly not obvious, is not a claim that should cause much controversy. A sufficient degree of well-orderedness is a prerequisite of justice. And since we owe justice to each other regardless of national affiliations and existing institutional ties, we must be under some kind of duty to contribute to the well-orderedness not only of our own society, but also of other societies. Moreover, in the light of what I have said in Section 1 about the implications of reasonable pluralism, we may expect the duty of assistance to hold good not only for burdened societies drawn to liberal well-orderedness, but to all decent societies with an allegiance to nonliberal but reasonable conceptions of the good and the right.

The principle of mutual aid would then seem to be something analogous to a "natural duty" in the sense in which Rawls uses this term in *A Theory of Justice* (97–99). More specifically, the principle may be seen as an extension and further specification of the natural duty of individuals "to support and to further just institutions" (TJ 293).[7] Unlike obligations, natural duties apply regardless of the voluntary actions of individuals and

---

[7] Cf. TJ 97–99, 293f., 297f. Alyssa Bernstein interprets Rawls's principle of mutual aid in this way (cf. Bernstein 2000, 178–82). I find Bernstein's interpretation suggestive, though it is not without complications. One should also wonder why Rawls himself did not even mention the concept of natural duty when drawing the line between the duty of assistance and the Difference Principle in LP.

irrespective of institutional ties between them. Unlike institutional principles (such as the Difference Principle), they regulate the actions of individuals rather than the workings of collective agents and institutions. To be sure, literally speaking, the duty of assistance to burdened societies cannot be a "natural duty" in the Rawlsian sense. The term "natural" in connection with rights or duties suggests among other things that the norms in question apply directly to natural individuals in virtue of their being *moral persons*, that is, human beings that have some natural properties in common (e.g., certain cognitive and motivational capacities and dispositions). And sure enough, institutionally structured collective agents like societies, states, or peoples are not the kind of entities that share natural properties with human beings. Still, there are two features of the intersocietal principle of mutual aid that suggest that it may be analyzed along the lines of the concept of natural duty. First, though peoples are institutionally organized collective agents, from the viewpoint of international cooperation within the global community they may be seen – and as a matter of international law they are seen – as individual agents with specific rights and duties. At any rate, that is the Rawlsian view (LP 23). The duty of assistance may then be said to apply to the individual agents of international cooperation. Second, following Rawls's account, the duty of assistance to burdened societies obtains without regard to the existence of cooperative relationships between the peoples involved that is, it obtains even in the absence of an international institutional basic structure.[8]

Besides the conceptual difference between natural duties and distributive principles of background justice, there are other structural dissimilarities between the principle of mutual aid and the Difference Principle which are relevant for the assessment of Rawls's argument as to why the one, unlike the other, is not a valid principle of global justice – is not part of the Law of Peoples. "Give to those who are in need of help!" and "Give to the least privileged!" in practice often amount to pretty much the same. As a matter of ethical theory, however, it is essential that the two precepts are worlds apart. The differences I have in mind are partly reflected in the three guidelines for the fulfillment of the duty of assistance stated in LP (106–12), and Rawls is certainly right in maintaining that to endorse this duty does not yet commit oneself to an egalitarian principle of distributive justice.

First, the duty of assistance is a value-based norm in a way that the Difference Principle is not. The duty of assistance involves a notion of *publicly recognized want* that gives rise to specific claims of need, which are alien to the Difference Principle and its justification. Indeed, the application of this principle presupposes either the absence or the adequate satisfaction of all valid claims of need. A person is in a situation of publicly recognized want if she needs certain goods (food, clothes, shelter, a well-ordered society) to realize a specific value (health, protection, self-respect) that, from a moral point of

---

[8] This point will be taken up in section IV below.

view, is of high importance and if she is not able to provide these goods for herself. Not to meet the legitimate claims of need of a person is a moral wrong – and a breach of duty – exactly because of the high importance the values in question have for the life of this person. And to acknowledge such a duty in a particular situation means to acknowledge that what is at stake is a value that, from a moral point of view, has high priority and urgency.

Transfers meant to maximize the income or wealth of the least-privileged members of a society (be it of individuals or of peoples), on the other hand, are not morally required to satisfy specific claims of need related to particular substantive values. In an affluent society, the Difference Principle would have us maximize the economic prospects of the least privileged, even though the members of this group may not be in a state of publicly recognized want. Individuals (or groups of individuals) cannot claim these transfers as necessary to realize specific important goods or values. The Difference Principle requires transfers on purely egalitarian grounds. Indeed, as long as there are differential claims of need (some need expensive medical treatment that others can do without), these have to be met before we may properly distribute goods in accordance with the Difference Principle. This principle presupposes equal claims on all sides, and sure enough, those who are in a situation of publicly recognized want have stronger claims than those who are not. What justifies the application of the Difference Principle is the very absence of differential moral claims (like differential claims of need or desert) for more than an equal share of goods, and the underlying idea is that among parties with equal claims, only mutual advantage can publicly justify economic inequalities. Transfers required by the Difference Principle are, then, simply necessary to eliminate inequalities of income or wealth that, if we take equality as a baseline, do not meet the reciprocity criterion of mutual advantage and thus would not be capable of being publicly justified. There is no question of whether or not people need these transfers to realize something that has high importance independently from the reasoning behind the Difference Principle, as in the case of transfers required by the duty of assistance.

Second, the duty of mutual assistance is a threshold norm, whereas the Difference Principle is a maximizing norm, notwithstanding the fact that the conception of publicly recognized want is a partly relational conception. Some goods we need because other members of our group have them, and some of these goods are, from a moral point of view, so important that a person who is not capable of providing herself with them has a valid claim of need on others who could help her. Dress codes illustrate the point in question. You may need a black suit to go to the burial of your great-uncle in order not to offend the other family members and to be regarded by them as a respectable relative.[9] Now, dress codes are conventional, and

---

[9] In the commentaries to the German *Sozialhilfegesetz* and in the practice of German courts, black suits are explicitly mentioned as goods that a male person needs to attend a

part of the reason why a person needs a black suit for a burial is simply that others wear them on such occasions. Being able to keep up with others is important for us as social beings, and for that reason, some inequalities give rise to valid claims of need and impose duties of assistance.

There is, however, still an important difference between eliminating existing inequalities in order to satisfy claims of need, and eliminating them in order to conform with an egalitarian principle of justice like the Difference Principle. In the first case the aim is not to eliminate the existing inequality as such, but only insofar as and to the extent to which its persistence would impose morally unacceptable burdens on somebody. The good to be realized through the help of others is not equality, but something else – in this case, the self-respect of the person who has to attend the burial and does not have the means to buy suitable clothes. Since the value of equality in these cases of need is only instrumental, there is no question of maximizing equality as such. Instead, the degree of equality aimed at is determined by what is necessary to realize the morally relevant background value (in our case, self-respect), and normally, less-than-full equality is necessary to realize this value up to the point beyond which there is no longer any moral claim of need that is to be publicly recognized. Thus, in our example there is a sound claim of need to be decently dressed for the burial, but there is no claim to be dressed exactly as nicely and as expensively as perhaps the other family members are. Hence, even in those cases in which claims of need require the provision of relational goods – like the good of being adequately dressed – in order to realize certain moral values, there is a threshold above which no further equalization is required in order to fulfill our duties of mutual aid.

Even though the Difference Principle likewise does not presuppose that we ascribe intrinsic value to equality as such, it does not operate in such a threshold fashion. As I have already said, the reason why transfers of income and wealth to the least privileged are required is not to enable them to realize specific values like health or self-respect, the realization of which empirically presupposes these transfers. What we are supposed to do is to minimize unjustified inequalities as such, or, more precisely, to minimize those inequalities that cannot be justified either in terms of differential moral claims (of need or desert) or in terms of mutual advantage for all parties involved. In a situation of equal claims on all sides, this turns out to be equivalent to maximizing the economic advantages of the least-privileged (cf. Hinsch forthcoming, Chap. 9).

Third, the claims of need underlying our duty of mutual assistance vary in kind and strength depending on the specific circumstances of those who must rely on our help. Some need clothes, others medical help; some need help very badly or urgently, others not. Given that people in publicly recognized situations of want typically have different needs of varying strength depending on their personal preferences, capacities, and circumstances, claims of need are typically differential claims. Hence, they are potential reasons to justify unequal distributions of goods or resources. The claims presupposed by the argument for the Difference Principle, on the other hand, are equal claims, and they are of a much more abstract character. At the most basic level we start out with equal claims of persons to live in accordance with principles and rules they can reasonably accept in the light of their fundamental interests and well-considered beliefs. As we proceed to the justification of principles of distributive justice, we make the assumption that prima facie nobody can reasonably claim more than an equal share of the goods to be distributed. The argument for the Difference Principle, given, for instance, by Rawls, relies on "equality as a baseline" and can do so only on the assumption that there are no longer any differential moral claims of need or desert to be taken into account.[10] As long as there are claims of that kind to be taken into account, they have to be satisfied before we can proceed to distribute goods in accordance with the Difference Principle.

Now, given these structural differences between the duty of assistance and the Difference Principle, and given their clearly distinct ranges of application in terms of the moral claims they are responsive to, the real question is not whether we replace the duty of assistance by the Difference Principle, or, as Rawls does, the Difference Principle by the duty of mutual aid.[11] Rather, it is whether our duties of mutual aid cover the whole ground of global distributive justice (claims of desert left aside for the moment), or whether they have to be complemented by a maximizing egalitarian principle like the Difference Principle, the application of which is not confined to publicly recognized situations of want.

IV. Rawls's Objections to a Global Difference Principle

In *The Law of Peoples* Rawls produces various reasons why he believes that the Difference Principle should not be applied on a global level and that it should be replaced by a more restricted and nonegalitarian duty of assistance to burdened societies. There seem to be two main arguments that carry the burden of proof. I call them the realistic-utopia argument and the collective-responsibility argument.

The realistic-utopia argument is nowhere in the book stated explicitly, but it is implicit in what Rawls says about the duty of assistance and affinity (LP §15.5). Global redistribution in conformity with the Difference

---

burial of a family member or close friend. A person without the money to buy such a suit on his own is in a publicly recognized situation of want and has a valid claim of need which in Germany gives him a right to social assistance that courts do enforce (cf. Birk et al. 1994, commentary to §21, 266–304).

[10] A point that has not always been sufficiently appreciated. See, however, Strasnick (1976, 88) and Nozick (1973, 94).

[11] In any case, a defense of the Difference Principle presupposes a fairly articulated conception of the adequate satisfaction of differential claims of need, a point Arrow (1973) has stressed early on in his criticism of Rawls's theory.

Principle, the argument says, cannot be part of a realistic utopia, because the moral psychology of normal human beings, as we know it, would not allow development of a sense of international justice strong enough to support a scheme of global redistribution that maximizes the collective wealth of the least-advantaged people. One reason to be skeptical in this regard is the low visibility of international institutions and the diffusion of their impact on the daily life of ordinary citizens. As a consequence, a worldwide sense of fellowship is widely lacking, and emotional ties between distant peoples on the globe are weak. Given this background, it may indeed seem dubious whether an effective and stable sense of international justice could possibly develop. Moreover, from a historical point of view, only the nation-state has yet proven to be capable of effecting large-scale redistribution to mitigate the various burdens of social and economic inequalities for its less privileged citizens on a regular basis – not to speak about far reaching egalitarian programs.

In my view the realistic-utopia argument is sound, and I agree that psychological principles set "limits to what can sensibly be proposed as the content of the Law of Peoples" (LP 112, n. 44). Still, the argument is of limited strength. Our identification with global institutions will become stronger as international cooperation and communication increase, which in turn will gradually strengthen our emotional ties with peoples in other parts of the world – a point Rawls himself stresses in support of his duty of mutual aid: "The relatively narrow circle of mutually caring peoples in the world may expand over time and must never be viewed as fixed" (LP 113). Aiming too short, then, may be as much a mistake as aiming too far. Moreover, to claim that the Difference Principle is an adequate principle of global distributive justice in a philosophical discourse is not the same as to claim, as a matter of practical politics, that we should try to establish it here and now. The latter would be foolish, while the former may be right. I shall not further discuss the realistic-utopia argument, taking it as a serious reminder not to fall victim to romanticism in political practice.[12]

The collective-responsibility argument against global application of the Difference Principle, though not without intuitive plausibility when taken by itself, is in various ways puzzling. It is subject to strong and more or less obvious objections, and it seems plainly inconsistent with many things Rawls said in *A Theory of Justice* and elsewhere about the narrow limits of desert-based arguments in identifying principles of distributive justice.

Rawls develops the argument in order to explain why he does not follow Charles Beitz's approach to international justice (LP §16.2). In a first step, he rejects Beitz's "resource redistribution principle." Relying on David Landes's study *The Wealth and Poverty of Nations* (1998), Rawls

---

[12] For an early discussion and more elaborated statement of what I have called the realistic-utopia argument, see Charles Beitz (1979, 155–58).

argues that since "the crucial element in how a country fares is its political culture – its members' political and civic virtues – and not the level of its resources, the arbitrariness of the distribution of natural resources causes no difficulty" (LP 117). Rawls claims that every people is (independently from the natural riches of its country) in principle capable of realizing a well-ordered society, with the exception, perhaps, of the Arctic Eskimos and other peoples in similar situations (cf. LP 108f. together with n. 34). In the second step of the argument, Rawls rejects Beitz's global principle of distributive justice. Following his argument, in a hypothetical world in which all duties of assistance among societies have been fully satisfied, Beitz's principle would lead to unacceptable results.

To substantiate this claim Rawls produces two examples, both of which involve the notion of a people's collective responsibility for its economic wealth. In both examples we have two well-ordered societies with the same population size that are initially at the same level of wealth. Then, in the two societies, different collective decisions are taken that lead to different levels of wealth in each of them. In the first example, one people decides to industrialize and to increase its rate of real saving, while the other does not ("preferring a more pastoral and leisurely society" [LP 117]). Some decades later, the first people is twice as wealthy as the second. Since we assume that both societies are already well ordered, the duty of mutual assistance does not apply, – that is, no transfer of funds is required to satisfy valid claims of need. Employing the Difference Principle, however, would, in the absence of incentive effects, lead to an egalitarian redistribution of funds until both societies are at equal levels of wealth. And this seems unacceptable.

In the second example, one society stresses fair equality of opportunity for women, who then begin to flourish in the political and economic world. As a consequence, the society gradually reaches, zero population growth, which in turn gradually increases the level of wealth in that society. The other, though also granting elements of equal justice to women (as is necessary to its being well ordered), does not pursue a policy of fair equality for women because of its prevailing religious and social values, which, we suppose, are freely accepted not only by men, but also by women. As a consequence, the rate of population growth in this society remains rather high, and gross national product per capita remains low. Again the duty of assistance *ex hypothesi* does not apply, and an egalitarian redistribution of wealth in accordance with the Difference Principle seems unacceptable, once we assume that population growth in the second country is voluntary, as suggested by the given description of the example.

There is no point in denying that both examples are intuitively suggestive. Still, they do not provide a reliable basis for a sound argument against a global application of the Difference Principle or similar egalitarian precepts. Typically, intuitive responses to hypothetical or real-life examples can be explained in various ways, and Rawls's interpretation of our reactions to the case at hand – namely, a global difference principle would yield unacceptable results – may not be the best one.

As they are stated, the two examples clearly do not illustrate cases of social cooperation among societies. They look very much like the two-island sort of examples that some critics have produced in order to discredit egalitarian conceptions of domestic justice. There is no joint production of commodities involved and not even an exchange of goods or resources across borders. Moreover, there is no unified scheme of international cooperation embracing the two peoples, with public rules effectively regulating their mutual affairs. At least, nothing of this kind is mentioned. It looks as if there were two separate peoples living on islands thousands of miles apart with no externalities whatsoever between them to be taken into account. *In this case*, it may indeed be wrong to apply the Difference Principle or any other egalitarian principle effecting redistributions with unilateral net benefits. Given the circumstances of the two examples, the principle simply does not seem to apply. The justification of the Difference Principle, as well as its practical employment, implicitly presupposes (1) that there are positive and negative externalities between individuals and groups of individuals, (2) that we have a unified scheme of cooperation, and (3) that the parties involved (be they individuals or societies) conceive of each other as partners with prima facie equal claims to share the fruits of cooperation. Since none of these conditions seems to be met in Rawls's examples, our intuitive responses are not very telling as regards the acceptability of a global difference principle in a world like ours, with an abundance of positive and negative intersocietal externalities and ever increasing international economic cooperation.

One might argue that the setup of the two examples chosen by Rawls deliberately reflects the idea that the principles of the Law of Peoples specify requirements of "natural duty" rather than demands of global economic distributive justice.[13] Indeed, the very fact that Rawls modeled the two examples in the way he did strongly supports the view that he presents the principles of the Law of Peoples as principles analogous to principles of natural duty. However, following this line of thought, there seems to be a problem of relevance regarding the two examples. It is uncontroversial that a global difference principle cannot be a principle of "natural duty" and certainly does not need to be established by two more or less fictitious examples. If we take it for granted, on the other hand, that the Difference Principle is a principle of distributive background justice, it seems obvious that the two examples, as they stand, do not provide us with adequate material to scrutinize the intuitive plausibility of this principle.

Of course, this problem can be taken care of. Rawls's counterexamples

---

[13] I am grateful to Alyssa Bernstein for making me aware of this interpretation. See note 7 above.

can be easily elaborated along the lines indicated so as to provide appropriate conditions for the application of the Difference Principle. Let us, then,
assume that there is political and economic cooperation between the two
societies on the basis of mutually agreed upon rules, and that the flow of
resources, goods, and services between them is sufficiently dense to give
at least prima facie plausibility to the idea of adopting an intersocietal principle of distributive background justice. Still, we assume that both countries are politically sufficiently autonomous to make different collective
decisions regarding economic and social policies that affect their respective future social productivities in the ways described by Rawls. May we,
under these circumstances, reasonably expect the representatives of the
two societies involved to adopt a global difference principle?

It may still be difficult to give a definite answer to this question because
we may still know too little about the normative beliefs of the members of
both societies. However, let us, for the sake of argument, assume that in both
societies the Difference Principle is adopted to regulate the domestic distribution of income and wealth. And let us further assume that, more generally,
the members of both societies endorse the following principle of reciprocity:
unless there are special claims of need or desert, inequalities of wealth can
be justified only if they are to the mutual advantage of all parties involved.
This being said, our question is whether people who accept the Difference
Principle and its underlying rationale in matters of domestic justice can
reasonably reject it as a principle of international justice, once there is a
sufficiently dense system of international economic cooperation.

A global difference principle strikes Rawls as unacceptable, because in
the two cases at hand the inequality of social wealth exists only because
of conscientious and reasonable collective decisions and efforts in one
country that could have been effected in the other country as well. There
seems to be a justified moral claim of desert on the side of those who
acted in more productive ways to get more than an equal share of the joint
social product[14] (keep in mind that, unlike Rawls in his setup of the two
examples, we assume intersocietal economic cooperation).

Now, obviously, we have to take into account the incentive effects that
in a public system of domestic or international justice go with the
Difference Principle, and we also have to consider the possibility of Pareto
improvements. Given realistic background assumptions about productivity
and motivation, applying the Difference Principle would still reward superior social productivity with superior social wealth, provided only that the
less productive partner also receives an additional share. Hence, differential collective wealth would not be reduced to zero, and a global difference

---

[14] Note that the claims of desert involved here are not *entitlements* but noninstitutional
moral claims based on a notion of individual or collective merit. They do not presuppose the
existence of established social rules or practices. The notion of moral and noninstitutional
desert is explained in Feinberg (1970, 56, 85–87); Kleinig (1971, 71); and Miller (1976, 91f.).

principle would be consistent with different levels of wealth among societies. In this regard, there is no difference between applying the principle on the domestic level and applying it on the international level. Once this is accepted, it is easy to see why Rawls's two counterexamples derive their intuitive plausibility from a misconception of the nature of productivity-based claims of desert.

Productivity-based claims of desert are intrinsically relational. In a situation of strictly equal capacities and opportunities, an agent (be it an individual or a group) who, in a joint scheme of production, is more productive than another may be said to deserve a higher reward than his or her less productive partner. In order to honor justified claims of desert, we have to set up a ranking of the productive contributions of all agents who are involved in a given scheme of cooperation and then reward them, in accordance with this ranking, with smaller or larger shares of the total product of their joint activities. This, however, does not mean that any participant has a desert-based claim to receive a particular share, or rather, to receive a share with a specific absolute value. Indeed, given a fixed total product, an indefinite number of classes of individual shares will normally be ordinally consistent with the relative strengths of the agent's productivity-based claims of desert. As a consequence, applying the Difference Principle under realistic conditions is not incompatible with honoring productivity-based claims of desert, as long as those who are more productive end up with a higher share of goods than those who are less productive. And given the economy of incentives, this will normally be the case in international cooperation no less than in domestic cooperation.

All we have to do in order to uphold a global difference principle in the presence of legitimate collective claims of desert is to deny that more-productive societies may legitimately claim not to be taxed for redistributive purposes at all, because they properly deserve the full marginal benefit of their superior social productivity. To hold that they can legitimately claim that, however, would imply a serious misunderstanding of the nature of productivity-based claims of desert. In a situation of sufficiently dense economic cooperation, no single agent can reasonably claim his full marginal product, and no society can claim its full domestic product, as the only appropriate reward for his or its meritorious productivity, simply because (among other reasons) the value of this product is largely determined by economic factors beyond the agent's control. Thus, in our examples, it depends on aggregate demand and supply of resources and commodities in the two societies, on the terms of trade between them, and on domestic and international traditions, practices, institutions, and the like, which in one way or other may be undeservedly more favorable to one society than to the other.

To conclude: even though in both cases the more productive people may have a collective claim of desert to end up with greater wealth than the other, the more productive group cannot reasonably claim its full domestic product. And since a global difference principle will normally reward superior productivity of peoples with superior economic rewards, it cannot be rejected on the basis that it is incompatible with honoring just collective deserts.

V. Justice between Generations

There is one final comment that I want to make with regard to the second of Rawls's two counterexamples. It clearly involves a problem of inter-generational justice worthy of attention – a problem which is merely implicit in the first one. The society that – due to its high rate of popula-tion growth – ends up less wealthy than the other may be seen as deserv-ing a lower level of social wealth. *Ex hypothesi*, it freely chooses (in the light of sincerely and not unreasonably held religious views of its members) not to pursue policies of fair equality of opportunity for women. It may, indeed, seem reasonable if those who voluntarily choose not to pursue policies of equal opportunity that would increase their collective wealth are held responsible for their decisions and if a claim on their side to receive egalitarian transfers is denied. There is, however, a serious problem with doing this, which Rawls does not discuss, even though in his earlier writings he is acutely aware of it (TJ 63ff.; cf. Scanlon 1996, 8f.): end-states of one period of economic activity (in our case the levels of wealth attained by the two peoples after "some decades") are at the same time starting conditions of the next period. As a matter of distributive justice, therefore, a given distribution of wealth has not only to be acceptable as a set of possibly deserved results of what has happened in the past, but also as a starting condition for what will happen in the future. Otherwise, future transactions and their prospective results will not meet the requirement of procedural justice of fairly equal-ized starting conditions.

As long as we are talking about the same group of people acting contin-uously over time, there still may be no problem. If we can reasonably hold them responsible for their past decisions, they may deserve a lower level of wealth, not only as an end-state of one period of activity, but also as a starting condition for the next period. This simple model of an agent's responsibility, however, collapses once we have a change in the group of actors, as is the case in our example involving population growth. Once we have more than one generation, the end-states of one period – possibly deserved by the generation responsible for decisions in that period – will be starting conditions for another generation of people, who have not been active in the first period and thus cannot necessarily be held responsible later on for decisions taken in that period.[15] As a matter of intergenerational

---

[15] The disclaiming qualification in "cannot *necessarily* be held responsible" is meant to avoid too narrow an interpretation of individual responsibility for collective decisions in this

justice, a comparatively low level of wealth may appear (in the light of just deserts) fair to one generation, and still be clearly unfair to the next. Given the overlap of generations (children grow up with their parents or, at least, during the lifetime of their parents' generation, drawing on this generation's funds), there may be no way to treat children fairly other than by giving their parents more than they supposedly deserve. Whether fairness to children (in terms of fair starting conditions) in a global scenario actually requires an egalitarian distribution of resources conforming to a global difference principle is an open question, but it clearly requires more than giving them what their parents deserve, because the parents took political decisions with which the children themselves may not be willing to identify with later on.

VI. Conclusion

I take it – though I have not argued for it – that a scheme of global social justice appropriate from a liberal point of view will have a two-tier structure, distinguishing between domestic and global justice. There will be a plurality of reasonable principles of domestic justice, some of which are egalitarian and some of which are not. Still, there will be an overarching global principle – or a set of such principles – regulating the intersocietal distribution of global wealth. In my view, this most likely will be an egalitarian principle, and a global difference principle strikes me as a strong candidate. In any case, a "duty of assistance" to burdened societies, though not to be denied, by no means covers the ground of distributive global justice. Given the kind of arguments that, from a liberal point of view, support egalitarian principles of domestic social justice, any attempt to deny the appropriateness of an egalitarian conception of global justice is bound to backfire domestically, in some way or other. In particular, desert-based arguments, like those employed by Rawls in *The Law of Peoples*, prove to be incapable of undermining principles of global egalitarianism as long as these principles allow for different levels of social wealth which – though not for desert-based moral reasons – respond to differences in the social productivity of peoples. These arguments seem to involve a misconception of the relational character of valid claims of desert. Moreover, they

context. In my view, under certain conditions a person may reasonably be held responsible for a collective decision – in the sense of having no claim to be compensated for unwelcome consequences of that decision – even though she was not personally involved in the decision-making process. If she accepts the normative authority of the decision-making body and if she also endorses the reasons for the decision upon due reflection, this would make it seem at least not unreasonable to deny her compensation for unwelcome consequences. If the children of the religiously inspired nonegalitarians in our example turned out to be true believers in their parents' creed, they certainly would not have a claim on other peoples to compensate them for the detrimental economic consequences of their nonegalitarian normative beliefs.

employ dubious notions of responsible agency, implying, for example, that children may be held responsible for decisions of their ancestors with which they may no longer want to be identified, merely because they belong to the same people.

Acknowledgments

This chapter owes much to the ideas and comments of Alyssa Bernstein, who read two earlier versions of it and with whom I had an illuminating exchange about the issues discussed in the text. Moreover, I am greatly indebted to her for kindly correcting my English. I am also grateful for helpful comments by Peter de Marneffe, Thomas Pogge, and Markus Stepanians.

References

Arrow, Kenneth. (1973). "Some Ordinalist-Utilitarian Notes on Rawls' Theory of Justice." *Journal of Philosophy*, 70, 245–63.

Barry, Brian. (1999). "Statism and Nationalism: A Cosmopolitan Critique." In *Global Justice*, edited by Ian Shapiro and Lea Brilmayer, 12–66. *Nomos* 41. New York: New York University Press.

Beitz, Charles. (1979). *Political Theory and International Relations*. Princeton, N.J.: Princeton University Press. Second edition published 1999.

Bernstein, Alyssa. (2000). "Human Rights Reconceived: A Defense of Rawls' Law of Peoples." Ph.D. diss., Harvard University.

Birk, Ulrich-A., et al. (1994). *Bundessozialhilfegesetz: Lehr- und Praxiskommentar*. Baden-Baden: Nomos.

Feinberg, Joel. (1970). *Doing and Deserving*. Princeton, N.J.: Princeton University Press.

Hinsch, Wilfried. (Forthcoming). *Gerechtfertigte Ungleichheiten*. Berlin: de Gruyter.

Kleinig, John. (1971). "The Concept of Desert." *American Philosophical Quarterly*, 8, 71–78.

Landes, David. (1998). *The Wealth and Poverty of Nations*. New York: W. W. Norton.

Miller, David. (1976). *Social Justice*. Oxford: Clarendon Press.

Nozick, Robert. (1973). "Distributive Justice." *Philosophy and Public Affairs*, 3, 45–126.

Pogge, Thomas. (1989). *Realizing Rawls*. Ithaca, N.Y.: Cornell University Press.

Rawls, John. (1978). "The Basic Structure as Subject." In *Values and Morals*, edited by Alvin Goldman and Jaegwon Kim, 47–71. Boston: Reidel Publishing.

———. (1999a). *The Law of Peoples*. Cambridge, Mass.: Harvard University Press.

————. (1999b). *A Theory of Justice*. 2nd ed. Cambridge, Mass.: Harvard University Press. First edition published 1971.

Scanlon, Thomas. (1996). "The Diversity of Objections to Inequality." The Lindlay Lecture. Lawrence: University of Kansas.

Strasnick, Stephen. (1976). "Social Choice and the Derivation of Rawls's Difference Principle." *Journal of Philosophy*, 73, 85–99.

6

CONTRACTUALISM AND GLOBAL ECONOMIC JUSTICE

LEIF WENAR

The statistics on global poverty and inequality are so dramatic that theories which ask little of us and our institutions risk the charge of complacency in the face of obvious injustice. Here I focus on John Rawls's and T. M. Scanlon's contractualist theories, and the surprisingly undemanding principles that – it is claimed – each yields. In each case, I argue that the theories may require more of us than the theorists believe. My aim is to indicate work that needs to be done concerning what morality demands of our personal resources, and concerning what global institutions we should support, by those who find these contractualist theories compelling.

I. Contractualist Demands on Individuals

In Scanlon's contractualism, what we owe to each other is to act in accordance with principles that no one could reasonably reject (Scanlon 1998). One ground for reasonably rejecting a principle, Scanlon says, is that its being in effect would render some people badly off, and there are other principles available which would render no one that badly off (Scanlon 1982, 111). So, for example, a principle allowing gratuitous deception is reasonably rejectable because under it some people would be badly off (namely, the deceived), and there is another principle available (forbidding deception) under which no one is as badly off as the deceived would be were such deception allowed. Essentially, this principle is reasonably rejectable because the deception it allows would make the deceived worse off than a principle forbidding deception would make potential deceivers. Since any principle of gratuitous deception is reasonably rejectable, gratuitous deception is morally wrong. Scanlon uses this form of argument to account for the main so-called "negative" moral duties, such as duties against deceiving, injuring, promise breaking, and the like.

The form of argument is general, so it bears on our "positive" duties of assistance as well. Here the form of argument should generate pressure for redistributing material resources toward equality. For each principle P that allows A to control more resources than B, there is a more egalitarian principle under which no one is as badly off materially as B is under P. So those who would be rendered worse off by less egalitarian principles have grounds for rejecting such principles in favor of more egalitarian ones. And the marginal diminishing value of resources should further intensify this pressure toward redistribution.

This is why what Scanlon actually says about duties to the distant needy is so unexpected. Scanlon presents what he calls the "Rescue Principle" for situations in which one can alleviate someone's dire plight like starvation.[1] He says this Rescue Principle is not reasonably rejectable: it does impose moral requirements. Yet, according to the Rescue Principle, assistance is required only if it can be given at a "slight or moderate" cost – one is required to help when one "can very easily do so" (Scanlon 1998, 224–5). Given the egalitarian tendency of his theory, this is a surprisingly undemanding principle for Scanlon to endorse.

Thomas Nagel offers the following guess as to why Scanlon is so lenient:

> While no one could reasonably reject some requirement of aid from the affluent to the destitute, the cumulative effect on an individual life of an essentially unlimited requirement to give to those who are very much worse off than yourself, whatever other affluent people are doing, would simply rule out the pursuit of a wide range of individualistic values – aesthetic, hedonistic, intellectual, cultural, romantic, athletic and so forth. Would the certain abandonment of all these things provide reasonable ground for rejection of a principle that required it – even in the face of the starving millions? The question for Scanlon's model would be whether it could be offered as a justification to each one of those millions, and my sense is that perhaps it could, that one could say: "I cannot be condemned as unreasonable if I reject a principle that would require me to abandon most of the substance of my life to save yours." (Nagel 1999, 12)

Yet can one's "hedonistic" and "athletic" projects really weigh much in the scales against the misery of the destitute? A contractualist must not take up Nagel's suggestion for resisting more significant duties of assistance, because of the relative triviality of these values. If disruption to personal projects were reasonable grounds for rejecting a principle of assistance, it would equally be grounds for rejecting principles forbidding aggression, coercion, or deception. But no one thinks that disruption to personal projects of the kind that Nagel mentions should weigh heavily in considering, for example, a principle forbidding the infliction of serious injury. If Nagel's sort of appeal is to have any force in limiting the demandingness of contractualism, it cannot work by focusing solely on the amount of "donor sacrifice."

The real cause for a contractualist concern is that "donor sacrifice"

---

[1] "Rescue," with its connotations of transient emergency and restoring people to a level they have formerly attained, seems an inapt term to use in the context of global poverty.

might diverge from "recipient benefit." Before deciding to give his resources, a donor needs confidence that these resources will be used and not wasted, that they will be used for the most urgent projects, and that these projects can reasonably be expected to work toward the long-term good of the recipients and their progeny.

It is currently difficult for the average potential donor to have such confidence. This is especially true given popular stories about global aid and development where, in a cruel inversion of Mandeville, private virtues have turned into public vices. Certainly it would seem less compelling to abandon "the substance of one's life" if what one sacrificed were to be used in ways that merely increased population pressure, or furthered some bureaucrat's career; or if one's money merely freed up resources to buy weapons for a pointless war, or freed up funds to pay off loans that would have been forgiven anyway. To a contemporary rich individual, his or her relation to the global poor may not appear at all analogous to being able simply to hand meals across the railroad tracks. It may seem more like having to throw food across the tracks through the open windows of speeding trains.

Were this kind of causal disconnect to obtain, it would make a real difference to the demandingness of contractualist morality. For it is not simply our duty to spend a certain amount of money or seconds or calories in trying to help others, independently of the efficacy of the channels of transmission. It must be reasonable to reject a principle of assistance on the grounds that the sacrifice demanded of one is very much greater than the benefit it provides to the other person, even if the other is very much worse off. Bill Gates could not be morally required to give up his entire fortune to provide just one penny for even the neediest soul. This "comparative benefit" grounds for rejection will generate a counterpressure against redistributive equalization within any plausible contractualism.

Given this, I believe that the main work for a Scanlonian contractualist to do on the question of direct action by the global rich is not philosophical, but empirical. If the causal links are good – that is, if rich individuals can in fact improve the long-term well-being of the poor and their descendants through direct action with their time and money – then contractualism may place on rich individuals quite significant demands. The worse the links are, the less this form of contractualism will require. The important work for theorists is, therefore, to investigate (what is not well documented in the normative literature) how much rich individuals can help at what cost.

II. Why Do Institutions Need Special Justification?

Individuals face a daunting causal nexus, but institutions have a causal efficacy that individuals lack. Hegel epitomizes this familiar thought:

> Intelligent, substantial beneficence is . . . in its richest and most important form the intelligent universal action of the state – an action compared with which the

action of a single individual, as an individual, is so insignificant that it is hardly worth talking about. . . . The only significance left for [individual] beneficence . . . is that of an action which is quite single and isolated, of help in need, which is as contingent as it is transitory. Chance determines . . . whether it is a "work" at all, whether it is not immediately undone and even perverted into something bad. (1978, 255–6)

Institutions often have greater skills in predicting consequences, more accurate and systematic memories, greater ability to carry through plans, and more power to influence others' decisions (O'Neill 1986, 37–8).[2] One would think, therefore, that more could be expected from them.

To the extent that institutions with global reach are or can become causally efficacious channels for the rich to get their resources to the poor, a Scanlonian contractualist will say that the rich individuals who can control these institutions must use them as instruments for fulfilling their individual obligations. This follows directly from the "positive" duties of assistance described above. No connection here is assumed between rich and poor beyond the causal.

However, some have thought that global institutions have a moral significance that goes beyond their instrumentality for carrying through the positive duties of the rich (e.g., Pogge 1998, 504–7). For global institutions, it is claimed, generate their own species of unfairness. Since many of the statistics cited in discussions of global economic justice are set in terms of collectivities and their institutions, it is worth isolating exactly which phenomena are supposed to show that institutions have this extra moral significance.

It cannot be simply the fact the those who live under some national institutions are on average materially better off than those who live under others. Given the immense expansion of world product, "zero sum" reasoning is obviously inappropriate here. It is not the case that if some are advancing, it must mean that others are declining, or that if some have more, others must have less. Different national institutions might just produce different average levels of material wealth, and if national societies were not sufficiently connected to each other, there would be no special cause for moral concern (Miller 1999, 188–91).

However, national societies are, of course, connected to each other by many global and transnational institutions. Moreover, it is very plausible that the well-being of the worst off is significantly affected by the actions of the better off through these institutions; and, of course, the worst off are very badly off in comparative and absolute terms. Still, one may wonder whether these facts alone are sufficient to establish a special problem of institutional justice.

[2] Moreover, because they can coordinate individual action, institutions may be able rightly to impose on individuals demands that it would be unreasonable to expect individuals to place on themselves (Beitz 1983, 599; Nagel 1999, 13).

The literature is interestingly divided in its emphasis on this point. The right tends to stress that all humans once lived at subsistence, and that poor countries are as materially well off and as populous as they are today mostly because of their contacts with developed countries (e.g., Bauer 2000; Hayek 1988, ch. 8). The left tends to point out how rich countries use their overwhelming power to skew international institutions to work in their own favor (e.g., Pogge 1992; 1994, 223; 1998, 506; 1999, 360).[3]

Both sides can be correct here. Interaction with richer countries may have made poorer countries materially better off than they would have been, but not as well off as they could have been. This kind of situation obtains in a wide variety of cases (for example, with parents and children, or universities and professors). In such situations the question is always whether the one party has done enough with respect to the other. So we must determine the type of relationship the parties are in, and the responsibilities of the parties in relationships of that sort.

And here we do hit the kind of phenomena that give rise to a distinct problem of international justice. For, it is claimed, international institutions do not just connect people and influence their fates. International institutions are coercively imposed, especially by the rich on the poor (Pogge 1998, 276). This is the sort of fact that a contractualist would claim necessitates a separate treatment of global institutional justice, such as the Rawlsian account that will be examined in the following sections. Coercion requires special justification.

Now before simply assuming that international relationships are coercive, we should be careful to specify what coercion causes the concern. The World Trade Organization (WTO), for instance, presents itself as an international "fair and stable trade club," accepting applications from anyone who agrees to the club rules. To assent that there is coercion here, one should want to be precise about who is threatening whom and why these are threats and not offers. But there can be little doubt about the coercive imposition of the basic system of limited state sovereignty and international relations that the West has imposed on the world, and which continues to be upheld by the economically and militarily dominant countries (Hurrell 1999, 248–55; Pogge 1989, 276; 2001). If it is correct that this state system is coercively imposed by some on all, or by all on all, then the standards for judging its rules and outcomes become much stricter. A club must merely ensure that all subscribers are held to its agreed terms; but an inescapably coercive system of rules must prove itself fair to all – and especially to those who do worst by it.

The dominant contractualist theories of fair coercive global institutions derive from the work of John Rawls. In the next section I contrast Rawls's own global theory with the cosmopolitan egalitarian interpretation of justice as fairness. This contrast will reveal why Rawls holds a theory of

---

[3] Both emphases are found in Doyle's (1997, 423–52) survey.

global economic justice that is surprisingly undemanding of richer countries. In the following section I canvass what can be said for and against the path that Rawls takes. Finally, I propose a new original position argument as one way of making up for an important defect in Rawls's account.[4]

III. Why Is Rawls Not a Cosmopolitan Egalitarian?

Rawls's fundamental norm is that coercive political power is only legitimate when exercised in accordance with ideas that all who are coerced can reasonably accept (Rawls 1993, 136–7). This norm of legitimacy bears obvious similarities to Scanlon's contractualist criterion discussed above. It is also crucial for explaining why Rawls – perhaps our leading egalitarian individualist – propounds a theory of global justice that is neither egalitarian nor individualistic.

Rawls's theory of justice for the institutions of a modern democratic society, "justice as fairness," is well known (Rawls 1971). The basic structure of such a society is a set of coercive institutions that greatly influence citizens' life chances by the ways that it divides up the benefits and burdens of social cooperation. A just basic structure will be a fair scheme of cooperation among citizens regarded as free and equal. Rawls draws out the implications of these fundamental ideas with his original position thought experiment, which places representatives of free and equal citizens in fair conditions for choosing the terms of social cooperation. The representatives deliberate behind a veil of ignorance that hides from them morally arbitrary facts about the citizens they represent, such as their economic class. Rawls holds that two principles would be selected in this original position: the first affirms that familiar rights and liberties should be strongly protected; the second proposes a progressive principle of equal opportunity and the radically egalitarian difference principle. According to the difference principle, inequalities of wealth and income between citizens should be allowed only insofar as these inequalities benefit the least- advantaged citizens.

Charles Beitz (1999, 1983) and Thomas Pogge (1989, 1994) have proposed a cosmopolitan reformulation of Rawls's justice as fairness as the solution to the problem of global justice.[5] The global basic structure is, they claimed, also a scheme of coercive institutions that significantly affects individuals' life chances by dividing up the benefits and burdens of worldwide social cooperation. It likewise should be a fair scheme of cooperation, amongst "citizens of the world" viewed as free and equal. A global original

---

[4] I try to integrate Rawls's published works together, as indicated in the next section, in my paper "The Unity of Rawls's Work" (forthcoming). I give a more detailed explication of Rawls's Law of Peoples and the supplementary original position argument in my 2001.

[5] I paper over substantial differences in their presentations here. Pogge is no longer an unqualified supporter of the Rawlsian approach, although I believe he would welcome Rawlsians' support for his Global Resource Dividend proposal. See Pogge (1999).

position can be constructed to represent these "world citizens" fairly by
veiling from their representatives morally arbitrary features such as country of citizenship. The result is a globalized version of Rawls's two principles of justice, and in particular a global difference principle that would
require economic inequalities to work to the advantage of the world's
worst-off individuals.

When Rawls finally published his own theory of global institutions, "the
Law of Peoples," it surprised many readers and disappointed the cosmopolitans (Rawls 1999). First, and contrary to the cosmopolitan interpretation,
Rawls stipulated that the parties in the global original position should not be
thought to represent individual human beings. Rather, each party in the
global original position should represent a whole society – or a "people," as
Rawls prefers to say. Moreover, the principles that Rawls claimed would be
agreed upon in such a global original position are quite dissimilar to the two
principles of justice as fairness. They are instead closer to familiar and
conventional principles of modern international relations.

Specifically, Rawls's principles of the Law of Peoples state that peoples
have rights to self-defense, and should obey the rules of war; that peoples
should abide by their treaties, and should respect basic human rights; and
that peoples should set up cooperative organizations like a world bank, and
should ensure fair trade. Beyond this Rawls does include a limited "principle of assistance" that requires wealthier countries to help "burdened"
peoples in developing and maintaining decent and stable domestic institutions. But he includes no principles of economic egalitarianism whatsoever
– that is, he includes no principles aimed directly at narrowing the
economic gap between richer and poorer countries. As Pogge remarked in
discouragement on an early version of Rawls's theory of global relations,
"I am at a loss to explain Rawls's quick endorsement of a bygone status
quo" (1989, 246).

The puzzle of Rawls's rejection of cosmopolitan egalitarianism deepens
when we see why he does *not* reject it. Rawls does not reject cosmopolitan egalitarianism because he worries about foisting international egalitarianism on the deeply inegalitarian cultures of the world – for he claims that
he would abjure global egalitarianism even amongst peoples all of which
accepted justice as fairness (1999, 119–20). Nor does he doubt that fellow
feeling amongst the citizens of different countries could grow strong
enough for the global rich to support continuous redistribution to the
global poor (1999, 112–13). Nor does he argue that global institutions
could never be adequate to carry out an egalitarian program (1999,
112–20). Why, then, does Rawls reject cosmopolitan egalitarianism?

To understand why, we must first examine why Rawls populates his global
original position with representatives of peoples instead of people. Here is
where Rawls's norm of legitimacy becomes crucial: coercive political power
is only rightly used when exercised in accordance with ideas that all who
are coerced can reasonably accept.

This norm first appears in *Political Liberalism* (Rawls 1993). In this book Rawls says that the pluralism of modern democracies rules out drawing the ideas that will serve as the basis of coercive *domestic* institutions from the "comprehensive doctrines" of any group of citizens (1993, 36–40). Muslims, for instance, could reasonably reject the Lutheran tenets of their neighbors as a basis for ordering the basic structure of their society. The only other source of ideas for grounding social institutions, Rawls says, is the society's *public political culture*, understood as the political institutions of the regime and the public traditions of their interpretation, as well as the historic texts and documents that have become part of common knowledge (1993, 13–15). All citizens can reasonably accept coercion on the basis of concepts and principles found in the public political culture, because all can acknowledge that the public culture is a focal point of "implicitly recognized basic ideas" that are most likely to be "congenial to [citizens'] most firmly held convictions" (1993, 8).

In a liberal democracy, the public political culture will contain, at the deepest level, the ideas that citizens should see each other as free and equal and as cooperating fairly with one another. So domestic coercive institutions will be legitimate only if they are based on these fundamental ideas of freedom, equality, and fairness. This constrains legitimate domestic institutions to those that assure priority for basic rights and opportunities, and provide assurance that all citizens will have adequate means to take advantage of these (Rawls 1993, 6). (Justice as fairness is, then, one theory for constructing a legitimate basic structure.)

Turning now to the Law of Peoples, Rawls's fundamental norm of legitimacy requires that principles for coercive *global* institutions must be worked up out of ideas that are reasonably acceptable to all who will be coerced by them. Analogously to the domestic case, we will have to look in the global public political culture to find these ideas. That is, we will have to look to *global* political institutions and the public traditions of their interpretation, as well as to the historic global texts and documents, to find the ideas on which to base principles of global justice.

And this is precisely, I believe, where Rawls balks at cosmopolitanism. For, while documents in the global public political culture like the *Universal Declaration of Human Rights* proclaim the freedom and equality of all men, such declarations mainly concern how domestic governments should treat their own citizens. They are not primarily about how citizens of different countries should regard and relate to each other. Moreover, while citizens of different countries are bound in their dealings with each other by international criminal law and the Geneva Conventions, in the main the political institutions of international society work in terms, not of individual citizens, but of states, or (as Rawls would have it) "peoples." Peoples, not people, are the main actors in the public political culture of international treaties, conventions, and organizations.

There simply is no robust global public political culture which emphasizes that the citizens of different countries ought to relate fairly to one
another as free and equal. There is no focal point comparable, that is, to the
ideas of free and equal citizenry contained in the public political culture of
a liberal democracy. It is peoples, not citizens, that international political
institutions regard as free and equal, and so it is these ideas of peoples that
Rawls thinks he must use to develop his global political principles.

Rawls, no doubt, believes as much as anyone that all humans should be
regarded as free and equal to each other. But he believes more deeply that
people should not be coerced, except according to a self-image reasonably
acceptable to them. In this way, Rawlsian politics is identity politics. Since
"global citizens" cannot be assumed to view themselves as free and equal
individuals who should relate fairly to each other across the board, we
cannot build coercive social institutions which assume that they do.[6]

This explains why Rawls is not a cosmopolitan, but not why he fails to
be an egalitarian. After all, the global public political culture does contain
the ideas that *peoples* should be regarded as free and equal, and that the
society of people should be fairly regulated. But these are just the ideas
that led to the domestic difference principle. Since the fundamental ideas
of a global society of peoples so closely resemble those of the liberal society of citizens, should Rawls not advocate that economic inequalities
between peoples are only permissible if they work to the advantage of the
least-advantaged *societies*?

The answer is no, for one striking reason. As Rawls sees them, peoples
and individual citizens simply have different fundamental interests. To put
it bluntly, citizens in a liberal society have an intrinsic interest in gaining
greater wealth and income, since these are all-purpose means for pursuing
their various goals. Peoples, on the other hand, as such have no interest in
greater wealth. For a people, material prosperity is optional: if a people
desires more wealth, it is free to pursue this through international trade or
loans. But as such, peoples only have interests in protecting their territorial integrity, securing the safety of their citizens, maintaining their independent and just social institutions, and sustaining their self-respect as
peoples (Rawls 1999, 24, 34). As Rawls defines them or discovers them in
the relevant public political cultures, citizens as such want more wealth,
while peoples as such do not.

Therefore, peoples as such are indifferent to the economic distribution
of wealth, unless this has some secondary political impact. A people must
be concerned with its level of wealth if, for example, this is insufficient to
support a free and just political order (and from this interest will spring
Rawls's international duty of assistance to burdened societies). Yet, above

---

[6] For the view that peoples should be treated as free and equal regardless how they view
themselves as represented in the "public political culture," see Beitz (1983, 596); Pogge
(1989, 270); and Føllesdal (1997, 152–3).

the goal of internal justice, and given no political knock-on effects, a people as such is blissfully indifferent to its economic status relative to other peoples. This is why the distribution of wealth is a problem for citizens, but not for peoples. There need be no principles for distributing *adiaphora*.

Rawls's characterization of the interests of peoples raises many questions. For example, how can it be that each citizen that makes up a people has an interest in more wealth, while the collectivity of citizens has no such interest? It might also be wondered whether Rawls's characterization simply loses touch with reality, as a drive for material prosperity seems a fixed point in the motivation of the world's nations. Instead of considering these specific questions, I want to take a broader view of whether there are lessons to be learned from contrasting Rawls's and the cosmopolitan egalitarian approaches to global economic justice.

IV. For and Against a Law of Peoples

In practical terms, Rawls's Law of Peoples may be closer to egalitarianism than he makes it seem. His "principle of assistance" demands that richer countries do whatever they can to see that all countries can stably maintain decent governments that respect basic human rights. This will require significant effort by the richer countries to improve the situation of the world's poorest nations – a noteworthy implication. Moreover, if Pogge is right, the chronic destabilizing corruption inflicted by rich politicians and businesspeople on poor nations' governments cannot be overcome without reducing the huge differentials in per capita gross national product (Pogge 1994, 214; 2001). Finally, Rawls may be forced after all to admit that poorer peoples will want a more equal distribution of national wealth – not because peoples want wealth in itself, but because they are concerned to maintain their own self-respect as peoples.

Yet what are we to make of Rawls's theoretical strategy, and especially his anticosmopolitanism? My view is that Rawls demonstrates that theorizing in terms of peoples (or states or nations) has real advantages, but that it also leaves at least one important topic out of reach.

One real advantage to Rawls's rejection of cosmopolitanism is that, in addressing peoples (or their close equivalents), it addresses agents that have crucial roles in the world as it is. The importance of this is one major theme in Onora O'Neill's work on poverty (O'Neill 1986). To be a guide to action, arguments must be accessible to those who are to be guided by them. And an exclusively individualist picture of agency will be inadequate to problems of world poverty because it fails to address the institutional and collective agents that make vital decisions about what is to be done (O'Neill 1986, 32–5).[7] Agencies such as peoples have practical

---

[7] For contrast see Beitz (1983, 598).

perspectives of their own, and how they reason is a significant (indeed perhaps the most significant) factor in how the world is run.

The payoff for Rawls's working in terms of peoples is that the principles that he says are derived from his global original position include many that are absolutely essential for keeping the world order even minimally tolerable. Consider principles such as that nations have a right to self-defense, but not to aggressive war; that nations should abide by the rules of war and keep their treaties; and that they should trade fairly with each other. These principles are no less important because they are part of a familiar "status quo," or because they are often honored in the breach. They are principles that the world lives, or should live, by, and we should be lost in global affairs without them.

Indeed, Rawls's mild "principle of assistance" gains much of its force because it is derived from an argument (Rawls's global original position) that also endorses these basic principles of global justice that we already condone. Original position arguments work, after all, not just because they are built from compelling premises, but because they *both* "accommodate our firmest convictions and . . . provide guidance where guidance is needed" (Rawls 1971, 200). Recall that in justice as fairness our approval of the principle of equal basic liberties is meant to wash over our uncertainty about the difference principle. Similarly, in the Law of Peoples, our endorsement of Rawls's principles of a peaceful, stable world should spill over to his principle for aiding "burdened" societies. So far as I know, cosmopolitan theories have proposed radical economic principles without yet showing that their form of original position reasoning can "accommodate our firmest convictions" on global justice. So cosmopolitan egalitarians need another horse to put before their cart.

Nevertheless, cosmopolitans are dead right in their charge that theorizing exclusively in terms of peoples appears to be lacking because of the absence of "normative individualism" (Føllesdal 1997, 151). It is striking that Rawls's Law of Peoples evidences no direct concern for individual well-being whatsoever. A people's motivation to act on the principles Rawls proposes does *not* spring from any ground-level concern for individual welfare. When one people intervenes in another people's affairs – for instance to stop human rights abuses or to provide food aid – the intervening country does *not* do this for the sake of the well-being of the tortured or the starving individuals in the other country (Pogge 1994, 209–10). Rather, the intervening country is trying to bring the other country (back) to legitimacy so that it can play its role in the society of peoples. And the criterion of legitimacy itself is not based in concern for individuals; rather, it simply defines the minimal standard for a people's moral agency. It is as if societies were humans, with their individual members as merely the cells of their bodies, and one society gave health care to another in order to enable it to rejoin the scheme of social cooperation. This failure of people's concern to "trickle down" to individuals seems peculiar, even if it has no untoward consequences in the theory.

Even more importantly, some crucial interests of individuals cannot, in Rawls's structure, "trickle up" to become the concerns of their peoples. This does have untoward consequences in the theory, as we can see from looking at Rawls's account of fair trade.

Rawls's principles for trade are meant to be fair amongst free and equal peoples who have decided to increase their wealth through exchange. These principles state that nations should keep their economic treaties, that there should be a world bank, and that obvious market imperfections like monopolies and oligopolies should be discouraged (Rawls 1999, 42–3). What is notable is that these are all provisions that allow *peoples* to relate to each other fairly. Indeed, Rawls could have added all of the main WTO rules to his list, such as the rules that nations not distinguish amongst trading partners, the rules demanding national laws to give equal treatment to foreign and domestic products, the rules against subsidies (one nation trying to boost its own industries), and the rules against dumping (nations exploiting market imperfections to knock out another country's industries). These provisions all seem sensible as far as they go; what they lack is any concern for *individuals'* economic interests. They are not the sort of rules that could, for instance, help Indonesian factory workers in a labor dispute with a multinational corporation; or help the victims of the Bhopal industrial accident.

And of course individuals do have their own independent interests in gaining economic goods and avoiding economic bads. Justice as fairness (Rawls 1982, 166) tells us, for example, that individuals want income as a generic resource for pursuing their life plans – and there is no reason to think that individuals have an interest only in domestically generated income. Individuals have interests in income, employment, economic opportunities, good working conditions, clean air, and more. And the structure of the coercive institutions that regulate international economic activity can affect these interests significantly. Yet within a Law of Peoples, these individual economic interests cannot percolate up into the theory, since the theory is exclusively about how peoples should relate to each other. This is why Rawls's type of theorizing about global justice needs supplementation.

V. A Cosmopolitan Economic Original Position

Original position arguments are simply a way of moving from a conception of agents and their moral relations to definite principles. What is needed to supplement Rawls's global original position is an argument that relates individuals fairly to each other regarding the effects they have on each other through international economic activity.

The materials we have to work with in constructing this new original position argument are limited, since (as argued above) we must stay within the bounds of legitimacy by using ideas and conceptions that are reasonably acceptable to everyone who will be coerced. We can maintain such reasonable acceptability, I believe, by drawing on ideas and conceptions from three sources. First, there is the global public political culture of international institutions (such as the United Nations) and documents (such as the *Universal Declaration of Human Rights*). Second, here possibly going beyond Rawls, we may draw on common knowledge of human beings and their interests. Third, and definitely extending the Rawlsian approach, we may add what those who take part in the international economic order must reasonably presume about the other people who participate in this order. For example, consumers must reasonably presume that there are producers, and polluters must reasonably presume that any consumers of their pollution may be damaged by it.[8] Drawing on even this limited range of sources may yield enough material to get some definite results.

The new original position can be laid out in this way. The conceptions of persons that we use are of the consumers, producers, and owners of internationally generated economic goods and bads. We can define these persons by their interests. Consumers have interests in consuming more goods and services, but less pollution. Producers have interests in job opportunities, income, employment stability, decent working conditions, and so on. Owners have an interest in maximizing return. And human beings in all these roles have interests in long-term health and in developing and maintaining at least basic abilities rationally to direct their own activities. We can also assume a partial hierarchy in these "primary goods," for example, that basic physical health is more important than consumption of luxuries.

The moral relations we assume amongst persons so conceived is also minimal. We assume that these persons should relate fairly over time. This gives us a thin veil of ignorance. Representatives of our economic agents have veiled from them only the economic roles of those they represent, and to which generation those they represent belong. So the parties do not know whether they represent consumers, producers, or owners, and they do not know when in the lifespan of humanity those they represent live.

This veil also embodies the simple but powerful idea – which I believe is found in the global political culture – that all individuals' lives are equally important. But we cannot knit a thicker veil from the assumptions that, for example, individuals are more robustly "free and equal." Nor can we rightly assume that individuals' class positions are arbitrary from a moral point of view. These ideas are not a deep part of the international political culture, so it would not be legitimate to coerce people in accordance with them.

What principles will this original position yield? Some principles will arise from commonalities of interests among the individuals represented. For instance, all economic agents have interests in economic predictability – so

---

[8] For the idea of a normative presumption of agency, see especially O'Neill (1996, 91–123).

we should get prohibitions on theft and fraud, provisions for enforcing contracts, and the goal of maintaining price stability. Some principles will flow from the hierarchy of human interests. We should expect prohibitions on slavery and child prostitution; penalties for industrial negligence; requirements for minimally decent working conditions; and provisions for employment (if not job) security. But, since we cannot assume that the current distribution of income is morally arbitrary, we cannot in this original position generate an argument for the difference principle by assuming a baseline of economic equality. This seems to me appropriate.

It may seem to some, in contrast, that this original position is biased in favor of labor over capital. But capital is represented through its owners, and also, importantly, through the interests of future producers and consumers. We should, therefore, expect restrictions on international capital, but not a strangulation insofar as we can expect that it will be laying golden eggs in the future.

As for institutional instantiation of the principles, much is already in place or easily implementable within current national laws or by existing international bodies. For some provisions – such as on working conditions – institutions for enforcement are less clear. Yet the project of representing individual economic interests fairly in the international realm seems important and plausible enough for further work to be considered.

References

Bauer, P. (2000). *From Subsistence to Exchange*. Princeton: Princeton University Press.

Beitz, C. (1983). "Cosmopolitan Ideas and National Sentiment." *Journal of Philosophy*, 80, 591–600.

———. (1999). *Political Theory and International Relations* (with new afterword). Princeton: Princeton University Press. First edition published 1979.

Doyle, M. (1997). *Ways of War and Peace*. New York: Norton.

Føllesdal, A. (1997). "The Standing of Illiberal States, Stability and Toleration in John Rawls' 'Law of Peoples.'" *Acta Analytica*, 18, 149–60.

Hayek, F. A. (1988). *The Fatal Conceit*. Chicago: University of Chicago Press.

Hegel, G. W. F. (1978). *Hegel's Phenomenology of Spirit*. Trans. A. V. Miller. Oxford: Oxford University Press.

Hurrell, A. (1999). "Security and Inequality." In *Inequality, Globalization, and World Politics*, edited by A. Hurrell and N. Woods, 248–72. Oxford: Oxford University Press.

Miller, D. (1999). "Justice and Inequality." In *Inequality, Globalization, and World Politics*, edited by A. Hurrell and N. Woods, 187–210. Oxford: Oxford University Press.

Nagel, T. (1999). Review of *What We Owe to Each Other*, by T. M. Scanlon. *London Review of Books*, 21:3, 10–13.

O'Neill, O. (1986). *Faces of Hunger*. London: Allen & Unwin.

——. (1996). *Towards Justice and Virtue*. Cambridge: Cambridge University Press.

Pogge, T. (1989). *Realizing Rawls*. Ithaca, NY: Cornell University Press.

——. (1992). "Cosmopolitanism and Sovereignty." *Ethics*, 103:1, 48–75.

——. (1994). "An Egalitarian Law of Peoples." *Philosophy and Public Affairs*, 23:3, 195–224.

——. (1998). "A Global Resource Dividend." In *Ethics of Consumption*, edited by D. A. Crocker and T. Linden, 501–36. Lanham, MD: Rowman & Littlefield.

——. (1999). "Human Flourishing and Universal Justice." *Social Philosophy and Policy*, 16:1, 333–61.

——. (2001). "Priorities of Global Justice." *Metaphilosophy*, 32:1/2.

Rawls, J. (1971). *A Theory of Justice*. Cambridge: Harvard University Press.

——. (1982). "Primary Goods and Social Unity." In *Utilitarianism and Beyond*, edited by A. Sen and B. Williams, 159–86. Cambridge: Cambridge University Press.

——. (1993). *Political Liberalism*. New York: Columbia University Press.

Rawls, J. (1999). *The Law of Peoples*. Cambridge: Harvard University Press.

Scanlon, T. (1982). "Contractualism and Utilitarianism." In *Utilitarianism and Beyond*, edited by A. Sen and B. Williams, 103–27. Cambridge: Cambridge University Press.

——. (1998). *What We Owe to Each Other*. Cambridge: Harvard University Press.

Wenar, L. (2001). "The Legitimacy of Peoples." In *Global Politics and Transnational Justice*, edited by P. de Greiff and C. Cronin. Cambridge: MIT Press.

——. (Forthcoming). "The Unity of Rawls's Work."

7

JUSTICE AND NAKEDNESS

STÉPHANE CHAUVIER

Concepts of Global Distributive Justice

What conception of distributive justice, if any, is suited to the world as a whole? Most philosophers who deal with the question of global justice fall into one of two groups: either they deny the applicability of any conception of distributive justice at the global level, and are content with a simple refurbishment of the traditional Law of Peoples, or else they seek to apply at the global level the same method and the same principles as apply at the domestic level.[1] In this chapter I want to suggest a third alternative. The situation of the world as a whole does indeed fall within the purview of distributive justice; however, the appropriate conception of justice at the global level cannot simply replicate the conception that is suited to the domestic level. The morally relevant circumstances that confront us when we consider the distributive inequalities among individuals in different political states are unlike the circumstances we face in considering such inequalities among citizens of any one society. For this reason, applying to the world at large a conception of distributive justice suitable for domestic society would be not only unrealistic, but also ethically objectionable. In the following, I defend these claims and argue specifically against a global application of the Rawlsian Difference Principle. I subsequently introduce and defend some principles of global distributive justice that are unique to the international context.

Consider a simplified case in which there are only two kinds of states or peoples: those that have a liberal constitution and a fairly high per capita income, and those that are despotic and poor.[2] Let us assume – in order to bracket the problem of cultural pluralism about conceptions of justice and

---

[1] For the former, see John Rawls (1999a, esp. § 16.2, pp. 115ff.); for the latter, see Charles Beitz (1999, 127–76 and 198–214) and Thomas Pogge (1994).

[2] In the following discussions, I shall not distinguish among the terms "peoples," "states," and "nations," though I am aware that distinctions can be made among these kinds of entities. What I have in mind is a political community, or a set of citizens, with their own political institutions.

other social values – that the members of every state prefer having a liberal constitution and the highest per capita income compatible with their chosen way of life.[3] According to what sort of ideal theory of global justice could we understand this situation as an instance of distributive injustice? Two kinds of theories might plausibly be proposed. The first would take the interests of states or peoples as primary and would maintain that a just global order requires that each state or people enjoy a certain kind of political constitution and meet certain economic standards. Insofar as our hypothetical case failed to satisfy these conditions, it would be a case of distributive injustice. The second kind of theory would take the interests of individual persons as primary and would maintain that each person – regardless of the state in which she lives – is entitled to political and economic conditions that our hypothetical case fails to provide. Each approach can be modeled by a Rawlsian-style procedure of deliberation behind a veil of ignorance (Rawls 1999b, 11); in the first case, the parties to the deliberation are representatives of states, while in the second case, the parties are representatives of the individual members of each state.

The Point of View of States

Consider first the approach that takes states or peoples as its basic units. What sort of principles could representatives of states agree to behind a veil of ignorance, in order to regulate affairs among them? Since our simplified case assumes that each state or people prefers a liberal constitution and affluence, it seems plausible that the representatives would, at a minimum, endorse some principle like the following, which I will call *the equal-opportunity principle*: the global order must be such that each state enjoys equally the opportunity – one that can be realized by its voluntary efforts – to become liberal and to become as affluent as any other. The question is whether the representatives would go further than this and endorse an egalitarian principle analogous to Rawls's Difference Principle.[4]

Let us first examine the political principle of liberalism for all, a demand that we can regard as having not only a logical, but also a psychological and procedural, priority over the economic demand. I believe we can regard it as a kind of analytical truth that the political constitution of a state is something that it must give to itself. There is no plausible sense in

---

[3] Rawls's rejection of principles of global distributive justice seems to be tied to his (plausible) assumption that not all well-ordered peoples have a dominant interest in political liberalism and economic affluence. I want to establish that even if we assume such a dominant interest, we should still reject egalitarian principles of global distributive justice. The basis of my argument is not the cultural pluralism of the world, but rather the value of its political pluralism.

[4] The analogous principle would apply to the distribution of wealth among states as such, and would not apply across borders to the individual members of states.

which we can speak of a supranational global institution that gives each of a plurality of states its (liberal) constitution – for in that case, we would be speaking not of genuine states at all, but of something like territorial departments of a global political state. Representatives of individuals might prefer such a global state, but representatives of states – situated behind a veil of ignorance and selecting principles on the basis of what each believes will be to his state's best advantage – could not consent to a political order in which states as such would cease to exist.[5] The global order that is implied by the political demand of liberalism for all must therefore focus on helping peoples to achieve liberal constitutions on their own. Thus, the representatives would agree at least to an institutional structure (1) that prevents any state from thwarting the will and the efforts of any other to achieve a liberal constitution and (2) that authorizes external intervention on behalf of a population that is struggling to achieve a liberal constitution against the efforts of a despotic internal minority.

These two conditions clearly suggest some of the traditional provisions of the Law of Peoples, with the addition of a special set of rules and procedures governing the right of intervention. Such rules would not bear directly on distributive justice, for their role is not to distribute some pool of scarce goods equitably among several entities, but rather simply to maintain a global environment favorable to the freedom of each people. However, it seems likely, as many have argued, that the very possibility of achieving a stable liberal constitution is tied to a certain level of economic development. Thus, on the basis of the political principle alone, we should grant that the parties would endorse as an entitlement of each state the minimum of economic welfare needed to achieve a liberal constitution (and we can reasonably assume that this entails a minimally decent standard of living for each of a state's citizens). While this is a demand of distributive justice, it is a modest one; the economic preconditions of liberalism hardly extend so far as to license the sort of egalitarian distributive demands that the domestic original position yields.

However, each state has a rational interest not only in a liberal constitution, but also in a high level of affluence. The economic preconditions of liberalism, whatever they are, are not likely to go far enough to

---

[5] Here I simply assume, provisionally, that states have an essential interest in their continued existence as states. Such an assumption is of a piece with a robust view of states as kinds of moral persons. While some will be naturally inclined to such a conception of states, others may prefer to regard states' interests as fully reducible to the interests of their constituent individuals. Such an analysis might or might not yield the conclusion that the continued existence of a state is among its essential interests. However, on such a cosmopolitan analysis of states' interests, the model that represents states in the original position collapses into the model that represents individuals. I consider and endorse the individual-based model in the section to follow. The present section is devoted to working out the consequences of the (apparently widely held) robust conception of states, according to which each state must be regarded as having an essential interest in its continued existence.

satisfy this economic interest. It might seem, therefore, that the parties would go beyond the modest distributive demands entailed by the political objective of liberalism for all, and would endorse an analogue of the domestic Difference Principle. If the representatives of individuals seeking to achieve their best rational advantage under a veil of ignorance would endorse principles of equality, why should the result be different when we deliberate from the point of view of the representatives of states?

In order to understand the crucial disanalogy between these two kinds of cases, we must take account of Hume's analysis (1975, 183–92) of the "circumstances of justice." Hume argued that the very idea of justice or injustice can arise only when a group of individuals share a specific kind of social context – one in which there are conflicting claims about the distribution of scarce resources. Hume may have been primarily or exclusively concerned with the *psychological* origin of the idea of justice, but his analysis of the circumstances of justice reveals that no mere comparison of the endowments of two representative individuals can warrant a judgment that those endowments represent a just or unjust distribution. The individuals must also be in a certain kind of social context for their situation to be one of distributive justice or injustice. Specifically, they must confront the same pool of scarce resources, and they must make conflicting claims to portions of it.

There is at least one important further condition prerequisite to any question of distributive justice, though this condition is only implicit in the Humean account. Imagine two persons – one with a high income and the other with a much lower one. Suppose that the latter does nothing to improve her standard of living, though she has the opportunity to do so. We do not say that the situation is unjust, because the less-well-off individual can improve her situation if she so chooses. To generalize: in order for the concept of distributive justice to gain a purchase on some set of circumstances in which individuals enjoy unequal endowments, it must be the case that the worse-off party or parties cannot, through their voluntary actions, achieve a level of endowment comparable to that of the better-off. In this sense, freedom or responsibility precludes the question of distributive justice. When individuals are completely responsible for their own economic endowments, there is no logical room for an application of the concept of distributive justice. Only when individuals are in a certain state of dependency toward their endowments can their situation be regarded as distributively just or unjust. With some rhetorical license, I will term this state of dependency *the condition of nakedness.*

The condition of nakedness provides the key to understanding the difference between the domestic and the international cases. An individual person is necessarily naked with respect to her political community; absent any social cooperation with others, she would be unable to achieve what even the poorest member of a human group can achieve. Her life would indeed be, in Hobbes's admonitory words, "solitary, poor, nasty, brutish and short" (1968, 186). By contrast, it cannot be said that a state, alone and apart from other states, must be comparably deprived and vulnerable. In this sense, while individuals are necessarily naked with respect to their communities, states need not be naked with respect to any community of states. Of course, some existing states may be naked in this sense – they may exist as the abject dependents of powerful states or powerful international institutions. However, we have already established that the representatives of states would endorse at least the equal-opportunity principle, and this principle, as we have seen, reliably precludes their nakedness. Each representative knows that his state, on its own, will be able to achieve a certain level of security, autonomy, and economic welfare.

From this there follows a further sense in which the nakedness of individual persons is not replicated among states. A state, finding itself in a position in which its essential interests are already adequately met, may seek to improve its endowments through cooperation with others; but it also has the genuine option of going it alone. By contrast, an individual person finds himself in a position of nakedness and must enter into cooperation with others in order to acquire the endowments necessary to satisfy his essential interests. States therefore enter into negotiations with other states with a real "exit" option: none need cooperate with the others. The terms of cooperation among them can therefore be worked out through a bargaining process that will reflect the value that each participant gives to the status quo. By contrast, individuals have no significant bargaining power and no exit option.[6] Each must accept whatever the going terms of social cooperation are, and those terms will determine the level of social endowment that each individual enjoys.

The difference that I am emphasizing between states and persons can be expressed as the difference between nakedness and responsibility. Unlike individual persons, states are responsible agents in the following sense: they are capable of subsisting and meeting their essential needs independently of one another, and the level of endowment that they enjoy will thus be owed in large measure to their voluntary efforts and to the terms of cooperation into which they enter voluntarily, from a position of bargaining, with other states. Of course, in explaining economic inequalities among states, it may never be possible entirely to disentangle what is due

[6] Of course, the citizens of a democracy can in principle collectively alter the basic structure of their society through a sort of bargaining political process. However, the institution of majority rule, the constraints of the existing basic structure, and the absence of a genuine "exit" option mean that the results of such bargaining could be unacceptably disadvantageous to some individuals, whose interests may be unfairly disregarded by the majority. This is the reason why a just social domestic structure cannot be determined by a bargaining process (see Rawls 1999b, 116n.).

It might be thought that a right of emigration may constitute a kind of exit option. But even then, the result is simply to make the immigrant naked with respect to another political community or with respect to the state of nature.

to the responsibility of the state from what is due to unfavorable conditions, including historical inheritance and the distribution of natural resources. In this sense, while states are responsible, they are only partially responsible agents. I shall return below to the matter of how unfavorable conditions and other contingencies bear on the question of global justice. For the moment, it is sufficient to note that the component of responsibility that states have for their economic status marks an important difference between them and individual persons.

It is crucial to note that this responsibility of states for their level of economic endowment is not simply a contingent feature of a state's system, but rather follows from the essential nature of states as such. I shall not undertake to enumerate all of the essential features of states, but one that seems to me indisputable is what I will call *political responsibility*. By this I mean that a society is a state only if it is a set of persons whose collective organization makes them collectively responsible for the fundamental terms of their social cooperation. If a community or set of persons is not collectively responsible for the basic rights and responsibilities of its members, and for the basic economic structures of its society, then it does not constitute a state. It seems to me that the (partial) responsibility of states for their level of economic endowment is a presupposition of their political responsibility. A "state" whose level of endowment was entirely dependent on a larger collectivity could not be a politically responsible agent. If that is correct, then an international analogue of the Difference Principle is logically incompatible with the political responsibility of distinct states; to apply an egalitarian distributive principle to states would be precisely to *denude them* of their political responsibility.[7] I conclude that the representatives of states could not consent to an egalitarian redistributive principle because to do so would undermine or destroy something in which each state has an essential interest – namely, its political responsibility.

What then are the appropriate principles governing the economic relations among states? What would their representatives endorse, when deliberating behind a veil of ignorance? If the preceding argument is correct, they would not endorse principles that could undermine their states' political responsibility; however, they would be concerned to hedge against unfavorable circumstances – the sorts of contingencies for which states cannot be responsible. The most conspicuous of such contingencies is the distribution of natural resources. Insofar as there is a link between the economic potential of each state and its access to natural resources, we may say that states are clearly in the circumstances of justice. They all

---

[7] This is more than a semantic claim about the meaning of the word "state." The crucial point is that under a global scheme of distributive justice, the political units that remained – whatever we were to call them – would no longer constitute distinct groups, each of which is collectively responsible for its own fundamental institutions.

want to maximize something that depends in part on their share of natural resources, so they will want to formulate a mutually acceptable principle governing the sharing of those resources. If, as seems undeniable, the natural distribution of resources among states is random, then – for the reasons that lead Rawls to reject the theory of natural liberty (Rawls 1999b, 62–63) – something must be done in order to compensate for the "natural lottery." A representative could not agree to a general right of states to the exclusive enjoyment of their territorial resources, since in that case, the representative's state might be excluded from access to natural resources that are necessary for its economic projects. Representatives would therefore demand, at least, a principle of equal access to resources. Natural resources must be treated as a *res communis*, at least in the sense that no state can view itself as the owner of the mineral resources that are located in its soil or subsoil. A more demanding sense of this requirement would involve allocating equally to each state negotiable rights to a much broader range of the earth's natural resources.

Suppose then that each representative knows that his state will have access to the natural resources it needs, enjoys the economic preconditions of a liberal state, and is secure against outside interference in its domestic life. If we could also assume that each state was economically closed, then its capacity to achieve affluence would depend almost entirely on its own legal and moral efforts. However, the assumption of economically closed states is too unrealistic. Each representative knows that his state is likely, if not certain, to be integrated into a global system of transnational exchanges and investments. This suggests augmenting the principle of access to natural resources with a principle or principles establishing fair terms of transnational cooperation.

It might be thought that such terms would replicate fair terms of cooperation in the domestic context. However, the quite important differences that I have already emphasized between states and individuals with regard to their nakedness or responsibility results in a different decision situation for the representatives of these respective agents, deliberating behind a veil of ignorance. An individual's representative knows that all of her endowments will depend on the basic structure of the society in which she lives, and that she will have no genuine exit option from those terms; thus, she formulates an egalitarian demand that constrains those basic structures. But a state's representative knows that it commands a level of endowment sufficient to satisfy its essential interests, and that it can therefore bargain for the terms that will govern its interactions with others. Moreover, a state's representative values this economic responsibility as a precondition of his state's essential political responsibility, and will demand only what does not undermine it.

The most robust principles that satisfy this condition, I believe, would provide for (1) access to capital resources at below-market terms for suitably qualified states and (2) fair bargaining procedures for the establishment of the terms of international transactions. The principles of fair bargaining do not themselves establish the terms of cooperation, as do the principles of justice for the domestic case; rather, the principles of fair bargaining constrain the second-level rules under which the rules governing the interactions of states are to be negotiated and renegotiated. Representatives would not, for example, consent to a procedure where the first-level rules are determined by the majority, without any guarantee for the interests of minorities; a state's representative deliberating behind a veil of ignorance would demand that the condition of equal bargaining power for each state be institutionally recognized in the various forums where rules are negotiated between states.[8] One of the main ingredients of global justice would therefore be a set of demands concerning the procedures for establishing the international or global rules – a demand which is clearly very different from the sort that an individual person would formulate when considering, behind a veil of ignorance, her position within a domestic society.

We can conclude that if we employ a model that represents states in its constructive procedure, and if we suppose states to be responsible agents with an essential interest in their status as responsible agents, then a just global order cannot simply replicate domestic notions of social justice; in the global context, the strongest egalitarian principles of distributive justice that we can assert may be characterized as principles of *equal access*, in contrast with the principles of *equal entitlement* in distribution that are appropriate in the domestic context. A principle of equal entitlement requires that each agent or each representative receive, through appropriate institutions, the same level of endowment as the others (or some level consistent with a maximin principle). By contrast, a principle of equal access requires only that each agent have equal access to what it needs to further its ends, should the agent choose to do what depends on its responsibility.[9] Something accessible is not given to the agent; rather, the agent must engage in voluntary effort to enjoy what is accessible to it.

To summarize the concrete conclusions of this section, a just global order is characterized by three sets of global institutions and rules:

1. *A set of institutions devoted to the application of the Law of Peoples, including a right of intervention.* No state may prevent another from giving itself the political constitution of its choice; the well-ordered states are to assist those that are despotically governed as they try to

---

[8] It is important to note that this is one of the strongest claims of the current developing states, because the rules of transnational exchanges and investments represent above all the interests of the industrially developed states.

[9] From an institutional point of view, the difference between principles of equal entitlement and principles of equal access amounts to the difference between, on one hand, institutions such as the Tobin tax or Pogge's general resource dividend and, on the other hand institutions such as the European Bank for Development, which offers capital resources to private investors at below market conditions.

achieve liberal constitutions; and each state shall be entitled to aid when necessary to sustain the economic conditions for a liberal constitution and a minimally decent standard of living for its population.

2. *A set of institutions devoted to a common administration of natural resources and to an adjustment of the market of capital resources.* Under public constraints concerning the conservation of resources and the ecological impact of their use, each state is to have access to the natural resources of the earth – access that could be organized through a suitable market of negotiable rights; and capital resources are to be made accessible at below-market terms to any state that chooses to shift from a form of life that is not oriented toward the maximization of affluence to a more intensive form of production.

3. *A set of procedural rules governing the adoption, revision, and amendment of the rules governing international transactions.* In these various institutional areas, each state's interests are to be taken into account – for instance, through the possession by each state of a weak veto right (its exit option) and by qualified minorities of states of a strong veto right.[10]

We can reframe these conclusions in terms of the Humean problematic introduced above. If an agent's endowments are entirely owing to its responsibility, then it is not in the circumstances of justice, and no principle of justice can be applied; if an agent's endowments are entirely owing to the basic structure within which it acts, then justice requires distributive equality. However, since economic inequalities among states depend in part on unfavorable conditions, and since in consequence states are partially – but only partially – responsible agents, justice requires only that each have the *capacity* to achieve the same level as the others, and not that each agent actually achieve the same level. Principles of justice appropriate to a distributive situation that is partly due to the responsibility of the agent will take the form of what I have called principles of equal access, in contrast with principles of equal entitlement.

A similar concern with the responsibility of states appears to be the motivation behind an important passage in Rawls's *Law of Peoples*. He invites us to consider the following case:

Two liberal or decent countries are at the same level of wealth (estimated, say, in primary goods) and have the same size population. The first decides to industrialize and to increase its rate of (real) saving, while the second does not. Being content with things as they are, and preferring a more pastoral and leisurely

---

[10] The relevant qualification of the veto-empowered minorities is not simply a matter of numerical proportion (say, one-third or one-quarter of states), but is intended to allow for certain classes of states to have an enhanced voice in decision making owing to such factors as high population size or low income (to offset the disproportionate political influence of the more affluent states). The idea is exemplified in the notion of "qualified majority rule" in the European Union.

society, the second reaffirms its social values. Some decades later the first country is twice as wealthy as the second. Assuming, as we do, that both societies are liberal or decent, and their people free and responsible, and able to make their own decisions, should the industrializing country be taxed to give funds to the second? According to the duty of assistance there would be no tax and that seems right; whereas with a global egalitarian principle without target, there would always be a flow of taxes as long as the wealth of one people was less than that of the other. This seems unacceptable. (Rawls 1999a, 117)

The unacceptability that Rawls finds in the egalitarian entitlement scheme does not appear to be grounded in considerations of cultural diversity or cultural pluralism about conceptions of justice; the ground of his objection here seems, rather, to be a notion of responsibility that is very close to what I have called political responsibility. Our commonsense understanding of justice, to which Rawls here appeals, reflects the tension between distributive justice and responsibility, and leads us to reject as unjustifiable an egalitarian entitlement principle for states because they are politically, and thus economically, responsible agents.

The Point of View of Individuals

Will the outcome of the construction differ if we take the second approach noted above to developing a theory of global justice – the approach that takes as its material units, not states, but rather the individual members of each state? Let me first introduce a distinction between two kinds of demands of distributive justice: those that I will call *absolute* and others that I will call *comparative*. An example of an absolute demand would be one that requires that each human person, regardless of her state, enjoy a certain set of basic rights, opportunities, economic entitlements, and so on. By contrast, an example of a comparative demand would be one that requires that each human person enjoy an *equal* endowment of social goods or of opportunities.

If we limit the choices of the parties to absolute demands, then the method of representing citizens rather than states in the original position could plausibly lead to the same sorts of principles as those that states' representatives could endorse. Representatives of equal citizens, deliberating behind a veil of ignorance, would no doubt endorse some principle to the effect that each person has an absolute right to some set of basic endowments,[11] but the universality of these rights and entitlements does not imply that a cosmopolitan institutional structure would be needed in order to secure them. A plurality of states could also do the job, so long as

---

[11] A complete account of these basic requirements cannot be developed here. I simply assume that it is possible to specify some universal basic social goods. The problem becomes more difficult when we cease to bracket the question of cultural pluralism, but I would hope that even then an acceptable account would be possible.

we add the requirement that appropriate international institutions be implemented in order to enforce the ethical duties of states toward their populations.

It also appears that individual citizens' representatives could rationally endorse the traditional provisions of the Law of Peoples governing the relations among states. The representatives of states will (given our earlier stipulations) have a rational interest in a world where each state is peaceful and well ordered; but a citizen's representative will have the same kind of interest. The choices of a citizen's representative would not be grounded in the interests of a state as such; still, there is an obvious proximity or convergence of the interests of states and of persons.[12] The former seek the preservation of their liberal constitutions and affluence, while the latter seek their basic rights; but these different demands call for, or are at least consistent with, the same kind of global order. So it appears that there is no substantial difference in outcome if we shift from a global theory of justice whose basic units are states or peoples to a theory whose basic units are the individual citizens of each state.

This conclusion is predicated, however, on our having considered only absolute demands, and not comparative ones as well. The outcome is different if we consider, for example, the demand for equality of opportunity, or equality of actual endowments. For in that case, the content of the claim made by a citizen of one state depends on the endowments of the citizens of other states. If we suppose that every citizen has a rational interest in his own economic welfare, it is difficult not to ascribe to the representatives the formulation of some highly egalitarian comparative demand, plausibly along the lines of the Difference Principle. Nevertheless, I will argue that we should resist the temptation to introduce such a principle. This is not because we must take into account the cultural pluralism of the world – for we have bracketed this problem – but rather because of the world's *political pluralism*, that is, its division into a plurality of distinct and autonomous political communities. I have already argued that a global analogue of the Difference Principle is incompatible with a plurality of states; thus, to defend such a principle is to reject political pluralism and to maintain that the political responsibility of distinct peoples should be subordinated to an egalitarian principle of distributive justice. The cost of such a position would be the rejection of the value of citizenship, conceived as membership in a distinct politically responsible community.[13]

<hr/>

[12] This convergence is arguably not contingent. As Kant argued (1968, 349–51), there is a link between the fact that a state takes the rational interest of its citizens into account and the fact that such a state has no interest in war and domination.

[13] Note that I do not necessarily assert, as some contemporary republicans (for instance, Pocock 1975) have, that citizenship has an absolute value or a value in itself. I would prefer to argue that citizenship has an instrumental value, that citizenship is a means for the implementation of justice among people.

In light of the foregoing considerations, the representatives of individual persons must choose, according to their rational expectations, not only between several different systems of states, but also between any such system on the one hand, and on the other, an institutional cosmopolitanism that would denude each state or people by depriving it of responsibility for its level of economic endowment. It is not implausible to maintain that the representatives of individual persons would reject institutional cosmopolitanism in favor of political pluralism. Various reasons could be advanced. For example, in order to demonstrate the rational desirability of a global state, it would have to be established first that such a state is even possible. After all, a state – or at least any just state – must be built on certain feelings or attitudes that are the conditions for the acceptance of the state's institutions by its citizens. It is not obvious that any single institutional structure could satisfy this condition for the world as a whole, and this is a consideration of which we may assume the parties are aware. In addition, there are a number of traditional arguments that cast doubt on the desirability of a global state, and we should suppose that the parties are aware of these arguments as well, or have the epistemic resources to construct them. For example, we find – in Aristotle (1944, 553–59), in Montesquieu (1951, 365), in Tocqueville (1991, 179), and in Rawls (1999a, 36) – the argument that the larger a state is, or the larger the number of distinct peoples it contains, the more despotic its government will tend to be. Other arguments could be grounded in the benefits of cultural diversity: it is plausible that, under a veil of ignorance, every rational person would prefer living in a world with cultural diversity to living in a culturally homogeneous world. Thus, the political plurality of the world can reasonably be regarded as part of the rational interest of each person.[14]

If this is correct, then the deliberation of the representatives of individual persons will be oriented toward what I will call *fair terms of cooperative separation*; for the representatives will agree that the primary condition for them to be able to form a well-ordered society is to form a plurality of societies. Thus, before every other investigation, they will look for the terms under which a pluralistic scheme can be acceptable to each, given that none knows the relative level of endowment of the state in which he will live.[15] Each knows that his state will, in principle, have the capacity to provide its members with their basic rights and entitlements (conceived as an absolute minimum standard) and to organize the collective life in a way

[14] The plurality of states is therefore not a good in itself, but its value is a necessary consequence of the fact that a world state would be culturally homogeneous and politically despotic, or at least paternalistic. For the latter distinction, see the Aristotelian difference between despotic authority, paternalistic authority, and authority among equals, in *Politics* 3.1278b30–1279a15 (1944, 203–5).

[15] If that procedure is correct, it implies that the determination of global justice is prior to the determination of any domestic rules of justice. The requirements of a global cooperative separation introduce a constraint on the conceptions of domestic justice that could be allowed.

that enables each people to be politically responsible. But each representative also knows that, because of historical and cultural circumstances, his people may not be fully able to exercise its capacity for political responsibility. Thus, the representatives of individual persons would be led to much the same international principles as would the representatives of states: a version of the Law of Peoples, augmented by principles governing justifiable intervention, by a guarantee of the economic preconditions of a stable liberal constitution, by a principle of equal access to natural and capital resources, and by a principle of fair international bargaining procedures.[16]

It should probably be acknowledged, however, that this still leaves too much to chance from the point of view of an individual's representative. For since none knows in which of the plurality of actual states he will live, and since each knows that the levels of affluence of different states can differ significantly, the decision in favor of political pluralism would carry for each representative the risk of ending up in a relatively disadvantaged position. Each representative would have to entertain the possibility that her relative distributive disadvantage could outweigh, for her, all of the other advantages of political pluralism, including the value of living in a politically responsible community. Unlike the representatives of states, the representatives of individuals would therefore have reason to adopt, as a safeguard, a rule according to which an individual who finds himself discontented by the relative disadvantages of the political community into which he has been born may elect to join a more affluent state by emigrating.[17]

Does such a rule, establishing a general right of emigration, imply that each state must also recognize a general right of *immigration*? The parties here must weigh the advantage of being able freely to join any state against the potential disadvantage of being a member of a state that any may freely join. This suggests what I will call a general rule of solidarity: if a state wishes to limit immigration (beyond whatever reasonable limits might be imposed by the capacity of its territory to support a population), then that state acquires a duty of assistance to those individuals who would otherwise have immigrated. Such a duty will require reasonable efforts toward eliminating the relative disadvantages that motivate the desire for immigration.

[16] We may extend the construction by adding a temporal dimension as well: since the representatives do not know at what time in history they are to live, none would agree to terms under which she might end up living in an era in which the world's natural resources have been severely depleted, its climate catastrophically altered, or its environment poisoned by previous generations. From these considerations we can derive international rules concerning the husbanding of natural resources by each generation for the one to follow.

[17] The method of representing states instead of individuals does not yield the emigration provision. Since the problems of emigration and immigration are central in our present world, the method of representing individuals may be better suited to the problems we face today. There are, of course, other substantial arguments in favor of such a method (see my 1999, Chap. 2).

A scheme of this sort is fully compatible with the principle of political responsibility, because each state (or each group of states, should some states decide to act collectively) is responsible for the immigration they have refused.

I am aware that these ideas are highly programmatic, but I hope that they suffice to indicate in general terms how we might work out a conception of justice for the global context, and why we should not simply apply to the world at large the same conception of social justice that we apply in the domestic case.[18] The crucial disanalogy is that the domestic conception necessarily presupposes the nakedness of individuals, while the international conception cannot presuppose the nakedness of states, since to do so would be incompatible with a state's essential political responsibility. Only by denuding states of their responsibility through the initiation of a global state could we satisfy at the global level the preconditions for applying the conception of distributive justice that is appropriate domestically. But if we acknowledge the ethical value of political responsibility, we must accept a plurality of states, and thus reject domestic conceptions of distributive justice in the global context.

The situation of the world at large raises theoretical and institutional problems that are unique to it and that have no clear analogues at the domestic level. Unlike the Humean circumstances of justice, in which naked agents must agree on terms regulating the distribution of scarce resources among them, the world at large represents circumstances of cooperative separation, in which partially responsible states or peoples must come to terms regulating their interactions with one another, their access to resources, and the emigration and immigration of their populations. Fair international bargaining procedures, universal access to natural and capital resources, and suitable rights of emigration and immigration are the main concerns of global justice.

Acknowledgments

I must thank Eric Cavallero for his substantial assistance with this chapter. I also thank Alain Boyer for his comments and advice.

References

Aristotle. (1944). *Politics*. Ed. and trans. H. Rackham. The Loeb Classical Library. Cambridge, MA: Harvard University Press.

Beitz, Charles. (1999). *Political Theory and International Relations*. Rev. ed. Princeton: Princeton University Press. First edition published 1979.

Chauvier, Stéphane. (1999). *Justice Internationale et Solidarité*. Nimes: J. Chambon.

---

[18] I have attempted a more complete justification in my 1999.

Hobbes, Thomas. (1968). *Leviathan*. Ed. C. B. Macpherson. London: Pelican Books.

Hume, David. (1975). *An Inquiry Concerning the Principles of Morals*. Ed. L. A. Selby-Bigge. Rev. P. H. Nidditch. Oxford: Oxford University Press.

Kant, Immanuel. (1968). *Zum ewigen Frieden*. In *Kants Werke*, vol. 8. Berlin: Walter de Gruyter.

Montesquieu, Charles-Louis. (1951). *De l'esprit des lois*. In *Oeuvres complètes*, vol. 2. Paris: Gallimard/Bibliothèque de la Pléiade.

Pocock, John. (1975). *The Machiavellian Moment: Florentine Political Thought and the Atlantic Republican Tradition*. Princeton: Princeton University Press.

Pogge, Thomas. (1994). "An Egalitarian Law of Peoples." *Philosophy and Public Affairs*, 23:3, 195–224.

Rawls, John. (1999a). *The Law of Peoples*. Cambridge, MA: Harvard University Press.

———. (1999b). *A Theory of Justice*. Rev. ed. Cambridge, MA: Harvard University Press.

Tocqueville, Alexis de. (1979). *De la démocratie en Amérique*. In *Oeuvres*, vol. 2. Paris: Gallimard/Bibliothèque de la Pléiade.

8

DOES GLOBAL INEQUALITY MATTER?

CHARLES R. BEITZ

Introduction

We live in a world whose massive inequalities dwarf those found within the developed societies familiar to most of us. This is most conspicuously true of inequalities in standards of living – measured, for example, in average per capita purchasing power, life expectancy, and under-five child malnutrition (Pogge 2001; Doyle 2000). Contrary to what one might think, these inequalities are mostly greater today than 50 or 100 years ago, and there is reason to believe that the gap will continue to grow.[1] Global political inequalities are also massive – both those found in the decision procedures of international political and financial institutions and those in the capacities of various agents to use their procedural leverage effectively (that is, in terms familiar from John Rawls, in the global analogs of political liberties and their worth). Global economic and political inequalities ("social inequalities," for short) are so great that one would think those who hold to liberal egalitarian principles in the domestic politics of the rich countries would be more concerned about them, and on different grounds, than many evidently are.

This last observation might seem naïve for either of two reasons. It might be that a plausible egalitarianism must be bounded – that is, that the reasons why we care about social inequalities are essentially connected to the structural or cultural characteristics of individual societies or states. Perhaps, for example, the distinctively rigorous demands of equality are conditions of the political legitimacy of the state – as Ronald Dworkin writes, "of the majority's right to enforce its laws against those who think them unwise or even unjust" (Dworkin 2000, 2) – rather than of any general moral principle, say, of beneficence or natural justice, that applies across boundaries. Or perhaps the normative force of egalitarianism is part

---

[1] This is due not only to differential rates of economic growth; the uneven distribution of control over intellectual property is independently significant. Consider, for example, the likely consequences for inequality of life expectancies of the continuing development of expensive, high-technology medicine in the rich countries.

of a culturally specific ideal, such as that associated with the tradition of social democracy in the west, rather than a consequence of any moral principle at all. If either view is right, then it might be overreaching to criticize the global order on the grounds that it contains so much social inequality.

Alternatively, someone might think that the idea of equality itself, properly understood, is so abstract or formal that it cannot contribute much to the resolution of substantive controversy about inequalities at *any* level of social organization. It is difficult to find anyone who disagrees that we should give equal consideration to each person's prospects, or that we should take each person's interests equally seriously. But, according to one version of the view I have in mind, the reason why agreement at this level can coexist with great disagreement at the level of policy is that a requirement of equal consideration does not amount to more than the familiar maxim that like cases should be treated alike – a maxim not without normative force, but unlikely, without more, to resolve many serious normative disputes (see, e.g., Westen 1982 and Frankfurt 1987 on economic equality, and Frankfurt 1999, ch. 13, on equality generally). A different, though related, view holds that, although we can imagine how an attractive egalitarian social ideal might be given substance, when we think about particular inequalities we find that our most powerful concerns arise from considerations "which are not essentially egalitarian" at all (Scanlon 1997, 1). Either way, the critique of global inequality would be naïve, not because the ideal of equality is out of place at the global level (though it might be that too), but because whatever (good) reasons we have to be moved by egalitarian social criticism appeal to values distinct from equality itself. Someone who accepted such a view might think that criticism of the global order would be more persuasive and less open to error if it avoided appeal to equality altogether and referred instead to the (non-egalitarian) reasons why social inequality is sometimes objectionable.

This is a crude summary of positions that deserve to be developed with more care. My purpose, however, is not to defend or criticize these views on their merits. I mean only to observe that there are various credible grounds for doubt that global economic and political inequalities should concern us for their own sakes. The problem I would like to explore is whether we have reasons for concern about global inequality that do not derive their force from the idea that social inequality is, per se, a bad thing. So I shall simply grant, for the sake of argument, that it would be naïve to complain about global inequalities on simple egalitarian grounds. The question is whether someone who wishes to avoid naïveté has other reasons to be concerned about these inequalities.

Direct versus Derivative Reasons

To frame the question this way is implicitly to distinguish between two kinds of reasons for concern about social inequalities. I shall call these *direct* and *derivative* reasons.[2]

Direct reasons are grounded on the idea that an inequality in the distribution of something – for example, income, health care, education, or political power, or at a more abstract level, welfare or resources – is a bad thing in itself, independently of the impact of the distribution on values distinct from equality. When Amartya Sen asks, "Equality of What?" and proposes, as his answer, equality in "basic capabilities," he is suggesting that *one* reason why a more equal distribution of these capabilities is to be preferred to a less equal distribution is that it is more equal (1992, ch. 1; cf. Sen 1980). He does not claim that equality in basic capabilities is desirable because this promotes some other good; instead, he regards equality (of *something*) as a fundamental ethical requirement, and treats the question, "of what?" as a challenge to produce a persuasive interpretation of this requirement.[3] Of course one might – like Sen – be a pluralist about value, and hold that equality is not the only fundamental requirement; other values might be involved as well, and in the end we might judge that an unequal distribution is better, all things considered, than an equal one. What directly egalitarian reasons assert is that equality should come into an all-things-considered judgment about the acceptability of a distribution as a separate value to be combined with whatever other values are at stake; it is not simply a convenient proxy for (some of) those values.

Derivative reasons, by contrast, treat a social inequality as a bad thing because of its consequences for values which are distinct from equality itself. Derivative reasons hold that these (nonegalitarian) values would be better served if steps were taken whose result would be to reduce the social inequality. For example, a welfarist who opposes inequality in the distribution of income on the grounds that a more equal distribution would result in greater aggregate social welfare (perhaps because increasing income is supposed to yield diminishing marginal utility) offers a derivative reason for equality: the desirability of a more equal distribution is due, not to the fact that it is more equal, but to the different fact that it is expected to generate more welfare for society as a whole.[4]

Derek Parfit, in his Lindley Lecture, distinguishes between a belief in equality and the "Priority View," which argues against certain social inequalities on the ground that "benefiting people matters more the worse

---

[2] The distinction is familiar. For example, Joseph Raz distinguishes between "strictly egalitarian" and "rhetorically egalitarian" principles (1986, 227) and Derek Parfit distinguishes between the "Teleological" (or "Telic") and the "Deontological" (or "Deontic") views of equality (1991, 3–4).

[3] Ronald Dworkin's (2000) construction of the basic question is similar, though, in contrast to Sen, Dworkin declines to apply egalitarian principles globally.

[4] The value of equality is not entirely absent from such a view, of course, since typically (though not necessarily) there is a sense in which each person's utility counts equally in the social welfare function. Nevertheless, the goal of social welfare is an aggregate for society-at-large; it is not a distributive principle.

off these people are" (1991, 19). The Priority View, as Parfit constructs it, furnishes a derivative reason for concern about inequality. He writes that "on the Priority View, we do not believe in equality. Though we give priority to benefiting those who are worse off, that is not because such benefits reduce inequality" (1991, 24). Whether this is correct depends on the reason why one adopts the Priority View. One reason, emphasized by Parfit, might be that the needs of those who are worse off are more urgent than the needs of those who are better off. We give priority to the needs of those who are worse off because we believe it is better for scarce resources to be devoted to the relief of more rather than less urgent needs. (As Parfit observes, this is a deontological analog of the utilitarian argument for distributive equality based on diminishing marginal utility.) But we might be moved instead by a different reason: we might think that everyone has an equal antecedent claim to a good, but that an inequality in its distribution would be justified if the inequality would be better for everyone in comparison with equality (this, of course, is part of Rawls's argument in the original position for the difference principle). This is a directly egalitarian reason for adopting a principle that behaves in the same way as Parfit's Priority View (for an example of such a view, see Nagel 1991, 66–70).

When I say that I shall set aside the egalitarian critique of global inequality, what I mean is that I shall bracket objections grounded on direct reasons for concern about inequality and consider only those grounded on derivative reasons. I bracket the former, not because I believe they are implausible – about that I am for the moment agnostic – but because they are more controversial and less widely accepted, and more easily portrayed as elements of a sectional or parochial political doctrine. I want to see how far the critique of global social inequality can proceed without benefit of directly egalitarian reasons. I want to know if, and if so why, global inequality should matter to someone who does not believe that global equality should appeal to us for its own sake.

Derivative Reasons Why Global Inequality Matters

To explore this question, I shall distinguish several derivative reasons for concern about social inequality at the domestic level and consider whether these reasons applied at the global level should trouble us as well. As I shall suggest, it does not appear *ex ante* that any of these concerns must be limited, by its terms, to inequalities arising within a single society; in formulation the concerns are quite general. Whatever reasons there might be to accord them greater weight within rather than among societies would arise, if at all, in connection with the substance of each concern. So we have two tasks – to understand the concerns, taken in general, and to ask whether they have force at the global level.

Two preliminary observations. First, I shall take "global inequality" as inequality among persons who reside in different societies from each other, not principally among societies themselves, taken as corporate entities; when I speak of inequalities among societies or states, unless otherwise noted, I shall mean this as shorthand for inequalities among the persons who inhabit them taken as a single group.

Second, the list of concerns is inspired by that suggested by Thomas Scanlon (1997) in connection with (presumably domestic) economic inequality. I note, however, that sometimes I interpret these reasons differently than Scanlon and that I concentrate on the respects in which they appeal to values distinct from equality itself.

Inequality and Material Deprivation
The most common and, morally speaking, usually the most powerful derivative reason for concern about much social inequality arises from its association with material deprivation. According to Scanlon, this objection holds that a social inequality is objectionable if some people are living in "terrible conditions" and it would be possible to alleviate their suffering by means of a transfer from the better off "without creating hardships of comparable severity" (1997, 2). What motivates this concern is plainly not any attachment to equality for its own sake, but instead a recognition of the lopsidedness of the comparison between the suffering that could be reduced for some and the opportunity costs to others of doing so.

Two aspects of this concern need comment, the first pertaining to the relationship between social inequality and suffering, and the second, to the reason why relieving suffering seems important to us.

With respect to the first aspect, it is important to see that the weight of the concern does not depend on believing that social inequality is the cause of suffering. It is not necessary, for example, that there be any sense in which the wealth of the rich was attained by exploiting the poor. The argument for relieving suffering is not about redressing a historical or structural injustice. As Scanlon says, the significance of the inequality is simply that it "provides an opportunity – a way of reducing the suffering of some without causing others to suffer a similar fate" (1997, 2).

But even this might be misleading. For the connection between the desirability of relieving suffering and the adoption of deliberately redistributive (or inequality-reducing) measures as a means to reach this goal is entirely contingent. If we look at the level of social policy rather than that of individual action, we can imagine at least three different schematic approaches aimed at improving well-being among the worse off: transfer, growth, and structural change. Only the first is redistributive in the familiar sense of requiring direct transfers of resources from some people to others. By contrast, under favorable conditions macroeconomic measures to promote the growth of output may result in improved living standards for the worse off without any direct transfers at all (though other forms of intervention might be required). Direct transfers might also be unnecessary if public investment in the development of economic infrastructure and the promotion of, say, labor-intensive industry were to relieve suffering by generating employment opportunities and increasing incomes among the poor. All three approaches involve a distribution of costs, of course, and over time all three might (though, in the second and third cases, also might not) result in a reduction in overall income inequality; but it is only in the first case that the reduction of inequality could be said to be the intended means of relieving suffering.

Let me turn now to the reason why the relief of suffering concerns us. Scanlon describes this as "at base a humanitarian concern" and suggests that its operation is limited to cases in which people are living in conditions that are "seriously deficient"; its force "fades away . . . as we imagine the situation of both rich and 'poor' to be greatly improved" (1997, 2). There is, however, a considerable distance between "seriously deficient" and "greatly improved," and in that region it seems that there is a continuing concern about individual well-being that may influence judgment about policy without being literally a concern to "relieve suffering" (or more generally, perhaps, a "humanitarian concern" at all). Scanlon speculates that this may be "a more truly egalitarian" value, but I am not sure this is true. Rather, it seems to be the concern described by Harry Frankfurt as that a person should "have enough" or "meet a standard" of well-being (1987, 37). This is not the same as "merely having enough to get along" or "to make life marginally tolerable"; rather, in Frankfurt's generous formulation, it is having enough for a (reasonable) person to be "content with what he has" or "to meet his expectations" (1987, 38, 39)[5] – to live a reasonably successful rather than only a minimally decent life. The proof that this is not a truly egalitarian concern is that there is no suggestion that inequality as such should be reduced: if everyone "had enough" this concern would not yield any objection to some people's having much more. As before, the existence of an inequality simply marks an opportunity to achieve a nonegalitarian goal.

It is doubtless true that the weight we attach to such an objection diminishes as a person's material conditions improve. This is because we assume (generally, but not always, correctly) that an improvement in material conditions is connected with a decrease in the urgency of the person's remaining unsatisfied needs and desires. The judgment about the urgency of these remaining needs may be partly comparative: we may think scarce resources are better used where they are located rather than be transferred

---

[5] Joseph Raz has written with great clarity about the content of such a notion of well-being and the sense in which we may be said to have a duty to promote it for others (though he does not explicitly consider the global context). See, for example, "Duties of Well-Being" (in Raz 1995, 3–28).

elsewhere. But the judgment may also be noncomparative: we may regard these needs as more or less inessential or unimportant for a reasonably successful life, and so to represent a less compelling claim on others, whatever their own circumstances might be.

These reflections suggest that there is no clear or sharply defined threshold of "serious deficiency" above which a concern to improve a person's material conditions simply ceases to operate. If there is a threshold, then, following Frankfurt, it might more aptly be described as "sufficiency" – though this, too, may be impossible to define sharply. When this latter standard has not been met, but we judge that further measures to improve well-being are not called for, it will not be because individual well-being does not matter, but because we judge, for any of a number of reasons, that it would be wrong or inefficient or otherwise undesirable to impose the costs of these measures on others.

On its face, this objection seems to apply with equal force to global as well as to domestic inequalities – that is, to foreign as well as to domestic deprivations – which are otherwise comparable. This is because whatever weight the objection carries is due to a recognition of the urgency of the interests of the worse off in comparison with the costs of satisfying these interests. Indeed, if the suffering of the globally worse off is more severe than that of the worse off in western domestic societies, then the objection may be even more pressing in the global than in the more familiar domestic cases.

Now, of course, in the global context even the goal of alleviating acute, avoidable suffering would require a more ambitious commitment of resources than anything seen so far. So in one sense it might be gratuitous to press the philosophical point that the concern underlying this objection to inequality is more demanding than terms like "suffering" and "serious deficiency" suggest. On the other hand, it seems no less a mistake in global than in domestic society to believe that improving the material conditions of life is a value for institutions and social policy only in situations of serious distress or extreme deprivation. That concern is more comprehensive, even if in some circumstances the impact of its extension may be offset by other considerations.[6]

If there is something special about the global context, it could have to do with either of two contrasts between the global and the domestic realms. The first trades on the fact that global society is composed of separate, if increasingly integrated, domestic societies, each with its own political culture and traditions as well as legal and economic arrangements. Because the locus of political capacity lies at the domestic level, one might think it pointless to seek measures at the global level that would contribute

---

[6] Among other things, this suggests a reason to resist the temptation to regard the "economic rights" found in international human rights doctrine as divided between "genuine" human rights, conceived as rights to the means of subsistence, and further claims which are categorically distinct and therefore less important.

to a sustainable improvement in individual well-being: in the long run, only domestic reform will relieve deprivation. If this is correct, then although we have reason to wish for improvements in the well-being of those who are relatively disadvantaged in global terms, the reason does not extend to a criticism of global inequality because the remedy must be local, not global.[7]

There is a good deal that might be said about this point, but since it would take us away from our philosophical subject I will simply note two observations.[8] First, there is a large, complex, and unresolved empirical question about the relative contributions of local and global factors to the wealth and poverty of societies. On any plausible view, local factors – for example, the extent and authority of the legal system, the character of the political culture and its traditions, the strength of commitment to the public interest among elites – are plainly of great importance. Second, however, it does not follow that the global environment is insignificant either as an element in the explanation of local political and economic phenomena (consider, e.g., the network of political forces that sustained corrupt governments of both left and right during the Cold War) or as a potential source of incentives and resources for domestic reform. The fact that local change is a necessary condition for a sustainable improvement in well-being does not imply that international contributions are not also necessary or would not accelerate the process if suitably deployed. So, even if we concede what should be conceded on the empirical point, we are still left with an objection to global inequality.

The other contrast involves the wider range of social and cultural factors that influence judgments about the sufficiency of the material conditions of life when these judgments range over a number of distinct societies. Sen notes, for example, that any application of the idea of equality of basic capabilities "must be rather culture-dependent, especially in the weighting of different capabilities" (1980, 219). To illustrate, consider Sen's suggestion that the idea of well-being can be described in terms of sets of capabilities to realize various basic human "functionings" (1992, ch. 3). These might include, for example, the capability to be well nourished, to avoid premature mortality, to have self-respect, and to take part in the life of the community.[9] Now some of these capabilities have relatively similar resource requirements across cultures (e.g., being well nourished), whereas the resource requirements of others may vary from one culture to the next (having self-respect, participating in the life of the community). Let us call the latter "culturally variable capabilities." Culturally variable capabilities

---

[7] See, for example, Rawls (1999a, 108–10). Although Rawls does not regard economic equality as a value to be pursued at the global level in the same way in which he could be said to do so in liberal society, he does advocate potentially significant international transfers to promote the development of poor societies.

[8] I have said more about this in Beitz 2000.

[9] These are Sen's examples (1992, 39).

may be more costly to achieve in relatively wealthier societies because doing so depends in part on reaching a norm that is determined by the realized ways of life of others. Looking across cultures, it might be that the goal of enabling everyone to live a "reasonably good" life, defined as achieving comparable sets of capabilities to function, would justify some degree of distributive inequality, with individuals in well-to-do societies having claims to larger minimum shares of resources than those elsewhere.

Once again, there are large issues here, this time philosophical rather than empirical. Again I cannot explore them here in detail. It seems to me true that there are such things as culturally variable capabilities, in the sense defined, some of which can reasonably be described as central to well-being on any plausible view, and so not easily dismissed as lacking in urgency. It is a question of considerable theoretical interest how, and on what basis, scarce resources should be allocated among individuals to help them realize capability sets of equal urgency, when the resource requirements of these capabilities vary.[10] It seems to me a plausible conjecture, however, that the feasible measures that might be undertaken at the global level to improve well-being among the globally worse off would not actually require depriving the better off of the means to achieve equally urgent capabilities. So the (theoretically correct) observation that it is more costly to realize certain capabilities in wealthy than in poor societies does not obviously count against the claim that existing global inequalities are objectionable because they are associated with remediable suffering.

Inequality, Humiliation, and Denial of Agency
Social inequalities can be objectionable for reasons other than that they may be associated with deprivation of the material means of life. Avishai Margalit writes, "In general, inequality symbolically expresses an attitude of downgrading – the view that the other is inferior in the social hierarchy" (1997, 148). I believe this is an overstatement (many inequalities do no such thing), but it is true that some social inequalities convey invidious distinctions of inferiority and superiority. This is most clearly the case for systems of caste and rank, which embed social distinctions in law, but it also applies to "informal" distinctions of class and status, at least where these are perceived to be deep and persisting. It may also be true, at least under some social conditions, of large differences in income and wealth, which, as Scanlon notes, may cause some people to "feel inferiority and shame at the way they must live" (1997, 3).

Why should we regard social inequalities that convey a sense of inferiority as objectionable? An obvious reason is that these inequalities are

---

[10] As Sen suggests, there is also a question about how the idea of "functionings of equal urgency" might be understood, particularly because a ranking of functionings by urgency might conceivably vary with social conditions.

incompatible with an ideal of society as an association of equals.[11] This is, in my terms, a directly egalitarian reason, so I must set it aside. But I believe there is also a derivative reason; to use Margalit's term, it is an objection to the *humiliation* associated with certain kinds of inequality (1997, 149–50). He takes the situation of outcastes to be exemplary: humiliation is "seeing humans as if they were in a permanent state of what may variously be called untouchability, defilement, impurity or pollution, so that it is religiously or morally necessary to keep away from them" (151). The humiliation of outcastes has a secular equivalent: it is a condition produced when social inequality effectively bars upward mobility and creates a permanent "'reject' status" in society (153). To be humiliated is to be made to feel unacceptable or unworthy of respect, as if one's life is not regarded by others as having significance or integrity of its own. Regarded in this way, humiliation is partly a noncomparative harm: it is objectionable because it undermines a person's dignity and self-respect and diminishes the capacity for independent agency.

It is surprising that this element has not been more conspicuous in global egalitarian thought, for it seems clear that the objection applies to global inequalities at least as forcefully as to their domestic analogs. It may be, once again, that too much weight has been placed on assumptions about the differences between the domestic and the global realms. One might think, for example, that differences of social position or standard of living produce humiliation for the worst off in domestic society as a result of their culturally induced awareness of the extent of these inequalities, reified in widely shared attitudes related to social class. But why believe that this dynamic does not also operate at the global level? It is true that not all deprivation, even severe deprivation, is humiliating: Margalit gives the example of the nomadic tribes of the Spanish Sahara, who live in extreme but egalitarian poverty, which they attribute to natural causes; he believes they therefore suffer no humiliation (1997, 149).[12] Most poverty, however, is not like this; more often it exists in societies where there are conspicuous local extremes of wealth. And, with the expansion and increased penetration of the global media, it cannot plausibly be held that global society is divided, as Rawls imagined a just domestic society might be, into a plurality of "noncomparing groups" that are either unaware of or indifferent to the standards of living found in other societies (1999b, 470–71; compare Scanlon 1997, 15). Nor can it plausibly be argued that the degrees of poverty found, for example, in many third-world cities are broadly consistent with a sense of oneself as an active agent, capable of taking effective command of the conduct of one's life.

The familiar relativist retort is that the capacity to regard oneself as an

---

[11] This is the source of a familiar argument for facially egalitarian procedures in democratic systems. I discussed this argument in Beitz 1989, 109–10.

[12] Margalit does not suggest that this is in any way a model of extreme poverty as it exists in most of the world.

independent agent is a parochial value, one not appropriately considered to be common among culturally diverse conceptions of human good. Thus, for example, it was argued in connection with "Asian values" that autonomy is more important for the educated westerner than, say, for the Asian farmer or worker (see, e.g., Kausikan 1993). This position has been widely discussed (e.g., by Sen 1999) so I shall simply note what seem to me to be the two main elements of a rejoinder without trying to defend them – a project that, in any case, is beyond our present scope. First, as a matter of fact, it is simply not true that cultures divide as the relativist claims; reality is more complicated, with divisions about values associated with individual autonomy typically occurring within cultures rather than between them. Second, as a matter of ethical theory, the fact of disagreement about a basic value cannot be, in itself, a reason to reject the value; disagreement can be found about virtually all values, even those we feel most confident in accepting, so if agreement were really a condition of acceptability we should reject most of the values we accept. If there are substantive reasons why independent agency should not be seen as a value for everyone, they need to be stated in a non-question-begging way. This the defenders of relativism seldom do.

What lesson should we draw from this? An important motive of egalitarian social thought has been concern about the debilitating effects of material deprivation on self-respect and the capacity for self-direction. In part this concern has derived from an ideal of society as a community of equals; but in part it also reflects a noncomparative conception of the minimum conditions of a decent human life, one most often framed as a concern about autonomy and self-respect. Holding other things constant, if this concern has weight at the domestic level, then it ought to have weight at the global level as well.

Inequality and Abridgement of Liberty
Some inequalities are objectionable because they express social relations in which the advantaged exercise an unreasonably large degree of control over others. As Scanlon writes, those who have greater resources "can often determine what gets produced, what kinds of employment are offered, what the environment of a town or state is like, and what kind of life one can live there" (1997, 3). Sometimes these determinations take place through institutional mechanisms – for example, as a result of a successful strategy of financial contributions to candidates for office. But control might be exercised directly in interpersonal relations as well – for example, by the feudal lord over his vassals or the sweatshop owner over his workers. In the institutional case, the objection seems to derive from considerations of political liberty, but as the subsequent examples suggest, this is an instance of a more general libertarian objection: large inequalities of resources can objectionably limit a person's capacity to determine the course of her life.

Is this really a derivative reason for objecting to an inequality? It might seem not, especially in the political case, where what is wrong with economic inequality appears to be that it enables some people to exercise greater influence than others over the outcomes of the political process. This is what is implied, for example, in the rhetorical claim that private political spending is equivalent to the casting of extra votes. Political equality seems to be appealed to as intrinsically desirable. There is something to this, but it is not the whole story. For when inequalities of wealth severely limit the choices effectively open to some people, their prospects are also set back in a noncomparative way. It is analogous to the case of humiliation: the deprivation of control is a further, separate harm.

And, as in the case of humiliation, if this is a legitimate ground of complaint about inequality at the domestic level, then prima facie it seems equally so at the global level. Why should it not be? Recall that the concern here is not that inequalities, for example, in access to the media, campaign spending, or public investment in education will impede participation in democratic politics (in which case the complaint would be parasitic on acceptance of a democratic egalitarian ideal and so might "reasonably be thought to apply only within the limits of a shared state" [Satz 1999, 79]). This may nevertheless be the case, but it is not the basis of the concern at hand. Instead, the concern is that prevailing inequalities will deprive some people of significant control over the conduct of their own lives by changing and narrowing the range of alternatives from among which they are effectively able to choose. Moreover, it is even less plausible here than in connection with humiliation that owing to cultural differences, the weight or urgency of the underlying concern varies among societies.

Of course, not all social inequalities, even large ones, are vulnerable to this objection. Much depends on the character of the institutions within which the inequality occurs, and particularly on the existence and effectiveness of institutional devices to protect against or compensate for the capacity of economic power to constrain liberty. The modern welfare state can be seen as embodying an array of such measures, from the protection of labor organizing to the social "safety net." Economic inequalities that would otherwise be objectionable might be acceptable when devices of this kind exist.

At the global level, however, there are no such devices. Members of economically vulnerable societies – particularly the worse off among them, who lack private means to fall back on – are exposed, without any effective recourse, to the consequences of decisions importantly affecting their life prospects which originate elsewhere. These range from the machinations of private foreign currency speculators to the macroeconomic "restructuring" conditions imposed on emergency lending by multilateral financial organizations whose decisions are dominated by the governments of wealthy societies. These might be seen as parallels at the global level of forms of action we are inclined to recognize in domestic society as involving the use of economic power to exercise excessive control over individual lives. Without effective restraining or compensating mechanisms, this dimension of global inequality is more, not less, troubling than its domestic analog.

Inequality and Procedural Unfairness
Sometimes what is objectionable about an inequality is not so much that it enables some people to exercise an unacceptable degree of control over others, but that it undermines or disrupts the conditions on which the fairness of many processes (like most competitions) depends. Scanlon observes that this and the previous objection can overlap in individual cases, significantly including the political one, but argues that the value of fairness is distinct from the value of liberty appealed to previously (1997, 4). I think he is correct about this: we can imagine decision processes (and not only those for the allocation of honors or opportunities, which he suggests as examples) which do not result in an agent's being deprived of substantial control over her life, but which nevertheless strike us for various reasons as unfair.

In the domestic case, we recognize procedural unfairness in several forms: as unwarranted exclusion from a decision-making process in whose outcomes an individual has an interest; as an asymmetry in the terms of participation in a process not justified by its aims; as reliance on irrelevant or partial information, or as exclusion of relevant information; or as "background conditions such as inequalities in training and resources" (Scanlon 1997, 4) that cause an agent's interests to be given either more or less weight than would be reasonable in light of their nature and urgency. It is not easy to say what these forms of procedural unfairness have in common, in virtue of which we regard their presence as tainting a decision. In some cases we identify the unfairness with reference to the purposes of the process; as a crude approximation, one might say that a rule-governed process is unfair if it employs distinctions which cannot be justified to reasonable participants who share an interest in achieving the process's purpose. But this cannot be all, for unfairness can also arise when there is no agreement as to a process's purpose or when the process is vaguely or incompletely determined by public rules; for example, we would normally (though perhaps not always) regard it as unfair to exclude an interested party from participation in a decision involving the provision of some collective good, even if the decision was reached outside of any rule-governed or conventionally defined process.

What might be the analogs at the global level of these forms of unfairness? The clearest cases involve well-established decision procedures embodying formal or constitutional inequalities. The U.N. Security Council, for example, has emerged in the post–Cold War world as the central international forum that authorizes humanitarian intervention. Its voting procedure accords vetoes to the five permanent members, but not to any representative of the class of states most vulnerable to intervention, and one might reasonably wonder whether such an inequality can be justified. A similar question arises about the World Bank, whose decisions concerning sponsorship of development initiatives primarily interest the less developed countries which are its clients, but whose board of governors cast votes in proportion to each country's ownership of capital stock in the Bank.[13] Both of these are examples of procedural inequalities that might be regarded as unfair because they do not seem to have any reasonable relationship to their institutions' purposes – though, of course, in each case the claim of unfairness is contestable.[14]

Analogs of another kind of domestic political unfairness might be found in the background inequalities that give rise to differences in bargaining power in international negotiations. In more and less obvious ways these differences are typically reflected in the negotiations' outcomes. Consider, for example, the most recent round of trade negotiations, which resulted, among other things, in an international intellectual property agreement that will raise the cost of technology to the poor countries.[15] It is arguable whether, from a global point of view, this agreement is the best that could be expected; this question I leave aside. What is clear is that the poor countries' inability to win more favorable terms of access to intellectual property was related to the lack of resources they could bring to bear in the negotiations. Their capacity to represent their interests effectively was impaired in a way that might be seen as analogous to the way the domestic poor are impaired when the political process is subject to the influence of extremes of private wealth. In both cases, inequality of resources distorts the process of political decision making by causing some interests to be weighted more heavily than they should be, given their nature and urgency, and others less. What is fundamentally objectionable is not the inequality per se, but its contribution to a distortion of the deliberative process of weighing and comparing of interests that issues in a decision. This is obscured in the international case by the tendency to see negotiations like the trade talks as free-standing cases of bargaining rather than as elements in an underinstitutionalized but evolving process of international governance. The latter view is encouraged by the concept of an international "regime" and seems to me the more realistic perception. If this is right, then the analogy with procedural unfairness in domestic politics is strengthened.

Responsibilities and Remedies

The preceding exercise consisted of distinguishing a series of ("derivative") reasons for concern about social inequality and asking whether those reasons

---

[13] To be more precise, each member country casts a minimum number of votes, increased in proportion to its ownership of stock.

[14] For example, as Michael Doyle pointed out in discussion, the great-power veto in the Security Council might be defended as part of a mechanism that prevents the United Nations from acting in ways that could reasonably be seen as partisan.

[15] This is the "TRIPS" agreement ("Trade-Related Aspects of Intellectual Property"). For a discussion see Oddi 1996.

might plausibly apply at the global as well as the sectional levels. This approach deliberately prescinds from theoretical problems concerning the meaning of global justice and the ethical significance of the boundaries between societies, and looks instead at the substantive grounds for objecting to economic and political inequalities like those that exist in the world today.

An advantage of this approach is to concentrate attention on the situation of those who are worse off and to emphasize the respects in which their circumstances interfere with their living what might reasonably be described as decent and satisfying lives. It shows that there are ethically significant reasons for concern about global inequality that do not depend on the prior adoption of a particular theoretical view about the moral character of the global community or of an egalitarian social ideal whose pertinence might be limited to the western liberal democracies.

There might also seem to be a disadvantage to this approach. In concentrating on the situation of the worse off, it postpones deciding which agents have responsibilities to remedy the objectionable features of global inequality. It also postpones asking *why* these agents should undertake sacrifices in order to improve the circumstances of others, and how they should choose when other responsibilities come into conflict. These questions, of course, are at the heart of disagreement about global justice. So it might seem that our exercise does not help much with the matters people actually disagree about.

I think this conclusion would be too quick, but can only gesture at the reasons why. There is dispute about whether we should understand global justice, so to speak, as an enlarged image of justice in one society – and as correspondingly demanding – or rather as a distinct construction, suited to a world that cannot be described as a single society, and therefore as demanding less than its domestic analog. In bracketing concerns about social equality per se, we leave aside the element of conventional conceptions of social justice that seems to generate its most exacting requirements. We are left with values whose importance does not derive from positional considerations, but rather from a noncomparative and fairly noncontroversial conception of human well-being. The fact that these values are weighty, and that satisfying them would be costly, suggests to me that even on the more restricted view about global justice, its aspirations must be ambitious.

Now, as I suggested, the idea of social justice has two faces. One looks toward the distribution of the benefits of social life; the other, toward the allocation of its burdens. Justice is about both distribution and contribution. The subject of social justice is difficult partly because the two problems interact and must be faced simultaneously, even though they implicate moral ideas that are to some extent distinct. For example, suppose that societies A and B contain equal numbers of suffering persons whose relief is of equal urgency; the question of whether the members of society A have equally strong reasons to relieve suffering in society B as in society A concerns contribution, not distribution – the allocation of burdens, not benefits – since, by hypothesis, the urgency of relieving the suffering is the same in both societies. Nothing I have said here will help solve this problem. On the other hand, if the analysis shows that the hard question is whether the well off have good reasons to withhold access to their resources from persons elsewhere whose well-being depends upon them, we have at least seen where the problem lies.

Finally, I note a more practical consequence of the exercise. Because philosophical discussion about equality so often proceeds at a highly abstract level, it is easy to fall into the error of supposing that any remedy for objectionable inequalities must involve some form of leveling – the transfer of resources from those who have more to those who have less. Concentrating on the substantive reasons for concern about global inequality reduces the temptation to error by directing attention to policy measures that specifically address these concerns – for example, relief of poverty, improvement of nutrition, empowerment of local communities, and so forth. Such measures may not involve leveling at all, or do so only as a by-product of acting on distinctly nonegalitarian aims. To see global inequality in this perspective may therefore not only underscore the urgency of transnational action, but also encourage a search for more realistic and potentially more effective remedies.

Acknowledgments

I am grateful to the members of the Bielefeld workshop for their comments on an earlier version of this chapter, and particularly to Andrew Kuper and Thomas Pogge, who provided helpful written suggestions and criticisms.

References

Beitz, Charles R. (1989). *Political Equality.* Princeton, NJ: Princeton University Press.
———. (2000). "Rawls's Law of Peoples." *Ethics*, 110, 669–96.
Doyle, Michael. (2000). "Global Economic Inequalities: A Growing Moral Gap." In *Principled World Politics: The Challenge of Normative International Relations*, edited by Paul K. Wapner and Lester Edwin Ruiz, 79–97. Lanham, MD: Rowman and Littlefield.
Dworkin, Ronald. (2000). *Sovereign Virtue.* Cambridge: Harvard University Press.
Frankfurt, Harry. (1987). "Equality as a Moral Ideal." *Ethics*, 98, 21–43.
———. (1999). *Necessity, Volition, and Love.* Cambridge: Cambridge University Press.
Kausikan, Bilahari. (1993). "Asia's Different Standard." *Foreign Policy,* 92, 24–41.

Margalit, Avishai. (1997). "Decent Equality and Freedom: A Postscript." *Social Research*, 64, 147–60.

Nagel, Thomas. (1991). *Equality and Partiality.* New York: Oxford University Press.

Oddi, A. Samuel. (1996). "TRIPS – Natural Rights and a 'Polite Form of Economic Imperialism.'" *Vanderbilt Journal of Transnational Law*, 29, 415–70.

Parfit, Derek. (1991). *Equality or Priority?* The Lindley Lecture. Lawrence: Department of Philosophy, University of Kansas.

Pogge, Thomas. (2001). "Priorities of Global Justice." *Metaphilosophy*, 32:1/2.

Rawls, John. (1999a). *The Law of Peoples.* Cambridge: Harvard University Press.

———. (1999b). *A Theory of Justice.* Rev. ed. Cambridge: Harvard University Press.

Raz, Joseph. (1986). *The Morality of Freedom.* Oxford: Clarendon Press.

———. (1995). *Ethics in the Public Domain.* Rev. ed. Oxford: Clarendon Press.

Satz, Debra. (1999). "Equality of What among Whom?" In *Global Justice*, edited by Ian Shapiro and Lea Brilmayer, 67–85. *Nomos* 41. New York: New York University Press.

Scanlon, T. M. (1997). *The Diversity of Objections to Inequality.* The Lindley Lecture. Lawrence: Department of Philosophy, University of Kansas.

Sen, Amartya. (1980). "Equality of What?" In *The Tanner Lectures on Human Values, 1980*, edited by Sterling M. McMurrin, 195–220. Salt Lake City: University of Utah Press.

———. (1992). *Inequality Reexamined.* Cambridge: Harvard University Press.

———. (1999). "Human Rights and Economic Achievements." In *The East Asian Challenge for Human Rights*, edited by Joanne R. Bauer and Daniel A. Bell, 88–99. Cambridge: Cambridge University Press.

Westen, Peter. (1982). "The Empty Idea of Equality." *Harvard Law Review*, 95, 537–96.

9

COSMOPOLITAN JUSTICE AND EQUALIZING OPPORTUNITIES

SIMON CANEY

One deep conviction shared by members of liberal societies is that individuals should enjoy equality of opportunity with their fellow citizens. Very few, however, think that there should be global equality of opportunity, where this requires that all persons throughout the world enjoy equal opportunities. I want in this chapter to present and motivate support for an ideal of global equality of opportunity. To do so I shall define and defend global equality of opportunity in Section I and then seek to respond to three powerful criticisms of this ideal (Sections II–IV).

I

1. Let me begin then by defining global equality of opportunity. To do so it is instructive to start by examining domestic (that is, state-level) equality of opportunity and noting that there are of course different interpretations of this ideal. Some, for example, adopt a purely formal conception, according to which those allocating positions (such as jobs or places at educational institutions) may not penalize someone because of features of his or her cultural identity such as race or creed. It operates at the stage at which positions are allocated and stipulates that positions go to the best qualified. It is, however, blind to the social and economic contexts in which people acquire qualifications. It is, for example, insensitive to the fact that people may be worse qualified because they were born into a less affluent class and therefore had less access to educational materials. For this reason, others adopt a more substantive conception which requires that resources be distributed to ensure that people's opportunities are not worsened by their race or class. Such a conception is, for example, affirmed by John Rawls. Rawls writes: "background social conditions are such that each citizen, regardless of class or origin, should have the same chance of attaining a favored social position, given the same talents and willingness to try" (1999a, 115; see also Rawls 1999b, 63, 72–73).

In what follows, I shall operate with this second conception of equality of opportunity. My claim is that this ideal should be applied at a global level. Persons should have the same opportunity to achieve a position, independently of what nation or state or class or religion or ethnic group they belong to. The ideal of equality of opportunity has received comparatively little attention from cosmopolitans, although we should record that there have been some exceptions: Brian Barry, for instance, once suggested it (1991b, 226, 237–39)[1] and, more recently, Thomas Pogge expressed some support for it.[2]

Two features of this ideal should be noted. First, it is important to emphasize that equality of opportunity does not require an equality of *outcomes* in which the ethnic, national, and class composition for each position mirrors the ethnic, national, and class composition of the population. It is a procedural rather than an outcome-related concept, requiring that persons do not have worse opportunities *because of* their nationality. This is not to say that outcomes are of no importance. They might serve as a useful indicator: where disproportionately few members of a profession come from one ethnic group, that might suggest that they have worse opportunities to attain that position. Second, global equality of opportunity is a claim about people's entitlements. A complete theory of justice must also speak to people's duties. What implications does this global equality of opportunity have for people's duties? This is a large question, but the appropriate line of reasoning would, I think, take the following form. We must start with an account of people's entitlements, and with this account in mind, we should design institutions that are most likely to bring it about that people receive their entitlements. From this we can then derive people's duties. Persons have duties to bring about and support those institutions required by the global principles of justice (Shue 1996, 17, 59–60, 159–61, 164–66, 168–69, 173–80). Clearly this needs to be developed at greater length. My aim here is just to provide a sketch of the implications of global equality of opportunity.

2. Having briefly explicated the concept of global equality of opportunity, I now want to turn to the question of why we should accept this ideal. The central reasoning for global equality of opportunity runs as follows: underpinning our commitment to equality of opportunity is the deep conviction that it is unfair if someone enjoys worse opportunities because of his or her cultural identity. Thus we think that it is unfair if a person enjoys worse chances in life because of class or social status or ethnicity. This deep conviction implies, however, that we should also object if some people have worse opportunities because of their nationality or civic identity.[3] The

[1] Barry connects this with global equality of natural resources. See Barry (1991a, 196–203). It is possible that something like global equality of opportunity underlies Hillel Steiner's affirmation of global equality of natural resources (Steiner 1999, 173–77).
[2] Pogge criticises "our current world order" because, *inter alia*, "[i]t fails to give equally talented and motivated persons roughly equal chances to obtain a good education and professional position irrespective of the society into which they were born" (1994b, 196).
[3] For this kind of point see Barry (1991b, 226); Beitz (1983, 593, 595); Caney (2000b,

core intuition, then, maintains that persons should not face worse opportunities in life because of the community or communities they come from. This point can be expressed negatively: people should not be penalized because of the vagaries of happenstance, and their fortunes should not be set by factors like nationality or citizenship. Or it can be expressed positively: people are entitled to the same opportunities as others. If, then, we object to an aristocratic or medieval scheme that distributes unequal opportunities according to one's social standing, or to a racist scheme that distributes unequal opportunities according to one's race, we should, I am arguing, also object to an international order that distributes unequal opportunities according to one's nationality (Carens 1987, 252, 256). In short, then, the rationale for accepting equality of opportunity within the state entails that we should accept global equality of opportunity.

3. Having presented the main argument for global equality of opportunity, I may now consider three supplementary considerations that provide further support for global equality of opportunity. The first two are evident if we compare global equality of opportunity with other cosmopolitan proposals. Let us compare it first with the view that global justice requires simply that each person has a basic right to subsistence. A powerful case for such basic rights has been given by Henry Shue (1996).[4] On their own, however, basic rights are insufficient since they allow some to have much worse prospects in life than others for no reason other than that, say, they are Somalian as opposed to Italian. Consider in this context a state which protects the basic rights of all its citizens but in which one race enjoys dramatically better opportunities than others. This is a liberal and humane system of apartheid. Notwithstanding its protection of subsistence rights, we would rightly consider such a system highly unjust. For the same reason, however, we should also object to a global order which protects the basic rights of all, but which skews opportunities to education, health, and employment to a privileged few who are favoured because of their national identity. Such a system is open to the objection that it is a system of liberal "global apartheid."[5] Global equality of opportunity thus fares well when compared to a basic-rights view.

It also fares well when compared with conceptions of global distributive justice from the other, more expansive end of the spectrum. This is

131, 144 n. 3); C. Jones (1999, 8); Pogge (1989, 247); and Pogge (1994b, 198). This reasoning is, I believe, either explicitly or implicitly present in almost all defences of cosmopolitanism, including, for example, those of Brian Barry, Charles Beitz, Thomas Pogge, Peter Singer, and David Richards. For exegetical evidence for this claim, see Caney (forthcoming, Section I). Cf. further Black (1991, especially 355–57).

[4] See also C. Jones (1999, Chapter 3). My argument in this paragraph should not be construed as a criticism of either, since both provide compelling vindications of basic rights and neither is committed to the rejection of anything more substantive.

[5] Richard Falk employs the concept of "global apartheid" to describe the existing global order (1995, 49–55).

the second supplementary consideration in support of global equality of opportunity. One objection levelled against cosmopolitan theories of distributive justice is that they are unduly arduous. This has most force against approaches such as Peter Singer's, which insist that individuals give until they are no better off than the most impoverished (1972). Such positions are vulnerable to the challenge that they are unduly strenuous (Cottingham 1983) and that this calls into question the realisability of this ideal and also its desirability, given the value of what Scheffler terms "agent-centred prerogatives" (1982). Now whatever the force of these considerations against visions like Singer's, they have little force against global equality of opportunity since its demands are relatively light. Analysis of the additional annual expenditure needed to bring about basic education, water, and sanitation for all provides indirect support for this. A recent report for the United Nations Development Programme (UNDP) records, for example, that 6 billion dollars per annum are needed to bring about "basic education for all" and that 9 billion dollars per annum are needed to bring about "water and sanitation for all." Meeting these demands is, however, not great if we also bear in mind that the annual expenditure on pet foods in Europe and the United States is 17 billion dollars, the annual expenditure on ice cream in Europe is 11 billion dollars, and the annual expenditure on cigarettes in Europe is 50 billion dollars (UNDP 1998, 37). Such statistics, of course, provide only indirect support, since global equality of opportunity requires more than meeting basic education, water, and sanitation for all. They nonetheless convey something about the low costs of global justice when compared to the existing expenditure on luxuries. Global equality of opportunity thus sits between the undue modesty of a basic-rights approach and the undue ambition of utilitarianism.

Global equality of opportunity enjoys a third advantage, namely, that equalising opportunities would contribute favourably to the alleviation of global poverty. It seems plausible to suggest that some persons are impoverished at least in part because they have not had a fair start in life and that had they had better opportunities, they could have been more likely to be able to earn a reasonable standard of living. It is, of course, true that those who, under the current system, enjoy more-than-equal opportunities because of their nationality would be worse off under a system of global equality of opportunity. But these persons, as residents of affluent states, already enjoy considerable benefits and are therefore not likely to be threatened with poverty.

4. At this point we should make one additional prefatory point. Lest my position be misunderstood, I should emphasize that I am not arguing that global equality of opportunity is the only global principle of distributive justice. One additional principle has already been suggested, namely, Henry Shue's affirmation of basic rights. Although it is insufficient on its

own, the introduction of global equality of opportunity does not render it redundant. To see this, consider someone who is presented with equal opportunities but who, through misfortune or disaster or lack of ability, ends up extremely impoverished. Without a basic right to subsistence, that person may be incapable of surviving. Global equality of opportunity should thus be supplemented with Shue-like basic rights. One might, of course, go further and argue that a world order characterised by global equality of opportunity and basic rights is insufficient. One might, for example, argue that we should also accept Derek Parfit's "Priority View," which states that "[b]enefiting people matters more the worse off these people are" (1998, 12; see, more generally, 1998, 11–15). I shall not evaluate such principles here: my aim is simply to make clear that global equality of opportunity may be supplemented by other principles.

5. Now that we have defended global equality of opportunity, it is appropriate to distinguish between two critical responses to this ideal. We should, in particular, distinguish between (1) *complete repudiation*, which denies that there are any global principles of distributive justice, and (2) *partial repudiation*, which does not deny that there are some global principles of distributive justice, but which does deny that there should be a principle of global equality of opportunity.

Both (1) and (2) reject global equality of opportunity, but the latter, unlike the former, allows for other global principles of distributive justice. Those who adhere to (2) are likely to reject global equality of opportunity because they think it too expansive. It is perhaps conceivable, however, that some may reject global equality of opportunity because they affirm a more expansive principle that requires abandoning global equality of opportunity.

Having presented the alternatives to global equality of opportunity, I may now analyse the type of argument that a critic must adduce in order to defeat it. If we assume (as I shall) that we accept the ideal of equality of opportunity within the state, we need, if we are to reject global equality of opportunity, an argument showing that the global context is disanalogous in some morally relevant respect – and hence that whilst equality of opportunity applies in the domestic context, it does not in the global context. Let us call such arguments *disanalogy arguments*. The latter identify some property, P, which exists in domestic contexts but not in transnational contexts.[6] A number of different properties might be identified. They include, among others:

- political factors: for example, that there is no state at the global level or that there can be no global cooperation between relevant parties to bring about just outcomes

[6] For an illuminating discussion which considers most of the possible disanalogies given below, see Beitz (1999a, 154–61, also 13–66) and Beitz (1999b, 521–24). See also Midtgaard (forthcoming) for an interesting disanalogy argument.

- psychological factors: for example, that individuals are motivated to comply with domestic principles of justice but not with global ones
- economic factors: for example, that economic interaction is qualitatively different at the global level as compared with the domestic level
- cultural factors: for example, that members of a state tend to share some cultural values with their fellow members, whereas members of the world as a whole do not share common cultural values

This list is not exhaustive and is intended merely to identify some properties that disanalogy arguments might invoke.

The disanalogy argument employed must take a different form depending on whether it is intended to sustain complete repudiation or partial repudiation. To sustain complete repudiation the disanalogy argument must identify some property, P_c, required for distributive justice and show that whilst present in domestic contexts, it is absent in the global context. To establish partial repudiation is a slightly more complex task. In such cases, the disanalogy argument must show that even though some principles of distributive justice apply at the global level, others (like global equality of opportunity) do not. As such it must identify some property, P_p, required for principles of equality of opportunity but not required for some other principles of distributive justice, and it must then show that P_p is present in domestic contexts but is absent in the global context.

II

Having sought to motivate some support for global equality of opportunity and having identified the logical structure that arguments must take if they are to undermine global equality of opportunity, I now want in the remainder of the chapter to consider three challenges to it. Let us begin by considering a challenge posed by Bernard Boxill (1987, 143–68). Boxill maintains that global equality of opportunity is an inappropriate ideal given the great cultural variety that exists in the world: "[t]he root difficulty [with global equality of opportunity] is that the world is made up of different societies with different cultures and different standards of success" (1987, 148). Put in the terms defined above, Boxill presents a disanalogy argument, claiming that equality of opportunity is applicable only when there is a degree of cultural consensus (property P) and then claiming that this condition does not obtain in the international realm.[7] This argument thus rests, crucially, on its moral assumption that equality of opportunity requires cultural commonality (as well as its empirical assumption about the multicultural nature of

---

[7] Since Boxill does not say whether he rejects all global principles of distributive justice or whether he rejects just some principles including global equality of opportunity, it is not possible to say whether he affirms *partial* or *complete* repudiation. This, however, does not affect the appraisal of his argument that follows.

the world). Let us call this the "calibration" argument since it points to the difficulty in calibrating people's opportunities, given people's very different values.

1. Boxill's argument comprises two considerations. The first is this:

> The principle of fair equality can be only imperfectly carried out, at least as long as different cultures exist. Thus, if, in some societies the pinnacle is occupied by the businessman and businesswoman, this is by no means always the case; in Hindu society it was occupied by the priest, in old China, by the learned man, and in other societies, by the soldier. For which of these standards are opportunities to be equalized? To choose one over the other seems invidious and presumptuous. (1987, 148)

The second consideration is this:

> Nor is it possible to get very far trying to make children of similar talent and drive in these different societies have similar prospects of reaching the standards of success in each society. First, there are the conceptual problems of devising criteria for the equality of prospects that are for radically different ends. And, if these can be overcome, there are the practical problems. The bright girl in New York is inevitably going to have better prospects of becoming a businesswoman in New York than the equally bright boy in Hindu society; and he will have better prospects than she of becoming a priest in his society. This is only partly because the education needed to be a success in business in New York is different from, and probably incompatible with, the education needed to be a priest in Hindu society. Even if schools offering both educations existed in both societies, the ethos of each society would ensure that the inequality remained. (1987, 148–49)

2. These two points do not, however, invalidate global equality of opportunity since they tell against some construals of that ideal but not others. Think about the first consideration. This has force against the following interpretation of global equality of opportunity:

> GEO$_1$: Global equality of opportunity requires that persons (of equal ability and motivation) have equal opportunities to attain the positions valued in one preferred society.

Boxill's point against GEO$_1$ is that it is obnoxious to choose one society's valued positions and to argue that there should be global equality of opportunity to achieve those valued positions.

Now think about the second consideration. This tells against the following construal of global equality of opportunity:

> GEO$_2$: Global equality of opportunity requires that persons (of equal ability and motivation) have equal opportunities to attain the positions valued in every society.

Boxill's point here (contained in the second quotation above) is, in part, that given the different cultural values that exist in different societies, it will always be easier for people in one society to acquire certain positions valued in their society than it will be for equally talented members of another society with different cultural values to do so.

An adherent to global equality of opportunity is not, however, committed to either of these versions. Consider, for example, the following:

> GEO_3: Global equality of opportunity requires that persons (of equal ability and motivation) have equal opportunities to attain an equal number of positions of a commensurate standard of living.[8]

This, I want to suggest, is not susceptible to Boxill's critique and represents an attractive and plausible interpretation of global equality of opportunity.

3. Let me begin then by noting that GEO_3 avoids Boxill's counterarguments. Since it requires neither that all have the same opportunity to the positions valued in one society (GEO_1), nor that all have the same opportunity to the positions valued in all societies (GEO_2), it is not vulnerable to the objections levelled against those two positions. Its claim that persons ought to have equal opportunities to gain positions of equal worth is not reliant on the assumptions criticised by Boxill's two arguments.

What of Boxill's more general concern about cultural plurality? Someone might protest that it is not possible to construct a fair metric to assess people's standard of living in a multicultural world.[9] GEO_3, thus, requires what cannot be provided. This challenge can, however, be met. There has, of course, been considerable discussion by many philosophers and welfare economists of how best to conceive of the "standard of living." One particularly promising approach has been developed by Amartya Sen, who construes the standard of living in terms of people's capacity to enjoy certain functionings (1982, 353–69; 1996, 30–53). Sen himself does not elaborate fully on what these capabilities are, but Martha Nussbaum does. Her plausible suggestion is that some goods are valued by all cultures, although the instantiation of them varies from one culture to another (1992, 216–23). Nussbaum thus outlines a list of important human goods including the capacity for (1) life, (2) health, (3) the avoidance of pain, (4) use of the five senses, (5) human relationships, (6) the deliberation about and pursuit of personal ideals, (7) relations of care for others, (8) access to the natural environment, (9) experiencing enjoyment, and (10) independence (1992, 222). Drawing on this, then, global equality of opportunity requires that people of equal talent have equal access to posi-

---

[8] Compare Pogge (1994b, 196).
[9] Compare Miller (1999, 192–93).

tions of an equal standard of living (where the standard of living is assessed in terms of their contribution to well-being). Cultural diversity thus does not undermine the possibility of constructing a fair index of the standard of living since it is possible to construct a transcultural metric by which to judge opportunities.

As well as avoiding Boxill's specific charges against GEO_1 and GEO_2, GEO_3 articulates the guiding principle of equality of opportunity, namely, that people of equal ability and equal willingness to try should have equal prospects. GEO_3 is faithful to the key point that persons should not have worse prospects in life because of their social position and, as such, is a plausible construal of global equality of opportunity.[10] Reflection on it, moreover, makes clear that Boxill is mistaken to assume that (global) equality of opportunity requires that each person have equal opportunity to exactly the same individual tokens. As GEO_3 makes clear, equality of opportunity does not require equal opportunity to identical *tokens*: it can be met where people have equal opportunity to positions of the same *type*.

Why, however, a critic might ask, should we accept a conception of equality of opportunity that calls for the equalization of opportunities to positions of a commensurate standard of living? To answer this question it is worth separating it into two questions: (1) Why make reference to the *standard of living*? and (2) Why stipulate that there should be equality of opportunity to positions of a *commensurate* standard of living? Let us consider question (1) first. The appropriate answer to this is simply that we value opportunities to a position because of the nature of the position and its benefits. If we seek to equalize opportunities, we should, accordingly, not be indifferent to the nature of those oportunities, and we should prefer a scheme of opportunities that protects human interests (as defined by an appropriate metric of the standard of living) to one that does not. To be blind to the nature of the opportunities available would be a form of fetishism.[11]

Let us now consider question (2). To see why the opportunities must be to positions of a *commensurate* standard of living, consider the following scenario: Imagine a state in which there are two people of equal ability and willingness to work hard. One (A) has the opportunity to become one of ten options, including being a doctor, a writer, and so on. The other (B) has the same opportunity to become one of ten options, including being a lackey, a worker in an asbestos mine, and so on. It would be highly implausible to claim this as an attractive conception of equality of opportunity because the opportunities that B is able to attain are much worse than those that A is equally able to attain. For equality of opportunity to obtain, then, persons of the same ability and the same industry should have the same chance to gain positions of an equal standard of living.

---

[10] Compare Rawls's conception of fair equality of opportunity (1999b, 63).
[11] My criticism here follows Amartya Sen's argument against primary goods (Sen 1982, 366, 368).

What these considerations suggest, then, is that GEO$_3$ represents a plausible and attractive conception of equality of opportunity. It is true to the intuition motivating equality of opportunity; it can explain why it is important to equalize opportunities to positions of a commensurate standard of living; and it avoids Boxill's objections.

4. A critic might reject GEO$_3$, however, on the grounds that the standard of living as defined by Sen and Nussbaum cannot be measured. It seeks to combine various different dimensions that cannot be quantified and hence cannot be used as a principle of distributive justice.

This revised version of the calibration argument is, however, unpersuasive. First, even if it is *hard* to measure some qualities (such as people's opportunities to certain goods), this fails to establish that they are of no moral significance and should be ignored by a theory of justice. The claim that persons are entitled to X should, thus, not be rejected just because it is hard to measure the extent to which persons possess X. It is, indeed, the wrong sort of reason for rejecting a claim about people's entitlements. Second, the objection exaggerates the problems involved in measuring the standard of living. There are many sophisticated assessments of the relevant indices (such as UNDP reports) which combine data on a multiplicity of different aspects (mortality rates, vulnerability to violence, literacy rates, proneness to certain diseases, access to healthy water, access to positions of responsibility, and so on). Of course, these can provide only good approximations, but as Amartya Sen wisely asks, "Why must we reject being vaguely right in favour of being precisely wrong?" (1987, 34). Third, although the Sen–Nussbaum metric is an objective one, one can get a good rough picture of whether people enjoy the same opportunities by simply examining the choices of well-informed people. This additional variant of the calibration argument is, thus, unsuccessful.

III

Others might resist global equality of opportunity for other reasons. In this section I want to consider a second challenge to global equality of opportunity. Whereas the first maintained that global equality of opportunity was impractical, a second response charges that it is inappropriate. It is often said, by philosophers who disagree on much else, that principles of distributive justice apply only to people who are interconnected in some way. John Rawls, for example, subscribes to one version of this claim (1999b, 6–10, especially 6–7). Charles Taylor, also, states that "*distributive* justice ... presupposes that men are in a society together, or in some kind of collaborative arrangement" (1985, 289). The central claim to be examined then rests on the ethical claim that some or all ideals of distributive justice are applicable only within a certain type of arrangement or framework and on the factual claim that there are no global arrangements or frameworks of this type. The terms employed (like "arrangements") are deliberately vague since they may take various forms.

Now, to defend complete repudiation and refute global equality of opportunity, the arguments to be considered must

1. provide a plausible account of a "system" or "collaborative arrangement"
2. establish that principles of equality of opportunity apply only within such systems
3. establish that there cannot be said to be a global system

Those who affirm partial repudiation must, in addition,

4. explain why their preferred principles of distributive justice apply outside of a system whereas equality of opportunity must apply within a system

These conditions are very strict and it is hard to think of an argument that meets conditions (1) to (3) – or (1) to (4). Let us consider some possibilities.

One fruitful way of addressing this issue is perhaps to employ H. L. A. Hart's analysis of special rights. To argue that there should be equality of opportunity within the state but not at a global level is to ascribe certain rights to a member of a society which are denied to those who are not members of that society. Since this right is possessed by some and not by all, it constitutes a special as opposed to a general right (Hart 1984, 84–88). On this analysis, then, British citizens, say, have a special right to *enjoy opportunities equal to those of other British citizens*, but those who do not enjoy British citizenship are not entitled to this particular right. To accept this special right, then, we should consider the justifications of special rights to see if they can support the special right to opportunities equal to those of one's fellow citizens. I shall concentrate on the two sources of special rights most likely to yield domestic equality of opportunity, where one of these sources generates two distinct variants.[12]

Argument 1: Mutual Restrictions
One standard way of acquiring special rights is what Hart calls "mutuality of restrictions" (1984, 85, more generally 85–87). Hart employs the term to refer to arrangements in which a number of people engage in a joint venture and thereby create benefits. Hart's plausible claim is that those

---

[12] I have omitted discussion of three of Hart's five sources of special rights – promises, consent, and "special liberties" – because it is difficult to see how any of these can vindicate the special rights discussed in the text. See Hart (1984, 84–85, 87).

who take part in this venture have rights to the produce, rights which only they enjoy and which are therefore special, as opposed to general, rights. This type of argument is often used to defend the claim that citizens have special rights to goods produced within a political system. In his book *Civic Virtues*, Richard Dagger, for example, draws on this Hart-ian reasoning to defend the special rights of citizens to economic entitlements (1997, 42–48 [esp. 46–48], 59–60).[13] Can one argue, in this vein, that equality of opportunity is defensible as a right that citizens possess as members of a political system?

I do not think so. The central problem is that those said to be the possessors of the right have not engaged in cooperation and produced a benefit. The putative bearers of the right to equality of opportunity are persons who have not yet participated in the economic system. No more than foreigners have they created the goods to be distributed as equal opportunities, and hence "mutuality of restrictions" cannot ground their right to (domestic) equality of opportunity.

In addition to this, those who endorse partial repudiation face an extra problem since they must explain why their distributive principle (a right to subsistence, say) should be treated any differently from the distributive principle of equality of opportunity. If the latter should not be regarded as a general right, then why should the former? And if the former should be treated as a general right, then why should equality of opportunity not be treated as a general right too? In other words, the "mutuality of restrictions" argument can vindicate partial repudiation only if it can explain why some principles of distributive justice apply outside of a cooperative framework but equality of opportunity does not.

Argument 2: Special Relationships (Part a)
Given the failure of the first argument, let us consider a second argument for treating the right to equality of opportunity as a special right that arises within a political community. Hart maintains that there are cases in which a special right "arises out of the special relationship of the parties" (1984, 87). Occupying a social role (parent, diplomat) brings with it certain special rights. Some argue, in this vein, that the social role of citizenship brings with it certain special rights, including welfare rights (Marshall 1950).

How might one develop this argument to defend domestic equality of opportunity but deny global equality of opportunity?[14] One version is given by David Harris, who argues that the special relationship of being a

---

[13] Although Dagger does not explicitly deploy this argument to defend the special right of citizens to opportunities equal to those of fellow citizens, it is nonetheless worth enquiring whether his argument does sustain that conclusion.

[14] For an incisive analysis of Harris's argument, see Fabre (1998, 121–24) and (2000, 61–62). See also her illuminating and comprehensive treatment of attempts to derive economic rights in general from citizenship (Fabre 1998; 2000, 57–65, 119–28).

member of a political community generates "citizenship rights," where "[c]itizenship rights, as their name suggests, are held by individuals in virtue of their membership of the society in question. They are ascribed to persons *qua* citizens rather than directly or exclusively *qua* human beings" (1987, 147). On this view, then, citizens have "social rights" (including economic rights) which "confer benefits to which an individual has a claim because he is a member of this community" (1987, 30). Harris adds, moreover, that these social rights include the right to the same opportunities as their fellow citizens (1987, 56–57, 86, 103–4). Harris's central claim then is the following: The social role of citizen brings with it an entitlement to opportunities equal to those of one's fellow citizens, and failure to provide equality of opportunity represents a failure to treat one's fellows as members (Harris 1987, especially 3, 27, 29–30, 37–38, 48–49, 53–54, 85–86, 101, 103–5, 145–65).

Harris's argument is vulnerable in a number of ways. First, it rests on the conceptual claim that part of what it means to be a citizen is to be entitled to opportunities equal to those of fellow citizens. This, however, is an unpersuasive line of reasoning since there are clearly other, nonegalitarian conceptions of citizenship which construe it simply in terms of having libertarian economic rights, the right to vote, and the right to receive the protection of one's rights by the state. Claiming that equal opportunity is part of what it means to be a citizen is not enough (King and Waldron 1988, 437).

Second, perhaps Harris's claim is the normative one that membership in a political society is a good and that distributing unequal opportunities to people within a regime denies some that good – the good of inclusion in a political society. But then the appropriate response to this is that although community is a good, it is not clear why this must take the form of being part of a "political community." People can enjoy this good of belonging in other ways (such as being part of a religious community). Political community is not then required, and hence, domestic equality of opportunity cannot be justified on the grounds that it is essential for political community.

Third, even if Harris's argument does provide a good case for domestic equality of opportunity, this, in itself, does not show that we should reject global equality of opportunity. At most, then, Harris's argument gives a reason *for* domestic equality of opportunity, but it does not give us an argument *against* global equality of opportunity. We may distinguish between a weak and a strong version of Harris's argument: the weak version states that *one* grounding for equality of opportunity is that it follows from the ideal of citizenship, and the strong version states that the *only* grounding for equality of opportunity is that it follows from the ideal of citizenship. To refute global equality of opportunity, the citizenship argument would have to take the strong form. But nothing that Harris says, however, shows what is wrong with non-citizenship-based arguments for equality of opportunity.

Argument 3: Special Relationships (Part b)
Other attempts to argue that the social role of citizenship generates special
economic rights (such as the right to domestic equality of opportunity) are
similarly unpersuasive. Consider, for example, one common defense of
civic economic rights. Many argue that being a citizen brings with it
certain civil and political rights and that these, in turn, require material
resources for their fulfilment. This second claim is grounded in a number
of considerations, such as that people will be independent citizens only if
they are financially independent.[15] Can one employ this line of reasoning
to argue that people have the right, *qua* citizens, to opportunities equal to
those of their fellow citizens? Does it show that equality of opportunity
should apply within states and not globally?

I do not think so for two reasons.[16] First, it is not clear to me that the use
of civil and political civic rights requires that persons have equal opportunities for positions. It may be true that they need material resources, but this
yields rather meagre rights (cf. Fabre 2000, 124–25) and does not entail that
persons must have equal opportunities to gain employment. The second
problem has been given in the discussion of the previous argument. If
successful, the argument under scrutiny gives us a reason to value equality
of opportunity within the state. But this is quite compatible with also calling for global equality of opportunity since the latter, by its very nature,
precludes there being inequalities of opportunity within a state. The argument thus does not tell against global equality of opportunity. To do that, it
must show that non-citizenship-based defenses of equality of opportunity
are unpersuasive – and this the argument has not done.

In short, none of the three arguments considered has established that
equality of opportunity is best construed as a civic right that applies within
the context of a sovereign unit.[17]

---

[15] See, for example, King and Waldron (1988, 425–31). See p. 427 for the specific point
about independence.

[16] I should make clear that King and Waldron's aim is neither to defend domestic equality of opportunity nor to undermine global equality of opportunity. My question is this:
given that this line of reasoning is often employed to defend civic economic rights, can it be
used to defend domestic equality of opportunity and to criticise global equality of opportunity?

[17] A critic might argue that a full defence of global equality of opportunity must do more
than criticise nonglobal conceptions of an institutional context. It must (1) provide an
account of a context in which principles of equality of opportunity apply and (2) establish
that there is a global institutional context which has this character. I would make two points
in reply to this. First, Beitz and Pogge have provided a plausible account of the type of institutional structure in which principles of distributive justice (including those of equality of
opportunity) apply *and* a persuasive argument to the effect that there is a global institutional
structure of this nature. See Beitz (1999a, 129–32 [esp. 131], 143–52, 200–205); Pogge
(1989, esp. 8–9, 11–12, 22–28, 33–36, 215, 226–27, 234–43, 240–41, 262–65, 273–80); and
Pogge (1994a, 90–98). See, further, O'Neill (1996, 101, 105–6, 112–21). Second, we need
to be given an argument for the claim that ideals of distributive justice apply only in an institutional structure. I have challenged this claim elsewhere.

IV

Having analysed and rejected two challenges to global equality of opportunity, we may now consider a third. This third argument is inspired by Rawls's *The Law of Peoples*, in which he defends a restricted set of principles of international justice, arguing that they would be endorsed by both liberal and decent nonliberal societies.[18] As such, they constitute a reasonable and fair international order. Rawls's eight principles include the independence and equality of peoples (nos. 1 and 3), the obligation to comply with treaties (no. 2), nonintervention (no. 4), self-defence (no. 5), and rules of *ius in bello* (no. 7) (1999a, 37). They also include two principles that bear on economic issues: Rawls's sixth principle states that "Peoples are to honor human rights," and his eighth principle states that "Peoples have a duty to assist other peoples living under unfavorable conditions that prevent their having a just or decent political and social regime" (1999a, 37).[19] Human rights, for Rawls, include the right to subsistence (1999a, 65, 78–81 [especially 65 n. 1]). Now Rawls's principle differs from the one canvassed in this chapter in two respects, the first of which is content. Rawls's principles are more minimal, and he clearly rejects more egalitarian principles such as global equality of opportunity. The second crucial difference is methodological: Rawls would reject the reasoning underlying global equality of opportunity. It would, in his view, be objectionably sectarian and intolerant since it rests on liberal egalitarian ideals that some reject (1999a, 18–19, 59–60, 63–79, 82–85, 121–22). As Rawls makes clear, it is inappropriate in his view to ground human rights on liberal moral ideals that ascribe to persons "certain moral and intellectual powers that entitle them to . . . rights" (1999a, 68, see further 119–20).

Prior to evaluating this Rawlsian argument, we may note that it is the right type of argument. It is a disanalogy argument: it focuses on one property that exists in some societies (commitment to liberal egalitarian values) and argues that since this property is not uniformly present on the global level, liberal egalitarian principles of justice (such as equality of opportunity) should not be implemented globally.

This is an important challenge. To meet it, a proponent of global equality of opportunity should, I believe, adopt a combination of conciliatory and combative points. Let me begin with two conciliatory points. First, the conviction at the heart of this argument, namely, that it is inappropriate to

---

[18] For Rawls's characterization of liberal peoples, see (1999a, 14, 49–51). For his characterization of decent hierarchical societies, see (1999a, 63–78). The latter are not aggressive (64). In addition, they affirm human rights (65), treat people as capable of bearing duties (65–66), and affirm a "common good idea of justice" (66 and more generally, 66–67). As a corollary, they include an element of consultation (71–75). For Rawls's typology of five types of society, see (1999a, 4).

[19] There is a footnote after the word "regime" which cites Rawls (1999a, sections 15 and 16).

thrust liberal principles on nonliberal peoples, does not establish that
equality of opportunity should not be pursued at the transnational level.
Rawls's argument has force (if it has any force) only against prescribing
liberal values for peoples who do not share those values. It can, however,
find no fault with the claim that there should be equality of opportunity
between all individuals who are members of liberal societies. In other
words, the "toleration" argument does not show what would be wrong with
establishing a regime in which, say, citizens of France enjoy the same
opportunities as citizens of Germany or Sweden (what might be termed
transnational, as opposed to global, equality of opportunity). This may be
inappropriate for other reasons, but the crucial point here is that it cannot
be criticised on the grounds that the underlying value (equality of opportunity) is one that is alien to those governed by it.[20]

Second, it is important to distinguish between those principles of
justice which should be entrenched in the global order (hereafter *structural principles*), on the one hand, and those principles which agents (like
individuals or social movements) are permitted, or obligated, to observe
(hereafter *agent principles*), on the other.[21] It is, one might argue, reasonable to suggest that the former must enjoy legitimacy and that this
involves securing the consent of all reasonable persons. Even if we accept
this conclusion, however, it does not invalidate individuals or social
movements acting on global equality of opportunity. It does not, that is,
invalidate those who adopt global equality of opportunity as an agent
principle.[22] It is even arguable that a state can honour Rawls's eight principles *and*, being consistent with this, adopt various policies designed to
equalize opportunities (such as allowing immigration or distributing
resources and technology). Global equality of opportunity (construed as an
agent principle) is thus compatible with the Rawlsian conception of the
international order.

The above two points have sought, broadly speaking, to accept Rawls's
strictures and to argue that they are compatible with some types of
attempts to equalize opportunities at a transnational level. I now want to
call into question Rawls's rejection of those cosmopolitan principles that
conflict with his principles. My criticisms focus on Rawls's account of
toleration and his account of the basic standards all societies must meet. I
begin with the former. Rawls's treatment of toleration is, I believe, problematic in three respects.

---

[20] For other Rawlsian considerations which would tell against it, see Rawls (1999a,
117–18). For criticisms, see Caney (2000b, 139–44).

[21] For a similar distinction, see Pogge (1994a, 90–91).

[22] Rawls allows that "persons in civil society may raise private funds for that purpose [to
induce people to become more liberal]" and may thus allow social movements to campaign
in this way (1999a, 85).

1. The first important point is that Rawls's toleration argument does not eradicate or invalidate the reasoning given in section I. Consider again the reasoning underlying global equality of opportunity. This maintains, in part, that if we object to persons having worse prospects because of their class or ethnicity, we should object to their having worse prospects because of their nationality or citizenship. Nothing that Rawls says invalidates this argument since it challenges neither the premises nor the analogy. It thus does not extinguish or dispel the reasoning, and it gives us no reason to abandon this claim. What it does, rather, is adduce a second, different consideration, the importance of tolerating decent alternative views. If we accept Rawls's intuition, then, the appropriate position is to accept both: global equality of opportunity and the value of not imposing values on peoples that they reject. The Rawlsian argument thus does not give us reason to reject global equality of opportunity: it gives us reason to accept an additional principle that is in competition with it (Caney 2000a, 541).

Another way of putting the point is this: Rawls's conclusion affirms that peoples are bound by what Raz terms an "exclusionary reason" (1975, 35–48).[23] In international politics, peoples must exclude from consideration certain convictions that they hold. My point is that Rawls's reasoning does not establish that there is an exclusionary reason; rather, it establishes that peoples are bound by two values: their convictions about justice (and the entitlements of all persons) *and* the value of tolerating decent peoples with whom one disagrees. Given this, the appropriate question, then, is how do we balance these two competing values when they conflict?

2. One consideration that should inform this decision – which is ignored by Rawls – concerns *who* dissents from the ideal being discussed. I want to suggest here that it is of great import *who* rejects a principle and that certain forms of rejection are not as morally significant as others. We can distinguish somewhat crudely between those who benefit from equality of opportunity and those who would not benefit from it. Let us discuss each separately.

a. The advantaged: suppose a beneficiary dissents from the ideal of equality of opportunity. Suppose, for example, that a woman denies that she ought to have opportunities equal to those of men. This gives us no reason to abandon equality of opportunity. What we should do is have equal opportunities, and if someone chooses not to avail herself of them because she disagrees with them, then she is free not to do so. Global equality of opportunity does not force the beneficiaries of it to take up the opportunity: it grants them *options* hitherto denied, which they are free not to take up.

---

[23] For another, different deployment of this concept to characterise an anticosmopolitan position, see Pogge (1998, 466). Pogge employs it to characterise the claim that governments may prioritise "the interests of compatriots" (466).

b. The disadvantaged: now suppose that those who would be disadvantaged by a principle reject it. Here it seems implausible to suggest that an ideal should be abandoned because some, who stand to lose by it, find it unacceptable. Consider in this light some domestic examples. Suppose, for example, that the landed aristocracy rejects redistribution within the state. This is not a conclusive reason to reject such redistribution. Or consider men who, whilst they affirm that women have some minimal rights, deny them equal status and deny them the suffrage. It seems implausible to maintain that we ought to abandon equal suffrage because of its rejection by the privileged and advantaged. The appropriate response here, surely, is to treat those who disagree with respect by listening to their objections, providing one's reasoning for one's decision, and acknowledging their good-faith dissent. It is not to abandon the entitlements of disadvantaged men and women and deny them a fair chance in life.

Neither type of rejection thus entails that we should reject global equality of opportunity.

3. The vulnerability of Rawls's treatment of toleration is further exposed when we note just how strong his conclusion is. For Rawls argues not just that liberal states should not seek to force liberal cosmopolitan values on others but also that they cannot even employ "incentives" to encourage peoples to embrace basic liberal values (1999a, 84–85). Given the first point made above, this conclusion is unsustainably strong. That is, given that we have two conflicting values, one promising way of balancing them is to pursue noncoercive ways of bringing about a world in which people are not denied their entitlements. Incentives thus represent an attractive method that respects people's autonomy and that yet may be deployed to encourage societies to respect the entitlements of their members and nonmembers.

None of the above, I should stress, should be construed as a reason to reject the importance of tolerating decent nonliberal views. My point is only that whilst we should recognise this value, it does not justify indifference to people's distributive entitlements and duties. To put the point succinctly: we have no reason to think that "cultural justice" should subordinate "economic justice."[24]

Let me now turn to Rawls's account of the basic moral criteria that all societies must meet (what, in other words, may not be tolerated). Rawls is, I believe, right to suggest that international justice requires that societies meet certain basic standards and that above that they may go their own way.[25] The problem with Rawls's account of these basic standards is both

[24] For these concepts, see Fraser (1997, especially 13–15).
[25] See on this Brown (1997, 292) and Miller (2000, 10).

that they are too low and that his rationale for them is unpersuasive. To see this, consider Rawls's theoretical framework. He argues that all societies must meet certain standards (even if they themselves do not recognise them). He thus defends certain human rights, arguing that they are legitimate because they are endorsed by decent societies, notably liberal peoples and decent hierarchical societies (1999a, 37, 69). But this is an unconvincing argument because these societies are *defined* in such a way that they will necessarily endorse his preferred list of human rights. This vindication of the minimum standards is thus question-begging and gives us no reason to accept his preferred account of the fair minimum (P. Jones 1996, 194–95). It also gives us no reason to reject an account of the basic framework that requires that all persons have equal opportunities. Expressed otherwise: if Rawls allows (as he does) the imposition of certain values on all societies even if some dissent from them, on what grounds can he reject global equality of opportunity?

Indeed, it is difficult to see how one can vindicate any given basic minimum without invoking the sort of ideals which Rawls insists that we should abjure, namely, ideas such as the moral status of persons (1999a, 68). How can one identify standards for a "decent" society and for human rights without invoking the dignity and worth of persons? Rawls's framework – unlike a cosmopolitan framework – lacks the theoretical resources required to establish a basic minimum, and, therefore, his rejection of competing accounts of the basic minimum (such as global equality of opportunity) lacks power. Rawls's account of the basic minimum, like his account of toleration, is thus unpersuasive.

V

It is time to conclude. This chapter has attempted to provide an argument for global equality of opportunity and to adduce three supplementary considerations in its support. It has also sought to meet three powerful objections. There are, of course, many other challenges that could be levelled against global equality of opportunity. What I hope to have done is to have met three of the most pressing.

Acknowledgments

I am very grateful to the participants at the conference on global justice, held at Bielefeld on June 26–28, 2000, for their comments, and in particular to Thomas Pogge for his helpful written suggestions.

References

Barry, Brian. (1991a). "Humanity and Justice in Global Perspective." In *Liberty and Justice: Essays in Political Theory,* 2:182–210. Oxford: Clarendon.

——. (1991b). "Justice as Reciprocity." In *Liberty and Justice: Essays in Political Theory*, 2:211–41. Oxford: Clarendon.

Beitz, Charles. (1983). "Cosmopolitan Ideals and National Sentiment." *Journal of Philosophy*, 80, 591–600.

——. (1999a). *Political Theory and International Relations* (with a new afterword). Princeton: Princeton University Press.

——. (1999b). "Social and Cosmopolitan Liberalism." *International Affairs*, 75, 515–29.

Black, Samuel. (1991). "Individualism at an Impasse." *Canadian Journal of Philosophy*, 21, 347–77.

Boxill, Bernard. (1987). "Global Equality of Opportunity and National Integrity." *Social Philosophy and Policy*, 5, 143–68.

Brown, Chris. (1997). "Review Article: Theories of International Justice." *British Journal of Political Science*, 27, 273–97.

Caney, Simon. (2000a). "Cosmopolitan Justice and Cultural Diversity." *Global Society*, 14, 525–51.

——. (2000b). "Global Equality of Opportunity and the Sovereignty of States." In *International Justice*, edited by Tony Coates, 130–49. Aldershot, England: Ashgate.

——. (Forthcoming). "Review Article: International Distributive Justice."

Carens, Joseph. (1987). "Aliens and Citizens: The Case for Open Borders." *Review of Politics*, 49, 251–73.

Cottingham, John. (1983). "Ethics and Impartiality." *Philosophical Studies*, 43, 83–99.

Dagger, Richard. (1997). *Civic Virtues: Rights, Citizenship, and Republican Liberalism*. New York: Oxford University Press.

Fabre, Cécile. (1998). "Social Citizenship and Social Rights." In *Communitarianism and Citizenship*, edited by Emilios Christodoulidis, 119–33. Aldershot, England: Ashgate.

——. (2000). *Social Rights under the Constitution: Government and the Decent Life*. Oxford: Clarendon Press.

Falk, Richard. (1995). *On Humane Governance: Towards a New Global Politics*. Cambridge: Polity Press.

Fraser, Nancy. (1997). *Justice Interruptus: Critical Reflections on the "Postsocialist" Condition*. New York: Routledge.

Harris, David. (1987). *Justifying State Welfare: The New Right versus the Old Left*. Oxford: Blackwell.

Hart, H. L. A. (1984). "Are There Any Natural Rights?" In *Theories of Rights*, edited by Jeremy Waldron, 77–90. Oxford: Oxford University Press.

Jones, Charles. (1999). *Global Justice: Defending Cosmopolitanism*. Oxford: Oxford University Press.

Jones, Peter. (1996). "International Human Rights: Philosophical or Political?" In *National Rights, International Obligations*, edited by Simon Caney, David George, and Peter Jones, 183–204. Oxford: Westview.

King, Desmond, and Waldron, Jeremy. (1988). "Citizenship, Social Citizenship and the Defence of Welfare Provision." *British Journal of Political Science*, 18:4, 415–43.

Marshall, T. H. (1950). "Citizenship and Social Class." In *"Citizenship and Social Class" and Other Essays*, 1–85. London: Cambridge University Press.

Midtgaard, Søren. (Forthcoming). "Rawlsian Stability and the Law of Peoples." In *International Distributive Justice*, edited by Simon Caney and Percy Lehning.

Miller, David. (1999). "Justice and Global Inequality." In *Inequality, Globalization, and World Politics*, edited by Andrew Hurrell and Ngaire Woods, 187–210. Oxford: Oxford University Press.

———. (2000). "The Good, the Poor and the Ugly: John Rawls and How Liberals Should Treat Non-Liberal Regimes." *Times Literary Supplement*, 24 March.

Nussbaum, Martha. (1992). "Human Functioning and Social Justice: In Defense of Aristotelian Essentialism." *Political Theory*, 20, 202–46.

O'Neill, Onora. (1996). *Towards Justice and Virtue: A Constructive Account of Practical Reasoning*. Cambridge: Cambridge University Press.

Parfit, Derek. (1998). "Equality and Priority." In *Ideals of Equality*, edited by Andrew Mason, 1–20. Oxford: Blackwell.

Pogge, Thomas W. (1989). *Realizing Rawls*. Ithaca, N.Y.: Cornell University Press.

———. (1994a). "Cosmopolitanism and Sovereignty." In *Political Restructuring in Europe: Ethical Perspectives*, edited by Chris Brown, 89–122. London: Routledge.

———. (1994b). "An Egalitarian Law of Peoples." *Philosophy and Public Affairs*, 23, 195–224.

———. (1998). "The Bounds of Nationalism." In *Rethinking Nationalism*, edited by Jocelyne Couture, Kai Nielsen, and Michel Seymour, 463–504. Calgary, Alberta: University of Calgary Press.

Rawls, John. (1999a). *The Law of Peoples with "The Idea of Public Reason Revisited."* Cambridge: Harvard University Press.

———. (1999b). *A Theory of Justice*. 2nd ed. Oxford: Oxford University Press.

Raz, Joseph. (1975). *Practical Reason and Norms*. London: Hutchinson.

Scheffler, Samuel. (1982). *The Rejection of Consequentialism: A Philosophical Investigation of the Considerations Underlying Rival Moral Conceptions*. Oxford: Clarendon Press.

Sen, Amartya. (1982). "Equality of What?" In *Choice, Welfare and Measurement*, 353–69. Oxford: Blackwell.

———. (1987). *The Standard of Living*. Cambridge: Cambridge University Press.

———. (1996). "Capability and Well-Being." In *The Quality of Life*, edited by Martha Nussbaum and Amartya Sen, 30–53. Oxford: Clarendon Press.

Shue, Henry. (1996). *Basic Rights: Subsistence, Affluence, and U.S. Foreign Policy.* 2nd ed. Princeton: Princeton University Press.

Singer, Peter. (1972). "Famine, Affluence, and Morality." *Philosophy and Public Affairs*, 1, 229–43.

Steiner, Hillel. (1999). "Just Taxation and International Redistribution." In *Global Justice*, edited by Ian Shapiro and Lea Brilmayer, 171–91. *Nomos* 41. New York: New York University Press.

Taylor, Charles. (1985). "The Nature and Scope of Distributive Justice." In *Philosophy and the Human Sciences: Philosophical Papers*, 2:289–317. Cambridge: Cambridge University Press.

United Nations Development Programme (UNDP). (1998). *Human Development Report, 1998.* New York: Oxford University Press.

10

THE GLOBAL SCOPE OF JUSTICE

STEFAN GOSEPATH

What is the scope of justice? Is justice global, universal, boundless? Or are there reasons of any sort, conceptual, normative, or pragmatic, to conceive of justice locally – to rather start at home, in a community or state-society and therefore require less from foreigners than from our fellow citizens? In order to find an answer to such questions, I will start in Part I by outlining what I see as a relatively plausible, and not uncommon, egalitarian conception of justice. According to this conception, justice is – at least prima facie – immediately universal, and therefore global. It does not morally recognize any judicial boundaries or limits. For many individuals, such a conclusion appears to be counterintuitive. In Part II, I will thus need to examine the question of whether there are moral and/or pragmatic grounds for rejecting or limiting the universal egalitarian conception of justice. This chapter is part of an ideal normative theory, since it is concerned with the abstract, philosophical, normative question of whether and why there might be a global dimension to justice. My conclusion that there is such a dimension will consequently lead to many normative-pragmatic questions belonging to nonideal theory, especially how best to construct and establish global (or international) institutions securing global justice. Regrettably, these questions cannot be further pursued in these pages.

I. An Egalitarian Conception of Justice

1. Given that we conceive of ourselves as moral persons, we owe justice to each other. We can best define the meaning of the unified, ahistorical concept of justice through recourse to Simonides' explanation of the concept as discussed in the first book of Plato's *Republic* and captured by Ulpian in the formula *suum cuique:* an action is just when it offers each individual his or her due. All justice thus appears related to that which is suitable or due.[1] This definition is entirely formal, since the decisive question of what is due

---

[1] One of the oldest definitions of justice is found in Plato (1998, 331e, 332b-c), paraphrasing the poet Simonides. The original reads as follows: the just is *to proshekon hekasto*

to whom remains open.[2] The formula, that is, the general concept of justice, contains a number of variables that need to be specified in order to arrive at specific notions of justice. In this way the concept of justice determines the problem for which the different conceptions of justice offer answers (Korsgaard 1996, 114). This first general definition of justice as suitability can be further specified through additional classical definitions, above all through a set of criteria that can be briefly summed up as follows: impartiality; the form of claim-rights laid by others; the specification of changeability and responsibility.

a. For justice, the criterion of impartiality is essential. On a first level, impartiality means the nonpartial application of a given norm. In contrast, on a second level, impartiality is demanded for the rules or norms themselves, in the sense of a ban on those based purely on subjective, egoistic factors. What is demanded, then, is an impartial justification or justifiability of the norms in question. The idea of impartiality is presented with its best model through the test of the "veil of ignorance."

b. At present, that which is adequately suitable to another person is understood to be that to which the other person has an individual moral claim or moral right: an idea sparked at the latest through the modern advent of natural law theory. What is primarily at stake in questions of justice is the adequate fulfillment of individual claims by different persons (Hinsch forthcoming, a). This additional defining trait of justice means the consideration of the rightful claims of others. Being just means satisfying claims that have the form of a subjective right in the sense of Hohfeld (1923): A has a right (or claim) against B that B do X precisely when B has a corresponding duty to A to do X.

c. The predicates "just" or "unjust" are only applicable when voluntary actions implying responsibility are in question. To be sure, prima facie, we could gain the impression that the basic conceptual opposition, fundamental for the adequate application of the concept of justice, is the opposition between fate on the one side and injustice with a human source on the other. But the basic distinction is not causal – whether human beings are or are not responsible for an event. The most general demarcating line does not run between man-made and non-man-made misfortune, but between an

---

apodidonai; Ulpian (1822, 10) renders this into the formula *iustitia est constans et perpetua voluntas ius suum cuique tribuendi.* Its brief form is: *suum cuique tribuere.* In recent years, this general definition has been taken up above all by Vlastos (1984, 60) and Tugendhat (1993, 367; 1997, 58–68).

[2] Notoriously, the formula "Jedem das Seine" ("to each his due") hangs cynically on the interior side of the entry gate to the Buchenwald concentration camp. But this fact merely underscores the formula being so general and vacuous that all and sundry political movements can make it their own.

injustice for which human correction and intervention is possible and sheer misfortune, or fate, in which case it is not (Shklar 1990; Rössler 1999; Temkin 1986, n. 2). One condition for the adequate application of the concept of justice is, thus, the presence of agents who are effectively in a position to alter institutional structures, practices, and actions corresponding to the principles of justice. Justice requires changeability and responsibility.

d. Justice is, hence, primarily related to individual actions. Individual persons are the primary bearer of responsibilities (ethical individualism). We are, first, all addressees of claims of justice, both individually and collectively, throughout the world. We are all primarily required to respect such claim-rights and to act accordingly. But establishing justice by oneself (ubiquitously and simultaneously) is beyond the individual's capacities. Personal moral responsibility is correspondingly small. Nonetheless, all individuals together have collective moral responsibility. In order to meet this responsibility, a basic order must be justly created. This is an essential argument of moral theory, or of justice, for the establishment of state institutions and fundamental state structures for political communities; with the help of such institutions and structures, the individuals can collectively fulfill this responsibility in the best possible manner.

From this vantage, institutions are only just in a derivative sense. The mainstream of current political philosophy regards institutions, especially the basic structure of societies, as the primary subject of justice. In the first sentence of the first section of *A Theory of Justice* Rawls (1971, 3) writes that "justice is the first virtue of social institutions."[3] But if the argument is correct that only individuals have claim-rights in their status as moral persons, justice can only derivatively apply to institutions, insofar as institutions help persons to realize their duty of justice. Any limitations of principles of justice to institutions or even states would contradict our ethical individualism.[4]

The introduction of law on the basis of justice is connected with this. Institutions (which must be justly created) are governed in modern complex societies by means of positive law. Through the implementation of moral rights as legal rights within a state, an additional important component emerges that is conceptually tied to the concept of a legal right:

---

[3] For Rawls it is crucial that "The principles of justice for institutions must not be confused with the principles which apply to individuals and their actions in particular circumstances. These two kinds of principles apply to different subjects and must be discussed separately" (1971, 54–55). A contrary monistic view to this dualistic view, but with the same universalistic and egalitarian spirit as Rawls (although utilitarian), is defended by Murphy (1998).

[4] I do not intend to imply that Rawls has this limitation in mind. He rather seems to see justice regarding personal actions, the basic structure of a society, and global justice as three distinct subjects of justice (Rawls 1999).

Having a legal right always means having an effectively enforceable entitlement to the protection of this right.[5] It is only on the state level that claim-rights become enforceable (Shue 1980, 13). This does not mean that they can never be factually violated, but mechanisms are in place ensuring to a reasonable degree that persons enjoy their rights.[6] Political communities structured by the rule of law[7] are hence the *political* addressees of justice (Pogge 1995). Claim-rights derived out of justice are directed at such states under the rule of law not merely for historically contingent reasons, but rather because moral persons are obligated to create and preserve central guarantees that can transform human rights from abstract moral claims into concrete, guaranteed legal entitlements. According to the best of our knowledge thus far, state-based rule of law is best suited to this task. The requirement of justice to collectively create and support just institutions that can, as effectively as possible, protect basic rights through the rule of law creates our natural duty to support and further the laws and institutions of a just state order.[8]

e. Last, but not least, justice requires various principles of equality. Besides the Aristotelian principles of formal equality – "treat like cases as like" – and proportional equality, justice today requires what is often called fundamental or basic equality. We all accept and recognize a universalistic and egalitarian morality of equal respect. According to this conception of morality, each person is to be treated as an equal and autonomous person from an impartial standpoint. People have a moral right to be treated with equal concern and respect (Dworkin 1977, 179–83).[9] The object of equal mutual respect is the autonomy of each and every person.[10]

This fundamental idea of equal respect for all persons and of the equal worth of all human beings is accepted as a minimal standard by all leading

---

[5] One generally speaks of "basic rights" only when human rights have been concretely localized in constitutional law or in the law of peoples. Civil liberties are then basic rights to which solely citizens of the particular state, and not foreigners, have a claim.

[6] What constitutes a reasonable degree of security is, in any particular case, primarily an empirical question. If guarantees are conceptually tied to the structure of a right, these can only be guarantees against standard threats, and not against all possible threats (Shue 1980, 29–34).

[7] This argument is neutral with respect to the scope, the sort of internal structure, and the historical, ethnic, religious, and communal situatedness of political communities structured according to the rule of law. This allows, as a borderline case, a single world state.

[8] This corresponds to what Rawls calls the "natural duty of justice" (1971, 114–17, 333–37). Cf. Waldron 1993 and Klosko 1994.

[9] Another even more vague formulation often found in legal constitutions is that of the equal moral worth of all persons (Vlastos 1984).

[10] Dworkin neglects the importance of autonomy (Gosepath 1995). Autonomy is meant here not as a narrow (moral) concept, in the way it continues to be used in the Kantian tradition (e.g., by Habermas), but rather as a broad concept of personal autonomy in the sense of general personal self-determination concerning the way in which one wants to lead one's life.

schools of modern Western political and moral culture. Any political theory making a claim to plausibility must begin with this notion of equality and cannot abandon it. In the postmetaphysical age, after metaphysical, religious, and traditional views have lost their general plausibility, it appears impossible to reach a general agreement on common political aims peacefully without recognizing the demand that persons be treated as equals.

The fundamental egalitarian principle supports and expands the material condition of impartiality,[11] according to which equal weight and equal consideration must be granted to each person. A Kantian argument for a principle of reciprocal justification results from this. Since it is immoral to force someone to do something of which he or she does not approve, only reasons acceptable to the other person can give one the moral right to treat the person in accord with these reasons. The impartial justification of norms rests on the reciprocity and universality of the reasons. Universal norms and rights enforced through inner or external sanctions are morally justified only if they, on the one hand, can be reciprocally justified – that is, one person asks no more of the other than he or she is willing to give (reciprocity) – and, on the other, if they are justified with respect to the interests of all concerned parties – that is, everyone has good reasons for accepting them and no one has a good reason for rejecting them (universality) (Forst 1994, 68).[12] In the end, only the concerned parties can themselves formulate and advocate their (true) interests. Equal respect, which we owe to one another, thus requires respect for the autonomous decisions of each noninterchangeable individual (Wingert 1993, 90–96). This procedural approach to moral legitimation sees the autonomy of the individual as the standard of justification for universal rules, norms, rights, and so forth. Only those rules can be considered legitimate to which all concerned parties can freely agree on the basis of universal, discursively applicable, commonly shared reasons. Equal consideration is, thus, accorded to all persons and their interests.

A certain kind of equal treatment can be derived from equal respect together with the principle of universal and reciprocal justification. Regardless of differences, everyone should be treated equally unless certain types of differences are relevant and justify, through universally acceptable reasons, unequal treatment or unequal distribution. Applied to the domain of political justice, this result represents a principle of prima facie equal distribution for all distributable goods. A strict principle of equal distribution is not required, but it is morally necessary to justify

[11] That is more than the purely formal impartiality already contained in the concept of justice, that is, the impartial application of a given rule and the requirement of a purely objective justification of a rule, since the condition to whom an objective justification is owed is now specified.

[12] Other current versions of "contractualism" are Rawls 1971, §4; Habermas 1983; and Scanlon 1998, esp. chap. 5.

impartially any unequal distribution. The burden of proof lies on the side of the unequal distributor. This presumption in favor of equality is the only principle that can be used to arrive at concrete, substantial results.[13] It follows from the justification requirement belonging to the morality of equal respect. This conception of morality is egalitarian, for it contains the claim of each individual to equal consideration in every justification and distribution. Every sort of public, political distribution is, in this view, in the first order to be justified to all relevantly concerned persons, such that they could in principle agree. If all individuals have an interest in the goods to be distributed, then the satisfaction of the preferences of each individual carries prima facie equal weight, since each person is of equal worth. Anyone who claims more owes all others an appropriate universal and reciprocal justification. If this cannot be provided, that is, if there is no reason for unequal distribution that can be recognized by all, then equal distribution is the only legitimate distribution. How could it be otherwise? Any unequal distribution would mean that someone receives less, and another more. Whoever receives less can justifiably demand a reason for his or her being disadvantaged. Yet there is, *ex hypothesi*, no such justification. Hence, any unequal distribution is illegitimate in this case. If no convincing reasons for unequal distribution can be brought forward, there remains only the option of equal distribution. Equal distribution is, therefore, not merely one among many alternatives, but rather the inevitable starting point that must be assumed insofar as one takes the justificatory claims of all to be of equal weight.

We must determine the political-moral rights we have by means of the justification principle and the prima facie equal distribution principle. The starting point for the determination of the content of political morality is the idea of (distributive) justice in its entire scope. *Moral* claim = rights arise out of the demands of justice, for humans are mutually obligated to establish just conditions and to distribute goods and burdens justly.

2. The presumption of equality provides an elegant procedure for the construction of a theory of distributive justice. The following questions would really have to be answered in order to arrive at a substantially full principle of justice.

• What goods and burdens are to be distributed (or should be distributed)? Which social goods comprise the object of distributive justice?
• What are the spheres (of justice) into which these resources have to be grouped?

---

[13] With different terms and arguments, the principle of justice is most strongly conceived as a conception of symmetry by Tugendhat (1993, 374; 1997, chap. 3); as a relevant-reasons approach by Williams (1973); as a presumption by Bedau (1967, 19); as a default option by Hinsch (forthcoming, b, chap. 5). For criticism of the presumption of equality, cf. Westen (1990, chap. 10).

- Who are the recipients of distribution? Who has a prima facie claim to a fair share?
- What are the commonly cited, yet in reality unjustified, exceptions to equal distribution?
- Which inequalities are justified?
- Which approach, conception, or theory of egalitarian distributive justice is, therefore, the best?

I cannot here deal thoroughly with these questions, but I would like to make at least a few short remarks regarding the relevant considerations for answering them. In any event, for the question that is in the focus of interest here, namely, "What is the scope of justice?" only the first two questions are of relevance.

Which goods and burdens should be distributed (Sen 1980 and 1992, chap. 1)? The goods to be distributed are often determined through a kind of contractualism that appeals to reciprocity and mutual use.[14] In this view, distributive justice applies only to those goods commonly produced, that is, produced through social and economic fair cooperation. The objects of distribution are the fruits of cooperation, to which everyone has a prima facie equal claim because everyone has participated in the production of these goods. This says nothing about other goods, for example, natural resources, which are not the result of common cooperation. This restriction to common cooperation is not particularly convincing.[15] It seems more plausible to consider, as goods to be distributed, all the desired goods and undesired burdens and all the advantages and disadvantages of human society that we control or are able to distribute. If particular goods are to be excluded, this must be universally justified by those who demand the exclusion. The question here regards the original (just) distribution of goods that are in some manner communal and have not yet been distributed, hence belong to no one, so that everyone has a basically equal claim to them (and correspondingly for burdens). (This brackets out previous claims to possession, as well as questions of just exchange and trade.) One could make the same point in a slightly different way, one that might be more realistic and realizable: All present ownership has to be justified. That requirement follows from the justification principle. If the owner of a good cannot give a universal and reciprocal justification for his or her claim of ownership that no concerned party can reasonably reject, then the good has to be redistributed. This allows for previous rights to possession as well as rights developed out of just exchange and trade. But these and other possible justifications have to be made against a background of a justified initial "appropriation" of the goods and

---

[14] At present, this is most apparent in Rawls (1971), and many of his adherents and critics follow Rawls in this respect. Cf., for example, Koller (1994).

[15] Cf. Nelson (1974, esp. 425ff.) on the question of whether rights to appropriate consideration in distribution are not in fact special rights which arise out of social cooperation.

resources in question. Thus, the chain of justifications might become quite long, reaching far back into the past.

Can the group of the entitled be restricted prior to the examination of concrete claims? Many theories seem to imply this when they connect distributive justice or the goods to be distributed with social cooperation or production. For those who contribute nothing to cooperation, such as the disabled, children, or future generations, would have to be denied a claim to a fair share. The circle of persons who are to be the recipients of distribution would thus be restricted from the outset. Other theories are less restrictive, insofar as they do not link distribution to actual coproduction, yet, nonetheless, do restrict it, insofar as they bind it to the status of citizenship. In this view, distributive justice is limited to the individuals within a society. Those outside the community have no entitlements. Unequal distribution among states and the social situations of people outside the particular society could not, in this view, be a problem of social distributive justice. Yet here too, the universal morality of equal respect and the principle of equal distribution demand that we consider each person as prima facie equally entitled to the goods, unless reasons for an unequal distribution can be put forth. It may be that in the process of justification, reasons will emerge for privileging those who were particularly involved in the production of a good (see below). But, prima facie, there is no reason to exclude from the outset other persons, for example, those from other countries, from the process of distribution and justification. That may seem most intuitively plausible in the case of natural resources, such as mineral resources, that someone discovers by chance on or beneath the surface of his property. Why should they belong to the person who discovers them, or on whose property they are located?

The goods and burdens to be distributed must be divided into various categories. Such a division is essential because reasons that speak for unequal treatment in one area do not justify unequal treatment in another. In order to reconstruct our understanding of contemporary liberal democratic welfare states, four categories seem essential: (1) civil liberties, (2) opportunities for political participation, (3) social positions and opportunities, and (4) economic rewards. For all four categories, distributive justice is the guiding aspect, the results of which can then be codified as rights.

After dividing social goods into categories, we must next ask what can justify unequal treatment or unequal distribution in each category. This approach results from the principle of equal treatment. The philosophical point of departure is a counterfactual, original distribution of common goods that have not yet been distributed and hence belong to no one, so that everyone has in principle an equal claim upon them. The following kinds of reasons must be taken seriously as candidates for justified unequal treatment in certain categories: (1) differing natural disadvantages (e.g., disabilities); (2) existing rights or claims (e.g., private property); (3) differences in the performance of special services (e.g., efforts or sacrifices for the sake of the community); (4) incentives (as in Rawls's difference principle); and (5) compensation for indirect or structural discrimination (e.g., affirmative action).

I cannot here discuss in detail the justification of these kinds of claims. I am not attempting here to provide a complete treatment of a theory of distributive justice based on the principle of prima facie equal treatment. The basic idea of the argument for social justice can be briefly described as follows: unequal shares of goods are fair when they are the result of labor and when they accrue to a person deservedly, that is, when they result from the decisions and deliberate actions of the respective agents. Such privileging or disadvantaging is, however, unfair when based on arbitrary and unmerited differences in social circumstances and natural gifts. Rawls's chief intuition rests on the distinction between choice and circumstances (Rawls 1971, § 12). Dworkin formulates this distributive criterion as follows: a just distribution must be both endowment-insensitive and ambition-sensitive (Dworkin 1981, 311). The natural and social endowment must not count, but the personal ambitions, intentions, and voluntary decisions of individual persons should. The individuals must, therefore, bear the costs of their decisions. This conception also tries to keep in mind the consideration that goods cannot simply be distributed, but that the production of the goods must first of all be supported and must secondly be justly ordered. The problem is not merely the prima facie right to the same share of goods, but also the right and, if necessary, the duty to make the elementary desired goods available.

The moral claim to a just portion of social goods and burdens worldwide – I claim – forms the principle for generating subjective moral or human rights that must be morally respected. The principle of prima facie equal distribution is thus, as a rule for the just distribution of social goods, a *generating principle of rights*.[16] One should conceive this principle of rights as the substantive guideline and source of justification for rights in general. Human rights are moral claims or demands of justice to something which must not be withheld from any human being. For the various categories of social goods, this principle should be able to give rise to more specific and precise rights. Moral claim-rights contain, in addition, the moral demand that these claim-rights be institutionalized and thereby protected legally. The human rights generated qua principle of justice must, therefore, be positivized in a further step as basic rights.

3. The particular conception of justice I have outlined so far is certainly a disputed theory. But for the question at hand, not so much depends on whether one agrees with this very conception of justice. Rather, what is important is that it belongs to a family of conceptions of justice seeming very

---

[16] This is intended in the way Kant understands his account of the sole human right as a principle of human rights.

plausible to the current mainstream in social, political, and moral philosophy. This family shares three central features: It is distributive, egalitarian, and universalistic. According to the first feature, it is assumed that justice has (among other things) to do with the justifiable reallocation or redistribution of goods and resources necessary for each individual to have his or her due (the distributional premise). According to the second feature, it is assumed that (at least) all human beings have an equal moral entitlement to equal respect and concern (the fundamental egalitarian premise). And the third feature is the premise that to be considered part of our modern morality at all, any norm of justice has to be justified with respect to the interests of all concerned parties – that is, all justifiable claims of (at least) all human beings have to be considered (the universalistic premise).

All theories that share these features have to conceive justice as global – or so I claim. I have argued in my 1998 against alternative, more limited conceptions of justice, such as the view that only freedom and the satisfaction of basic needs are to be protected as basic moral or human rights. I attempted to show that these views (must) always make use of the idea of distributive justice defined by the three mentioned features. If it is thus granted that these theories have to be considered members of the family of distributive, egalitarian, and universalistic conceptions of justice, their proponents – so I argue further – do not succeed in solidly grounding their respective restrictions on the scope of justice.

Distributive justice is applied in the context of social relations, in which various persons (for whatever reasons) have a common claim to certain goods or must together bear certain burdens. Insofar as these social relations are those of all human beings by virtue of their "membership" in the community of men, the appropriate burdens and goods must be distributed justly within the international community. On this view, these are demands of justice, which prima facie apply to all humans. The moral duties and claims emerging from distributive justice are, therefore, prima facie valid globally. According to the justification principle, all rules, actions, and relations or conditions for which responsibility can be imputed must be justified to *all* relevantly affected parties.

II. Possible Reasons for the Theoretical Limitation of Justice

Such a view has its definite advantages. By developing universalistic conceptions of justice, philosophy came up with a theory of global justice that was, and still is, running ahead of its time, since it corresponds to a process of globalization and diminishment of national-state power of which people are only now becoming aware. Philosophy is here not even too late. Minerva's owl must this time wait for daybreak, here not needing to start its flight only at night. Justice can no longer be conceived in terms of the nation-state when nation-states are increasingly losing their original power to supranational actors – when supranational political alliances such as the European Union and the North Atlantic Treaty Organization, and internationally operating corporations with enormous amounts of private money, are much bigger, stronger, and more flexible than many states could be. We seem to be moving towards a new, postnational constellation (Habermas 1998). For this challenge of globalization, a conception of global instead of national justice seems the most, if not the only, appropriate contemporary answer.

But, of course, it cannot be denied that such a universalistic theory has its disadvantages and problems. In the eyes of many, if not most people, global justice demands too much from individuals and their states.[17] The charge is one of excessive demands being made. If all human beings worldwide indeed had prima facie equal claim-rights to justice, this would require enormous redistribution from wealthy societies and their members to those living in poverty anywhere in the world. This may not correspond to the considered judgements of citizens throughout the world. Hence, on account of its radical consequences, global theory does not appear acceptable – this in relation to both its spatial and substantive dimensions. Apparently, too much is here being distributed to too many. These are the intuitive sources of strong objections to equating social justice with a prima facie requirement to secure justice globally. The requirement of global justice is exposed, in particular, to the objection that it cannot account for our intuition or our understanding of global (human) rights, according to which these rights comprise only particularly fundamental, especially important rights, but not the whole of justice. What are the reasons put forth for the more restrictive conception of universal justice held by many, according to which human rights can contain only a concept of minimal justice?

The charge of excessive demand remains, however, abstract and somewhat empty, as long as the opponents of global justice cannot specify other moral principles more compatible with our considered judgements. What are the possible principles or theoretical constructs, with the help of which these opponents of global justice can argue that the scope of justice has to be limited? A lot of the familiar objections and rival theories emerge from outside the distributive, egalitarian, and universalistic field, for example, libertarian, communitarian, and other views. They surely all require special consideration and refutations. Here, however, I will only be concerned with the question of whether there are plausible objections to the requirement of global justice solely on the basis of a distributive, egalitarian, and universalistic view of justice. For in the "universalist camp" as well, a general tendency can also be observed to give more weight to the claims of a state's members than to outsiders.

---

[17] For a nuanced critique cf., for example, Miller (1998), who criticizes the doctrine of moral cosmopolitanism as too demanding because of the content of the moral principles adopted and the scope of the doctrine. Miller opposes his views to those of Barry (1998), who holds a theory similar to, yet distinct from, mine.

In the present discussion, we can discern five universalistic objections, above all, to a generalization of redistribution claims so unrestricted as to transcend state boundaries. These objections invoke (1) the principle of "moral division of labor"; (2) the connection between cooperation and distributive justice; (3) the primacy of democracy; (4) the dangers of a world state; and (5) political-pragmatic factors. I would now like to briefly sketch and scrutinize each of the objections.

1. There are universalistic theorists who maintain the position that a state's special consideration of its residents can be justified in the framework of a "moral division of labor." Moral division of labor is possible in many different forms. As far as the principles of its shaping are concerned, however, one can generally differentiate between two fundamental models: the model of efficient duty assignment, and the model of relation-dependent responsibilities.

The *model of efficient duty assignment* is based upon the assumption that all people have the same mutual rights and obligations independent of their special relations; but that some of these rights, especially the more demanding ones, can be effectively fulfilled only through cooperation based on the division of labor – rather than through independent individual activities (Goodin 1988, 678ff.; Koller 1998, 104–9). In order to make these rights effective, an appropriate distribution of duties is required, in which certain persons or institutions are appointed to be in charge of fulfilling the respective rights of specific persons. The way in which this distribution of duties is to be arranged is simply a question of pure expedience. It should always be arranged in such a way that the moral claims of all persons can be fulfilled as well as possible. This can be clarified through the example by Schlothfeldt (1999) of how parents accept certain obligations vis-à-vis their children and, if occasion arises, may – and ought – to treat them preferentially vis-à-vis other persons. It does not have to be maintained that one's own children are to be given special consideration as a matter of principle. For a moral division of labor, it suffices that the duty to provide emotional and material sustenance is carried out especially well by parents.

The model of the moral division of labor as an efficient assignment of duty has its merits. The model, however, is inadequate as a basis for arguing against the global scope of justice, for it simply takes the sum of moral rights and obligations between people for granted and only deals with how the duties may be assigned to the individuals on the level of efficiency. It presupposes an independent criterion of global or local justice; and this presupposed criterion would need to carry the argument's burden, not the moral division of labor.

In contrast, the *model of relation-dependent responsibilities* only refers to the special social relationships between persons in order to differentiate their respective mutual rights and obligations, according to the degree of those relationships. Correspondingly, the closer persons are bound together by a relationship of mutual cooperation and dependence, the stronger their mutual responsibilities. Such a relationship exists if at least one of the following, ideally coinciding, conditions is met: first, a subjective awareness by the participants that they form a common enterprise of mutually advantageous cooperation or reciprocity, and second, the objective fact that the activities of the respective persons have actual effects on the lives of one another. The closer the interconnectedness of people, the stronger the moral responsibilities between them.

This model may explain better than the first model why the responsibilities between members of a family are stronger than those between the citizens of a state, and why these citizens may have more obligations to one another than do members of different societies. It thus offers the right basis for mounting an argument against the global scope of justice. Taken on its own, however, the model of relation-dependent responsibilities is not convincing. The model can easily be interpreted as reifying social relationships and adhering to normative communitarianism instead of maintaining normative individualism. It postulates the existing features of relationships between people as a given, without taking into consideration their appropriateness. But these features are contingent, and therefore it could be the case that other features would better accord with the demands of justice by and for various individuals. If moral obligations between persons depended only on their actual relationships, there would never be a reason to question these relationships from a moral point of view and, if necessary, reform them. That point of view and the circumstances of justice are not bound to existing personal relations; and they are normally not grasped that way in the considered judgement of most people.

Both models, however, have a common weakness. If the example of family duties is a good one for a moral division of labor, it only shows that the moral division of labor holds only as long as the party to which the duties are assigned can effectively guarantee their fulfillment. Otherwise other institutions have to step in. A federalistic system is required to secure the necessary help if the duty assignment turns out to be inefficient. An unqualified moral division of labor would be too risky and would place certain parties under possible unfair disadvantages they have not themselves chosen freely. The idea of a moral division of labor speaks instead in favor of a federalistic system of global justice (see more below).

2. Some philosophers argue that problems of distributive justice only emerge in the framework of *cooperation relationships:* as long as persons and groups do not function within conditions of institutionalized, mutually beneficial social cooperation, there can be no justified claims of one party upon the earned assets of another. But as already partially argued above, this limitation is implausible on a number of grounds. It represents only a

special case of distributive justice. The idea of such justice is not tied to an institutional framework of mutually supportive cooperation.[18]

First, the just distribution of nonproduced resources needs to be discussed. Second, there are claims on collectively produced goods that appear legitimated, not on the basis of cooperative accomplishment, but on that of needs; that is, even in a cooperative community, cooperative justice is not equal to the totality of justice. Alongside justice within a cooperative community, we find what might be termed the justice of solidarity (Kersting 2000, 22–26). Both possibilities are especially important precisely in the case of global distributive justice.

Third, according to the view under discussion, material entitlements can only be grounded as claims to the results of mutually supportive cooperation. Yet it is a matter of controversy whether current global relations represent such mutually supportive cooperation. One could maintain that the current global scheme is one of social cooperation analogous to that present in domestic states (Pogge 1988; Beitz 1999, 143ff.). Thus the conditions for the application of principles of justice, so conceived, would be at work on the international level. This view is, however, disputed. Its opponents claim that neither on the political, cultural, social, nor legal level is there enough cooperation on a worldwide scale for conditions of cooperative justice to be understood as present. The existing forms of cooperation are too weak and dispersed to justify the global application of principles of cooperative justice (Nelson 1974, 425ff.; Kersting 1996, 197ff.; Chwaszcza 1996, 173). This claim overlooks the common effects new realities now have on us: We internationally share the effects of war and peace, especially the threat of nuclear disaster. We also experience the globalizing effects of instantaneous worldwide communication. With its help, a process of worldwide financial and economic cooperation and information exchange is in the course of being established. We should also not underestimate the tendency towards a global moral consciousness, or at least a sense of injustice, as seen for instance in the social pressures and worldwide protests of an informed global citizenry regarding issues of human rights. The establishment of international law and international governmental and nongovernmental organizations has enormous effects on the realization of global justice. The dispute about the adequate factual description of current international relations does not, however, matter so much from a philosophical vantage. What really does matter, when it comes to the conditions in which justice is called for, are the so-called

[18] Nevertheless, a possible weakening of the claims to global redistribution emerges from considering the fact that in general, human beings do not work alone but in cooperation with others. For only the cooperative partners are entitled to the gains from mutual cooperation when two conditions are fulfilled: first, that all worldwide claims based on objective, physical – and possibly social – need are satisfied through the securing of minimum economic claims, and second, that the not implausible but still debatable premise is accepted that better situations are at least partially earned and thus justified.

"circumstances of justice" (Hume 1978, Book III, pt. 2, sec. 2; Hubin 1979; Rawls 1971, §22): it is called for whenever scarcity of resources is manifest. These conditions are universally given, since most of the desired goods are scarce, human beings having a general tendency to possess and develop ungratified and conflicting interests – a situation they cannot alleviate on their own. The conditions are thus, in any case, present universally at a global level. For this reason, and the other reasons mentioned above, the restriction of the scope of justice to functioning, institutionalized, mutually beneficial forms of social cooperation should be rejected.

3. As I take it, in our reflective judgements, "we" modern democrats all accept two political ideals (among others): on the one hand, universal moral claims of all human beings, worldwide, that must be respected by all other human beings and by social institutions; on the other hand, the conviction that democracy, as government by the people for the people, is the best form of government. There seems, however, to be a conflict between these two ideas. In politics today, we basically find two ways of dealing with this conflict: the "liberal" view defends the priority of justice and human rights against the "democratic-republican" view, which emphasizes the priority of popular sovereignty. For the liberal view (classically Locke [1980], today Rawls [1971]) liberal basic rights have priority over democratic participation. The "democratic-republican" view (classically Rousseau [1987], today Habermas [1992], most radically Rorty [1991]) claims the priority of public self-government of the citizens. Human rights should receive their legitimation as a result of the sovereign self-determination of the political community. According to this view, basic rights will be justified only as a function or a constitutive part of the democratic right to participation and discourse.

People often see global justice in deep conflict with other moral values, in particular democracy or self-government as the leading normative idea of collective organizations. They argue that the main or even sole natural human right is freedom. The basic legitimation for moral and/or legal norms comes, therefore, from the idea of and primary right to self-government. The historically most important argument for democracy is usually derived from the principle of self-government: It seems clear that, in the end, only the directly affected parties can formulate and advocate their (true or reasonable) interests. Equal respect, which we owe one another reciprocally, thus requires regard for the autonomous decisions of each unique and noninterchangeable individual. This procedural approach to moral legitimization regards the *autonomy* of the individual as the standard of justification for universal norms. Since we are morally obliged to respect one another's autonomy, such a conception of morality necessarily entails a personal right to reflective self-determination or self-government for each autonomous individual. This is the principle of equal individual freedom. Thus, people must not be coerced or forced under any regulation or government unless they can freely agree to it. *Consensus* is the criterion of legitimacy for collective decisions. If there is a consensus about an issue, for example, on institutional constraints or regarding a framework of rules, then each party will affirm this agreement freely for himself or herself, thus following the rule of "one will." In this way, each party will govern himself or herself. From these premises of autonomy and consensus, we can conclude that to be self-governing in the political realm entails participation in democratic discussions and enables decision making under certain conditions. As Joshua Cohen has put it: "Outcomes are democratically legitimate if they could be the outcome of a free and reasoned agreement among equals" (Cohen 1989, 22). If that argument is valid,[19] democracy has a moral grounding at least on par with, if not higher than, requirements of justice. We could thus confront a potential conflict between global justice requiring that certain actions be taken in certain areas and the outcomes of democratic decision-making procedures of a society governing the area in question.[20] The democratic decisions of a society or state might not, and often do not, conform to what we think the requirements of global justice are. Which side, then, has priority in case of conflict?

I would like to argue for the thesis that only a morally motivated priority of justice over democracy is plausible. If we search for a common moral basis for political ideals, the distinction between the two conceptions can be reformulated thus: The "democratic-republican" conception attempts to derive the primacy of processes of political self-legislation, and of the democratic legitimation of laws meant to guarantee justice, from the moral criterion of a general principle of justification and consensus. In contrast, the "liberal" conception interprets morality "constructively" as a canon of basic principles of justice and human rights that need to be the substantive basis for any legitimate legislation. In my view, only the "liberal" of these alternatives is plausible. Self-government, public autonomy that is, is itself a requirement of justice. Basic or human rights derived from global justice are morally justified, and as such they limit the realm of democratic decision making. They impose morally justified constraints on the sovereignty of the people. Positive law must be morally legitimate, that is, the justified claims of individuals to equal respect must not be violated. All legal compulsion must therefore be reciprocally and univer-

[19] The main difficulty with this schematic argument should, however, be clear: its strong dependence on the possibility of consensus. Constructed this way, the argument neglects the crucial phenomenon of disagreement or dissent. This is no accident. There is, in fact, considerable tension in this theory between the idea that an individual must be free to autonomously govern the world he shares in common with others and the claim that he must also afford this same freedom to every other citizen. Democracy, thus, would seem to be incompatible with *individual* self-government.

[20] The fact that international institutions are very often coercively imposed, especially by the rich on the poor, constitutes a distinct problem of international justice (Pogge 1998, 504–9; Pogge 2001).

sally justifiable and capable of being adhered to through reasonable insight alone. A state-structured community has a just basic order only when it is principally concerned with the establishment of just conditions. In this sense, the establishment of human rights as the moral core of legal rights must be an essential aim of the state. Yet this does not imply that all legal validity becomes purely moral validity. Moral arguments are necessary only for the justification of basic human rights, that is, for the abstract moral core, which must then be legally concretized and institutionalized (Forst 1994, 79). These fundamental human rights especially make their way into modern constitutions in the form of basic rights. Human rights comprise the framework that marks off the playing field for possible legitimate democratic decisions. Within this normative framework, it may be up to democratic processes both to carry out the necessary legal interpretation and concretization of human rights and to institutionalize and govern a political order in accordance with pragmatic, ethical, and moral reasons (above and beyond human rights). Moral rights remain "unsaturated" until they are codified and interpreted.[21] Human rights deliberately leave significant leeway open in the choice of a constitution or of economic or social rules.[22] Laws and programs are just in the sense of human rights if they remain within the acceptable framework and if they take on legal force through legislation in accordance with a just constitution. Political rule is thus normatively limited by the basic rights anchored in the constitution, and these are in turn limited by the moral human rights.

Both for pragmatic reasons and with a view to the theory of democracy, it makes sense to stipulate as basic constitutional rights securing global justice only particular, especially fundamental human rights. In this manner, the rights we do not wish simply to leave to the democratic decision-making procedures of particular states are singled out as especially worthy of protection. They include, first, those rights without whose guarantee the utilization of other rights is impossible. They include, second, and above all, those rights crucial to securing the core content of the morality of equal respect, that is, fundamental to the status of a person with equal rights. Thus, negative liberties, political participatory rights, and social rights to positive actions can be derived from this principle as legal claims to a particular distribution of specific goods; they can be thus derived through a demonstration that these very goods are especially central for the utilization of other rights. Yet the human rights derived from the universal principle of rights are, in essence, abstract. The necessary positivization and detailed concretization as basic rights in state constitutions must be reserved for the democratic procedures at work in specific

[21] Cf. Wellmer (1998) on the problem of determining the boundary between basic rights, which are morally fixed and more or less unalterable, and the interpretations we may stipulate through democratic processes.

[22] Hence, the moral and the political levels of justification overlap one another, yet only partially; they are not fully congruent (Forst 1998, 151).

historical and social situations, which are in turn safeguarded by means of human rights. The human rights making their way into constitutions as basic rights deliberately leave open a significant spectrum for the determination of specific rights. Thus, the affected parties can themselves, as morally autonomous individuals, determine how the moral claim = rights claims are to be understood in their specific historical circumstances.

4. In its basic tendency, global justice seems to lead – as Kant (1968) was afraid it would – towards a world state or – if that possibility can somehow be excluded – at least towards a kind of cosmopolitanism. This implication is seen, even by many universalists, as politically and morally dangerous. Prima facie, a great deal seems to speak for the danger of a super-state – a world-governing leviathan that cannot be stopped or constrained by other potentially equally powerful states. In addition, we value more local governments for good reason – and therefore a federalistic structure of larger nation-states and supranational, state-like organizations.

To answer this challenge, defenders of global justice distinguish between our *moral* requirement to treat every fellow human being worldwide with equal concern and respect and the *legal* requirement following from the moral requirement (Pogge 1992, 49; Beitz 1994; Beitz 1999, 199). The latter does not necessarily imply any legal cosmopolitanism, that is, a single overarching global political authority. Thus, it does not imply the demand for a world state. On the contrary, the demands of justice and moral rights can perhaps be realized in different states. Global justice is compatible with a system of dispersed political sovereignty. Moral claims and rights do not stop at borders, but are globally valid for all humans. But institutions people have to establish and support through fulfilling duties of justice might be organized locally, pluralistically; and for that purpose they might have borders that have no moral, but merely derivative significance. But it is necessary that such institutions themselves are just, that is, adhere to basic global principles of justly institutionalized organizations (Pogge 1992). By allowing for a federalistic community of institutionalized societies (it is not always necessary that these be ordinary states as we know them), global justice tries to account for what Rawls calls the "fact of pluralism." Global justice in a federalistic world structure can allow for a plurality and diversity of cultures, traditions, and comprehensive doctrines compatible with the universalistic egalitarian principles of justice. Thus, this objection, although not valid as stated, gives rise to a proposal of a supplementation and modification of the idea of global justice.

Connected with this is another objection to a legal cosmopolitanism that I rather take to be another supplementation. According to this "objection," "global" justice should be interpreted as the continuation of justice in a multistep model. That is, the primary focus of justice should be local institutions, and only those issues that cannot be regulated successfully on the local level should be dealt with on the next higher level, and so on up to the highest and most global level, that is, the world at large. This multistep model will, accordingly, not only restrict global justice to those issues with which smaller communities cannot cope, but also restrict global justice to structural measures and structural cooperation. Subsidiarity only demands cooperation between the smaller communities, to secure international justice for the sake of regulating relations between states in a fair way, thus guaranteeing justice for issues with which states cannot adequately cope. As something useless and harmful, the transferal of the legal model suitable for the state to the world community is thereby clearly rejected. On the one hand, this argument is based on the other argument, already partially refuted, that global states are dangerous. But on the other hand, it is based on the moral idea of *subsidiarity* (Føllesdal 1998; Höffe 1999, 126–34). Corresponding to ethical individualism, with justification having its starting point with the individual, this view holds that the individual remains primarily responsible for effectuating his or her responsibility. The individual must accomplish whatever can be accomplished on his or her own, and must not leave this to the wider society. The individual thus has both the duty of and right to self-help and self-responsibility. Correspondingly, this principle can be transferred to the level of societal hierarchy. Whatever the smaller, lower unit can accomplish, it must accomplish on its own. It can only hand things that overwhelm its capacities to higher units.

This fits well with the above mentioned principles of democracy and federalism. No centralized world state should be erected from above; but rather, a federal world organization or similar entity needs to be built up democratically from below, starting with local units. Only tasks not taken care of on a lower level remain to that organization. It complements the local federal institutional organizations where they need complementing, without dissolving them. All tasks, also those concerning justice, should remain on the lowest possible level, for example, those of civil and penal law.[23] That, however, will leave enough to do for institutions on a global level. But to be just, the principle of subsidiarity requires – and this should not be overlooked – an initial fair, global distribution of resources. To demand self-help from those who unfairly have less than others, but are still able to help themselves, seems itself unfair. For this reason, the developmental help offered by the "first world" to the "third world" for the sake of self-help tries to correspond to a proper moral criterion, without in any way realizing the fair background conditions necessary for it.

---

[23] If decisions are placed with subunits in a polity with subunit autonomy, some inequalities may arise for some individuals living in different subunits (Føllesdal 2001). The inequalities are justified only if they benefit those subunits in the worst condition. The trade-off that matters here, from the normative perspective, is the one between what these subunit poor stand to gain in terms of political autonomy, and what they sacrifice economically, under subunit autonomy compared to under a unitary political order.

5. As indicated, there are additional, political-pragmatic factors, and these are certainly good ones that any advocate of the cosmopolitan perspective should take seriously. I will mention only a few such factors, although the list can readily be extended.

For a start, how, precisely, responsibilities are to be distributed remains a crucial question. The moral rules meant to guide human actions must also reach those meant to be guided by them. An exclusively individualistic conception – according to this argument – here copes inadequately with the problem of international justice, because it does not address the collective and institutional agents who, in the real, existing world, actually make the important, influential decisions about what should be done.[24] But although the point is well taken, it remains true that theorizing exclusively in terms of collective bodies does not manifest the ground-level concern for the autonomy of individuals comprising a basic normative requirement in most ethical theories today.

At the same time, the expansion of justice is in inverse proportion to the remaining chances of realizing it. The more one packs into global justice and the human rights derived from it, the less one will achieve. One cannot currently attain the same emotional support from all persons for the whole of justice that a more restrictive conception of justice or human rights might indeed promise. Yet from the purely pragmatic argument, it only follows that one should not demand everything at once, but rather proceed in steps. The application of global justice must, perhaps, in reality amount to political compromise for the sake of attaining the desirable global acceptance. Nonetheless, such a compromise requires orientation around an ideal. And such a normative ideal is provided by the principle of distributive justice applied universally – a principle not devalued by political-pragmatic compromises.

These and similar objections cannot, in my view, undermine the strong normative approach of global justice.[25] To the extent that a global society currently exists, and to the extent that it has possibilities at its disposal, that is, to the extent it has control over and hence responsibility for social relations, all distributions of goods and burdens must be justified in the face of all interested parties. From the perspective of a distributive, egalitarian, and universalistic approach, it is not clear why the justified moral claim to a just portion of worldwide social goods should not be set down as global claim-rights.

Still we are left with the large problem of a lack of acceptance. Of what use can a conception of justice be if it is not accepted and supported by most

---

[24] The importance of this argument is one major theme in O'Neill (1986, esp. 32–35), and is seen by Wenar (2001) as one real advantage to Rawls's (1999) rejection of cosmopolitanism, in that in addressing people it is addressing agents who have crucial roles in the world as it is.

[25] However, this would surely have to be more thoroughly examined and discussed than it is here.

of our fellow human beings? Here many questions would appear to require answers: Is, for instance, the nonacceptance of principles of global justice really based on considered judgements? If yes, is there any solution or future prospect for setting a theory of justice and the considered judgement of all human beings into equilibrium on a worldwide basis?[26] Which side has to be changed, the theory or the basic intuitions? If no, it should be possible to demonstrate that cosmopolitan theories can accommodate the most solid convictions regarding matters of justice on a worldwide basis. Thus, even in the realm of abstract, ideal theory, much still needs resolution, not to speak of the many yet unclarified questions in the realm of nonideal theory.

References

Barry, Brian. (1998). "International Society from a Cosmopolitan Perspective." In *International Society: Diverse Ethical Perspectives,* edited by David R. Mapel and Terry Nardin, 144–63. Princeton: Princeton University Press.

Bedau, Hugo Adam. (1967). "Egalitarianism and the Idea of Equality." In *Equality,* edited by J. Roland Pennock and John Chapman, 3–27. *Nomos* 9. New York: Atherton.

Beitz, Charles. (1994). "Cosmopolitan Liberalism and the States System." In *Political Restructuring in Europe: Ethical Perspectives,* edited by Chris Brown, 123–36. London: Routledge.

———. (1999). *Political Theory and International Relations.* 2nd ed. Princeton: Princeton University Press. First edition published 1979.

Chwaszcza, Christine. (1996). "Politische Ethik II: Ethik der internationalen Beziehungen." In *Angewandte Ethik,* edited by Julian Nida-Rümelin, 154–99. Stuttgart: Kröner.

Cohen, Joshua. (1989). "Deliberation and Democratic Legitimacy." In *The Good Polity,* edited by Alan Hamlin and Philip Pettit, 18–27. Oxford: Basil Blackwell.

Dworkin, Ronald. (1977). *Taking Rights Seriously.* Cambridge, MA: Harvard University Press.

———. (1981). "What Is Equality? Part 2: Equality of Resources." *Philosophy and Public Affairs,* 10, 283–345.

[26] This might be the reason why Rawls (1999) balks at cosmopolitanism, as argued by Wenar (2001). Rawls's fundamental norm requires that the principles for coercive global institutions must emerge from ideas that are reasonably acceptable to all who are to be coerced by them. As Rawls (1993, 36–40) indicates in the case of one, particular society, the only conceptual source for grounding social institutions is the *public political culture,* understood as the political institutions of the regime and the public traditions of their interpretation, as well as the historic texts and documents that have become part of common knowledge. But are there such shared basic ideas in the global public political culture at all? If yes, do these ideas support cosmopolitanism? Rawls appears to decline cosmopolitanism because it does not correspond to the principles and implicit, basal ideas that can be framed by the public culture of international agreements.

Føllesdal, Andreas. (1998). "Subsidiarity." *Journal of Political Philosophy*, 6, 231–59.

——. (2001). "Federal Inequality among Equals: A Contractualist Defense." *Metaphilosophy*, 32:1/2.

Forst, Rainer. (1994). *Kontexte der Gerechtigkeit*. Frankfurt am Main: Suhrkamp.

——. (1998). "Die Rechtfertigung der Gerechtigkeit: Rawls' Politischer Liberalismus und Habermas' Diskurstheorie in der Diskussion." In *Das Recht der Republik*, edited by Peter Niesen and Hauke Brunkhorst, 105–68. Frankfurt am Main: Suhrkamp.

Goodin, Robert. (1988). "What Is So Special about Our Fellow Country Men?" *Ethics*, 98, 663–86.

Gosepath, Stefan. (1995). "The Place of Equality in Habermas' and Dworkin's Theories of Justice." *European Journal of Philosophy*, 3, 21–35.

——. (1998). "Zu Begründungen sozialer Menschenrechte." In *Philosophie der Menschenrechte*, edited by Stefan Gosepath and Georg Lohmann, 146–87. Frankfurt am Main: Suhrkamp.

Habermas, Jürgen. (1983). "Diskursethik – Notizen zu einem Begründungsprogramm." In *Moralbewußtsein und kommunikatives Handeln*, 53–126. Frankfurt am Main: Suhrkamp.

——. (1992). *Faktizität und Geltung: Beiträge zur Diskurstheorie des Rechts und des demokratischen Rechtsstaats*. Frankfurt am Main: Suhrkamp. Translated into English as *Between Facts and Norms: Contributions to a Discourse Theory of Law and Democracy* (Cambridge, MA: MIT Press, 1996).

——. (1998). *Postnationale Konstellation*. Frankfurt am Main: Suhrkamp.

Hinsch, Wilfried. (Forthcoming, a). "Angemessene Gleichheit." In *Subjektivität und Anerkennung*, edited by Barbara Merker, Georg Mohr, and Michael Quante.

——. (Forthcoming, b). *Gerechtfertigte Ungleichheiten*. Berlin: de Gruyter.

Höffe, Otfried. (1999). *Demokratie im Zeitalter der Globalisierung*. München: Beck.

Hohfeld, W. N. (1923). *Fundamental Legal Conceptions*. New Haven: Yale University Press.

Hubin, Donald. (1979). "The Scope of Justice." *Philosophy and Public Affairs*, 9, 3–24.

Hume, David. (1978 [1739–40]). *A Treatise of Human Nature*. Ed. L. A. Selby-Bigge. 2nd ed. Oxford: Clarendon.

Kant, Immanuel. (1968 [1795]). *Zum ewigen Frieden: Ein philosophischer Entwurf*. In *Kants Werke*, vol. 8, Akademie-Ausgabe. Berlin: de Gruyter.

Kersting, Wolfgang. (1996). "Weltfriedensordung und globale Verteilungsgerechtigkeit." In *Zum ewigen Frieden*, edited by R. Merkel and R. Wittman. Frankfurt am Main: Suhrkamp.

——. (2000). *Theorien der sozialen Gerechtigkeit.* Stuttgart: Metzler.
Klosko, Georg. (1994). "Political Obligation and the Natural Duties of Justice." *Philosophy and Public Affairs,* 23, 251–70.
Koller, Peter. (1994). "Soziale Güter und Gerechtigkeit." In *Theorien der Gerechtigkeit,* edited by H.-J. Koch, M. Köhler, and K. Seelmann, 79–104. ARSP Beiheft 56. Stuttgart: Steiner.
——. (1998). "Der Geltungsbereich der Menschenrechte." In *Philosophie der Menschenrechte,* edited by Stefan Gosepath and Georg Lohmann, 96–123. Frankfurt am Main: Suhrkamp.
Korsgaard, Christine. (1996). *Sources of Normativity.* Cambridge: Cambridge University Press.
Locke, John. (1980 [1690]). *Second Treatise of Government.* Ed. C. B. MacPherson. Indianapolis, IN: Hackett.
Miller, David. (1998). "The Limits of Cosmopolitan Justice." In *International Society: Diverse Ethical Perspectives,* edited by David R. Mapel and Terry Nardin, 164–81. Princeton: Princeton University Press.
Murphy, Liam. (1998). "Institutions and the Demands of Justice." *Philosophy and Public Affairs,* 27, 251–91.
Nelson, William. (1974). "Special Rights, General Rights, and Social Justice." *Philosophy and Public Affairs,* 3, 410–30.
O'Neill, Onora. (1986). *Faces of Hunger.* London: Allen & Unwin.
Plato. (1998). *Republic.* Trans. Robin Waterfield. Oxford: Oxford University Press.
Pogge, Thomas. (1988). "Rawls and Global Justice." *Canadian Journal of Philosophy,* 18, 227–56.
——. (1992). "Cosmopolitanism and Sovereignty." *Ethics,* 103, 48–75.
——. (1995). "How Should Human Rights Be Conceived?" In *Jahrbuch für Recht und Ethik,* vol. 3, edited by Joachim Hruschka, 103–20. Berlin: Dunkler & Humblot.
——. (1998). "A Global Resource Dividend." In *Ethics of Consumption,* edited by D. A. Crocker and T. Linden, 501–36. Lanham, MD: Rowman & Littlefield.
——. (2001). "Priorities of Global Justice." *Metaphilosophy,* 32:1/2.
Rawls, John. (1971). *A Theory of Justice.* Cambridge, MA: Harvard University Press. Second edition published 1999.
——. (1993). *Political Liberalism.* New York: Columbia University Press.
——. (1999). *The Law of Peoples.* Cambridge, MA: Harvard University Press.
Rorty, Richard. (1991). "The Priority of Democracy to Philosophy." In *Objectivity, Relativism, and Truth.* Cambridge: Cambridge University Press.
Rössler, Beate. (1999). "Unglück und Unrecht: Grenzen von Gerechtigkeit im liberaldemokratischen Rechtsstaat." In *Konzeptionen der*

Gerechtigkeit, edited by Herfried Münkler and Marcus Llanque, 347–64. Baden-Baden: Nomos.

Rousseau, Jean-Jacques. (1987 [1762]). *The Social Contract.* Trans. Maurice Cranston. Harmondsworth, England: Penguin.

Scanlon, Thomas. (1998). *What We Owe to Each Other.* Cambridge, MA: Harvard University Press.

Schlothfeldt, Stephan. (1999). "Migration als Problem der internationalen Verteilungsgerechtigkeit." Working paper no. 1, Interdisziplinäre soziale Gerechtigkeitsforschung. Berlin.

Sen, Amartya. (1980). "Equality of What?" In *Tanner Lectures on Human Values,* vol. 1, edited by S. M. McMurrin. Cambridge: Cambridge University Press.

———. (1992). *Inequality Reexamined.* Oxford: Clarendon Press.

Shklar, Judith. (1990). *The Faces of Injustice.* New Haven: Yale University Press.

Shue, Henry. (1980). *Basic Rights.* Princeton: Princeton University Press.

Temkin, Larry. (1986). "Inequality." *Philosophy and Public Affairs,* 15, 99–121.

Tugendhat, Ernst. (1993). *Vorlesungen über Ethik.* Frankfurt am Main: Suhrkamp.

———. (1997). *Dialog in Leticia.* Frankfurt am Main: Suhrkamp.

Ulpian, Domitius. (1822). *Fragmenta.* 4th ed. Ed. Gustav Ritter Hugo. Berolini: Mylius.

Vlastos, Gregory. (1984). "Justice and Equality." In *Theories of Rights,* edited by Jeremy Waldron, 41–76. Oxford: Oxford University Press.

Waldron, Jeremy. (1993). "Special Ties and Natural Duties." *Philosophy and Public Affairs,* 22, 3–30.

Wellmer, Albrecht. (1998). "Demokratie und Menschenrechte." In *Philosophie der Menschenrechte,* edited by Stefan Gosepath and Georg Lohmann, 265–92. Frankfurt am Main: Suhrkamp.

Wenar, Leif. (2001). "Contractualism and Global Economic Justice." *Metaphilosophy,* 32:1/2.

Westen, Peter. (1990). *Speaking of Equality.* Princeton: Princeton University Press.

Williams, Bernard. (1973). "The Idea of Equality." In *Problems of the Self.* Cambridge: Cambridge University Press.

Wingert, Lutz. (1993). *Gemeinsinn und Moral.* Frankfurt am Main: Suhrkamp.

11

TOWARDS A CRITICAL THEORY OF TRANSNATIONAL JUSTICE

RAINER FORST

I

The first question that has to be addressed when one thinks about issues of justice that transcend the normative boundaries of states is whether one is looking for principles of *international* or of *global* justice. Whereas the former view takes political communities organized into states to be the main agents of justice (i.e., who is asked to be just and who receives just treatment), the latter takes persons, regardless of their political membership, as the primary focus of justice (at least as far as the question is concerned of who receives just treatment). On the first view, principles of international justice are to regulate the relations between states in a fair way; on the second view, they are to regulate the relations between all human beings in the world and to ensure their individual well-being. I shall refer to proponents of the first view as *statists* and those of the second as *globalists*. These labels are of course artificial and comprise a number of quite different perspectives. For example, within the first camp we find liberals stressing the autonomy of peoples, communitarians emphasizing the integrity of cultural communities, nationalists arguing in favor of the priority of national ties of membership, and theorists of sovereignty defending the independence of states, as well as mixtures among these views.[1]

The main issue in this debate is to what extent the world as a whole is a *context of justice*, that is, a context characterized by conflicting claims that call for adjudication in light of principles of justice. For such a context to exist, there have to be identifiable authors and addressees of legitimate justice claims, whether they are rights claims or claims based on other grounds of justice. According to the globalists, the global context is the *primary* context of justice, and other, more local contexts can only be legitimate once the first one is well-ordered. To be sure, the statists do not deny

---

[1] This is why I do not follow Beitz's (1999b) suggestion to distinguish between "social" and "cosmopolitan liberalism" or Höffe's (1999, 296) and Thompson's (1992) usage of "communitarian" to denote this party.

that there are relevant justice claims in the international sphere. They merely argue for a restriction of their scope and hold that an updated version of the traditional *ius gentium* suffices (which may entail some components of economic justice).[2] The basic argument for this restriction is that, with respect to political and distributive justice, the globe is *not* the primary context of justice. Compared to the "thick" context of domestic justice, it is merely a secondary, "thin" one.

In my following remarks, I want to sketch briefly the main points of controversy between statists and globalists. I will then take up these points and develop an alternative analysis of the global context of justice. The basic idea is that a critical theory of *transnational* justice may provide resources for advancing the debate between international and global justice in both normative and empirical respects.

II

Scepticism among statists concerning global justice is fueled by the following considerations.

a. It is argued that a context of justice (especially distributive justice) exists only where there is a certain degree of institutionalized, mutually beneficial social cooperation that allows one to identify the goods that are to be distributed, the legitimate claims of the cooperating partners, and the addressees of those claims. And it is said that such conditions do not obtain on the international level, neither in economic, political, social, cultural, or legal respects (see Barry 1991, 194f.; Kersting 1996, 197f.; Chwaszcza 1996, 173). The weak and dispersed forms of cooperation existing at this level do not allow for a strong conception of distributive justice.

b. Building on this claim, statists argue further that national contexts of justice are already normatively structured in their own ways and that global principles would violate those structures (of property, for example) (see Kersting 1996, 195; Chwaszcza 1996, 174f.). The goods to be distributed are, on this view, already produced and distributed according to legitimate standards.

c. This leads to the statist charge that globalist theories imply the necessity of a global super-state. Such a state would – following Kant – be in great danger of becoming a "soulless despotism" or a "graveyard of freedom" (Kant 1968, 367)[3] because of the need of ever greater power and authority to govern such a large and differentiated territory.

---

[2] The most recent elaborate (and in a sense paradigmatic) normative theory in that respect is Rawls (1999a).
[3] See also Höffe (1999, 316), Kersting (1996, 198), Chwaszcza (1996, 173ff.), and Maus (1999).

d. Furthermore, statists argue that there is a danger inherent in applying a framework of global distributive justice that leads to a "depoliticized" view in which persons are seen only as parts of a large machinery of production and distribution without any political participation in that arrangement. Global distributive justice, then, would preclude political autonomy. In the words of Wolfgang Kersting, this means that some become "production slaves in a global impersonal distributive arrangement" whereas others are mere "clients of an anonymous global distributive agency."[4]

e. The globalist perspective is said to violate the normative infrastructure of given contexts of justice in another sense, for it turns the order of normative consideration on its head: it gives priority to obligations towards all persons equally considered, strangers as well as fellow members of one's nation. It thereby ignores the ethical significance of more particular memberships and attachments in favor of abstract, impartial, and decontextualized universal moral principles (see esp. Miller 1995, ch. 3; Kratochwil 1998).[5]

f. Globalists are further accused of starting with a false premise concerning the sources of inequality between political communities. Rather than a lack of natural resources or the unfairness of global political and economic structures, the main reason for underdevelopment and high degrees of poverty, illiteracy, and so forth, is the internal structure of those societies themselves. The cultural and political traditions of certain societies lead to a lack of social cooperation and organization that is the primary impediment to economic advancement and fair distribution (see Rawls 1999a, 105ff.).

g. The globalist enterprise, finally, is said to run into the dilemma of attempting to construct principles of justice for a world which comprises a huge plurality of cultures and traditions on the basis of fundamentally liberal normative premises. It therefore seems to disregard what John Rawls calls the "fact of pluralism" on the global level and is in danger of being intolerant towards nonliberal societies in general, requiring them to become members in a global liberal regime (Rawls 1999a, 82f.). Globalism, therefore, is a kind of veiled ethnocentrism and lacks a normatively neutral starting point.

---

[4] Kersting (1996, 201): "Produktionssklaven in einem globalen unpersönlichen Verteilungsarrangement" (and 192): "Klientel einer anonymen globalen Verteilungsagentur" (my translation).
[5] On this point, see my discussion of the communitarian critique of moral universalism in Forst (1994, chs. 3 and 4).

III

The globalist response to these claims and objections consists in a number of arguments which either directly refute or weaken the critiques. (Again, what follows is only a brief sketch.)

a. As far as the question of global cooperation is concerned, globalists argue in one of two ways. Either they maintain that there is at present a global scheme of social cooperation comparable to domestic ones which allows for the application of distributive principles such as Rawls's Difference Principle (Beitz 1999a, 143ff.; Pogge 1989, 241ff.); or they argue that in order to consider the global context as a context of (distributive) justice, it suffices to point out that, given the degree of globalization and interdependence, there is, in the words of Charles Beitz (1999a, 203), "*some* type of basic structure . . . both required and inevitable."[6] Following Hume's (1978, 494f.) and Rawls's (1999b, 109ff.) account of the subjective and objective "circumstances of justice," one can say that they do obtain to an important degree at the global level (see also O'Neill 1998, 515ff., and Habermas 1996b).

b. If the global context is one of justice, the question of domestic justice cannot take priority to, or be settled in advance of, the question as to what principles of global justice require. For even if a domestic society was internally just, it could still benefit from past or present injustices in the global sphere (Beitz 1999a, 149f.; Pogge 1989, §22). According to Henry Shue (1983, 603), "it is impossible to settle the magnitude of one's duties in justice (if any) toward the fellow members of one's nation-state . . . prior to and independent of settling the magnitude of one's duties in justice (if any) toward nonmembers. The magnitude of both sets of duties must be settled together."

c. Aware of the dangers of a global super-state, (most) globalists distinguish between "moral cosmopolitanism" – which according to Thomas Pogge (1992, 49) asserts that "every human being has a global stature as an ultimate unit of moral concern" – and "legal cosmopolitanism" (Pogge) or "cosmopolitanism about institutions" (Beitz 1999a, 199) – which implies the necessity of an overarching global political authority or world government. And it is argued that these two views are not necessarily connected. Even if, according to Pogge, an "institutional conception" postulates fundamental principles of justice for an assessment of institutionalized global ground rules, it is compatible with a system of dispersed political sovereignty that falls short of a world state.

---

[6] See also the revision of his view in Beitz (1983, 595).

d. Even though globalist views of distributive justice question the political autonomy of states, insofar as states are not seen as constituting primary and closed contexts of justice, and even though they do not emphasize an internal connection between distributive justice and self-government, some theorists do address the political autonomy of persons as self-determining members of political institutions. Pogge (1992, 64), for example, argues for a "human right to political participation," and Shue (1996, 71) for a "basic" right to "effective participation" in the most important political and social institutions determining the conditions of security and subsistence.

e. In a globalist framework "state boundaries have a merely derivative significance" (Beitz 1999a, 182), and accordingly the principle that "compatriots take priority" (Shue 1996, 131f.) cannot be accepted given the duties to others who are deprived of their basic rights. As a foundational moral thesis, the principle of giving priority to fellow citizens is to be rejected. Since the "moral cosmopolitan" demand of equal respect for every single individual is seen as basic, nationality appears only as a morally contingent fact (see Pogge 1989, 247). Yet on an "intermediate" (Beitz 1983, 597) level, such an individualist perspective also allows for the possibility of a contractarian agreement, of a Rawlsian kind, that would advocate a global system of states that, given fair background conditions, gives (limited) priority to citizens within each separate state. But this still presupposes that there is no independent moral significance to nationality or particular political membership.

f. Globalists reject, as an empirically false thesis of "explanatory nationalism" (Pogge 1999, 356), the diagnosis that the sources of global inequality and high degrees of underdevelopment in many societies are primarily domestic. They do not deny that internal factors lead to mismanagement and corruption, especially among political elites, but they argue that these phenomena are rooted in past and present systems of international political and economic relations. Hence the argument is not just that it is difficult to disentangle domestic and international sources of backwardness (Beitz 1999b, 525); it is also stressed to what extent the present situation benefits the rich states and is actively supported by them (Pogge 2001).

g. As far as the charge of ethnocentrism is concerned, globalists defend their universalist assumptions in a variety of ways. These responses range from the appeal to a global, "cross-cultural discourse" (Pogge 1989, 271) which will, so it is assumed, reach an overlapping consensus on basic principles of justice, to appeals to basic human rights to subsistence and security, which are assumed to be beyond reasonable normative disagreement (Shue 1996). Stronger forms of justification refer to substantive universal conceptions of human flourishing which form the moral core of every legitimate ordering of social life (Nussbaum 1990).

IV

Given this brief survey of arguments and counterarguments, I want to address the central issues of the debate by suggesting an alternative picture of the global context of justice (the first point of controversy) before then developing a conception of transnational justice that takes up the subsequent points of debate in a new way, one that ultimately leaves the confines of the controversy and leads to a third position.

On the one hand, it seems beyond doubt that a domestic political context of justice is marked by a degree of institutionalized (and noninstitutionalized) social cooperation that is not equaled on the global level – neither in political, legal, economic, nor cultural respects. This calls for a special consideration of these contexts when thinking about transnational justice. On the other hand, it seems equally clear that in the contemporary world the degree of globalized interdependence has reached a point where it is impossible not to speak of this context as one of justice: in addition to a global context of trade, there is now also a global context of production and of labor, and important actors in those spheres are to be characterized as "transnational" (especially large companies); there is a global ecological context with all the problems of scarcity of resources, pollution, and so on; there is a global context of institutions from the United Nations to the International Monetary Fund (IMF) as well as of nongovernmental institutions (Greenpeace and Amnesty International, for example); there is a global context of legal treaties and obligations, of technological interdependence (just think of the consequences of an aggressive virus emerging in the World Wide Web), of military cooperations as well as conflicts, of migration within and across continents; and there is, of course, an ever-growing global context of cultural production, consumption, and communication.[7]

But in order to come to a realistic global perspective when thinking about transnational justice, one must take a closer, critical look at these phenomena. For once one takes the history and concrete character of these multiple relations into account, it is a euphemism to refer to them as "cooperation" or "interdependence" without further qualification, since such terms imply relations of reciprocity that are obviously absent. Rather, what emerges is a complex system of one-sided and largely coerced cooperation and dependency rather than interdependence. In other words, one sees a *context of force and domination*. This does not mean that there is a simple and clearly structured field of power between, for example, "wealthy" and "poor" states; rather, it means that in most of the above named dimensions there are not just concrete relations of unequal power, but also more or less fixed patterns of domination. In order to speak of a

---

[7] For an extensive analysis of the developments named above see Held, McGrew, Goldblatt, and Perraton (1999).

"system" here, it is not necessary to see it as intentionally planned or as having a single center of power which fully controls it; it is sufficient to note that it does contain some stability and regularities and that it is intentionally upheld by various actors for the benefits they receive from it.[8] And even though the system of a global market is somewhat fluid, so that some countries or regions can gain in economic strength and political influence, they can only do so by playing by the rules of that system, which – if one thinks of the IMF requirements of economic stability – create enormous hardships internally. And apart from those few countries, the global system has the primary effect of forcing poorer regions and countries into a subordinate economic and political position where they can (at best) have some dependent standing as a provider of basic goods (be it natural resources or labor) for which they are scarcely compensated.[9] More than that, their debts constantly increase and have a paralyzing effect.

Therefore, if the discussion of principles of transnational justice is to start from an analysis of the present global context of *injustice*, it needs to see this context as one of a complex system of power and domination with a variety of powerful actors, from international institutions to transnational corporations, local elites, and so forth. Shifting perspective to that of the dominated, then, reveals that theirs is a situation of *multiple domination*: most often they are dominated by their own (hardly legitimate) governments, elites, or warlords,[10] which in turn are both working together and are (at least partly) dominated by global actors. Especially women and children are the subjects of even further relations of domination within the family and local community. A conception of justice must address such situations of multiple domination at various levels. At the global level, it must ask who benefits in the global market in what way, what are the terms of "cooperation," how are they fixed, and so on. At the micro-level, it must ask how these global structures support more local (and even traditional) structures of domination and exploitation. The various contexts of justice – local, national, international, and global – are connected through the kind of injustice they produce, and a theory of justice must not remain blind to this interconnectedness. In what follows, I can of course only outline such a theory and provide neither a proper analysis of injustice nor a normative construction of justice in detail.

V

It may be objected that the perspective just introduced, focusing as it does on phenomena of domination, fails to capture adequately what many

[8] I allude here (in a very general way) to Foucault's concept of power. See esp. Foucault (1990, 92–102).
[9] See, for example, the critical analysis by Altvater and Mahnkopf (1999, esp. ch. 6).
[10] This holds true especially for Africa, where at the moment a large number of states either have deteriorated and fallen into civil war or are in danger of deterioration.

regard as the main moral issue, namely, in the words of Pogge (2001, 22), "severe global poverty." But as he also makes clear, addressing global *economic* justice does presuppose that one is aware of the general system of injustice that produces and upholds a situation of inequality, of poverty, and hunger. To be sure, the existence of extreme poverty in a world rich enough to eliminate it calls for a strong moral reaction and for appropriate measures to alleviate suffering. Yet in order to criticize this situation as *unjust* and to appeal to duties of justice one must analyze it as the result of what Pogge (2001, 17) calls the "imposition of a skewed global order that aggravates international inequalities and makes it exceedingly hard for the weaker and poorer societies to secure a proportional share of global economic growth."[11] A judgment of injustice differs from moral judgments about human need and suffering or about inequality in that it not only identifies asymmetrical social relations as unjustified, it also locates the responsibilities for that situation. A context of justice is then a concrete context of justification and responsibility.

There are two reasons for a *critical theory of justice* to start with the "fact of multiple domination," as I want to call it. First, such a theory rests upon a comprehensive analysis of the phenomona of injustice and their deeper roots. If, for example, extreme inequality and poverty is a result of a complex system of domination and exploitation, a focus on only distributive justice may be insufficient and may even harbor the danger of leaving the unjust system basically intact by turning the hitherto dominated into mere claimants and recipients of goods. This is a kernel of truth in the worry mentioned above (II.d) that a conception of global distributive justice may leave out political autonomy (and, I should add, the question of power).[12] One can therefore say that the question of power is *the first question of justice*. It stresses the need for a theory that does not just focus on the justice of the distribution of goods, but on the justice of the "basic structure" of relations of political and economic power, that is, relations of government, of production, and of distribution.

Second, it is mistaken to assume that distributive justice and political justice, as freedom from unjustified domination, require distinct normative considerations. Both are guided by the overarching *principle of the justification of justice*, according to which, in a given context of justice, all social relations to which one is subject to and that can be changed by political action are to be justified reciprocally and generally to all those affected in a relevant way – be they economic relations or relations of political authority. Ultimately, in a context of justice a critical theory regards no social relations as "beyond justification," and its critique is directed against all those institutions, rules, or practices which either pretend to be

---

[11] See also Hurrell's (2001) analysis of the "deformity" of the current economic and political international order.

[12] The need for an analysis of power relations in the context of global justice is also stressed by Nielsen (1983) and, in a different way, by O'Neill (1991, esp. 300–304).

justified without being so or appear to be beyond justification in terms of being either natural or unchangeable. In both respects, ideology critique is necessary.[13]

The project of a critical theory of (in-)justice therefore consists of the following four points.

1. It contains an analysis of given social relations, that is, their historical genesis and their contemporary character, especially the inequalities and power asymmetries they contain.
2. It connects this with a critique of false justifications for these relations on the basis of the principle of justification – false justifications which hide social contradictions and relations of power.
3. Furthermore, it points to the necessity and possibility of justifications which can stand the test of reciprocity and generality. Reciprocity means that none of the parties concerned may claim certain rights or privileges it denies to others and that the relevance and force of the claims at issue is not determined one-sidedly; generality means that all those affected have an equal right to demand justifications. Given this basic right, this has to be a real and not merely hypothetical test: ultimately only those affected themselves can carry out the justification of their *own* basic social structures.[14] This is how critical theory links up with the claims and demands made by social actors themselves in concrete social contexts.[15]
4. Hence critical theory calls not only for justifiable social relations, but for a practice of justification. This is the first step towards justice.

The demand for reciprocal and general justification of all relevant social relations is based on the principle of justification, which itself is justified in a "recursive" way:[16] since in a context of justice the claim is that social norms, as well as the institutions and practices they supposedly justify, are reciprocally and generally valid and binding for every person affected by, and subject to, these norms, institutions, and practices, the criteria of their justification have to be the criteria of reciprocity and generality. The criteria of validity are criteria both for the justification as well as the authority of norms.

---

[13] This notion of ideology tries to avoid assumptions about "true" interests and identifies legitimate versus illegitimate claims based on the criteria of reciprocity and generality. Substantively, it calls for an analysis of the "justificatory" powers of the social actors involved and of the actual justifications that are being offered.

[14] This is an important argument of Jürgen Habermas's conception of critical theory, which, of course, calls for a theory of the social conditions under which such justifications as reciprocal and general can take place. In Habermas's theory, this leads to a theory of counterfactual "ideal" presuppositions of rational discourse as well as a theory of the modernization and rationalization of societies; cf. esp. Habermas (1984 and 1987).

[15] The need for an internal link between the concepts of critique and the interests and needs of social actors is stressed by Honneth (1994).

[16] I explain this kind of justification in my (1994, chs. 4 and 5) and in (1999c).

In accordance with the basic principle of justification, persons have a fundamental *right to justification*: a qualified veto-right against any norms and practices which cannot be justified reciprocally and generally – or, to use a modified version of Thomas Scanlon's (1998, 4f.) phrase, against norms that can reciprocally and generally be rejected. This is the basic moral right of persons which, in a given context of justice, takes on a substantive form and needs to be institutionalized. It forms the basis of human rights (see Forst 1999a)[17] as well as of any justifications of social basic structures (see Forst 1999b).

The claim I want to make is that this starting point for the construction of principles of justice allows for a reconstruction of the various dimensions of transnational justice (as well as a deconstruction of false assumptions): it applies to various aspects of justice in their specific justificatory quality (e.g., human rights or the specifics of distributive justice), and it achieves a comprehensive and complex view with respect to the contexts of domestic and global justice. For the basic right to justification lies at the core of both a justified domestic and a justified transnational basic structure. Hence, there is *one* "moral cosmopolitan" starting point which allows for an adequate consideration of the *various* contexts of justice as contexts of justification and self-determination, from the local to the global one. Speaking very generally, a "transnational" approach differs from a globalist view in considering particular political contexts as contexts of justice in their own right and in constructing principles of justice for the establishment of just relations between autonomous political communities. It differs from statist views by starting from a universal individual right and by considering the global context as an essential context of justice. Given the central aim of the realization of the right to justification within and between states in order to end the vicious circle of internal and external domination, a theory of transnational justice has to combine the various contexts of justice in the right way. In what follows I indicate the broad outlines of such a theory.[18]

---

[17] Even though I differ from Henry Shue in calling this right basic rather than rights to subsistence, security, or liberty, I agree with his understanding of basic rights as "everyone's minimum reasonable demands upon the rest of humanity. They are the rational basis for justified demands the denial of which no self-respecting person can reasonably be expected to accept. Why should anything be so important? The reason is that rights are basic in the sense used here only if enjoyment of them is essential to the enjoyment of all other rights" (1996, 19). But if a basic right is such a morally nonrejectable reasonable demand and the basis for further justifiable demands, then the very right to reciprocal and general justification must be the most basic right, for it stresses the equal, nondeniable claim of every person to be regarded as the author and addressee of reasonable demands in the first place. It is the right to be treated as a reason-giving and reason-deserving being.

[18] Another conception of transnational justice which differs from my own is O'Neill (1986 and 1991).

VI

One worry mentioned above needs to be laid aside first: namely, the charge of ethnocentrism (II.g). Is the idea of a basic right to justification a sufficiently "culture-neutral" idea for providing the basis for a theory of transnational justice? A few remarks have to suffice here regarding this important matter. First, it needs to be stressed that neither the statist nor globalist positions sketched at the beginning can do without universally valid normative notions. Even the statists assume that some form of state organization or political community is such a universal notion, as are notions of peace, cooperation, and even (more or less minimal) human rights. Thus, those advocating an individualist moral cosmopolitanism are not the only ones who make universalist assumptions; those who deny it do so too.

Second, one needs to take a close look at the arguments against a moral cosmopolitan, individualist starting point.[19] And here it seems that defenders of a statist view believe that a short-sighted application of a liberal concept of the person, for example, does not do justice to the cultural and political integrity of particular societies (organized into states). When this notion of integrity is examined more closely, the strongest claim one finds (made, for example, by some representatives of Asian countries and cultures) is that the state in question is a monocultural state and that its societal culture is, so to speak, a "fully integrated unity full of integrity." And since this is assumed to be the case (which, needless to say, is hardly realistic), "external" normative notions are foreign to it and potentially violate its integrity. Part of the claim for communal integrity is that it is constitutive of the integrity of the members of that community, so that their very integrity is violated by the application and intrusion of external standards. This, however, presupposes that the integrity of the whole community cannot be defended at the cost of the integrity of its members, and hence the claim for communal integrity depends on the plausibility of claiming that its communal structure is willingly supported by its members and not forced upon them. There is thus an internal criterion of legitimacy and acceptability built into this defense of communal and political autonomy, and it is a criterion that calls into question strong claims to integrity when there is internal dissent as to the question of how far the social structure is supported by its members and deserves their support. The claim of integrity depends upon a rather demanding form of acceptance, and as soon as, for example, human rights are claimed from *within* such a culture, they can no longer be seen as an external intrusion but are a challenge to the claim of integrity. Hence, if within such a culture or society a claim for justification arises, it cannot be answered except by persuasion and argumentation, by reasons acceptable in that context.

[19] For a fuller discussion of the following, see my (1999a, part I).

It follows, then, from this brief exercise of deconstruction, that rather than an alternative to the basic right to justification it is that very right which guides the arguments against an imposition of liberal values. This imposition is assumed to violate the rights of the members of a given society to determine their own social structure themselves in a way that does not undercut basic standards of equal membership and political influence. This also underlies Rawls's (1999a, 64ff.) argument for the qualified legitimacy of a "decent hierarchical society" as well as Michael Walzer's (1994) notion of a "thin" morality reiterated in "thick" contexts. In both cases, "self-determination" (Rawls 1999a, 61; Walzer 1994, 68) of a people or a community is the supreme standard.

One can say that the globalist defense of moral cosmopolitanism is based on that very right, too, but applies it differently, namely, with respect to one overarching global, distributive basic structure. This prepares the way for a "contextualization" of the basic right to justification that tries to do justice to both aims, that is, to the respect for communal political and social contexts and for the vital interests and claims of individuals. From a moral cosmopolitan standpoint there is no direct route to an institutional cosmopolitan standpoint which neglects more particular contexts (see above II.c and III.c).

VII

What is the correct way to situate the right to justification? What is its primary context? The first answer is that since the basic right to justification is the fundamental *moral* right to be respected as an autonomous moral person with the capacity for justification and the nonrejectable claim to demand justifications, the primary context in which this right is situated is the moral context of actions which affect other persons in a relevant way. Here the principle of justification calls for actions based on reasons not reasonable to reject given the criteria of reciprocity and generality. This is a noninstitutional perspective of moral rights and duties which apply to every member of the human moral community regardless of political settings.

But then the question arises as to which is the primary *political* context where this right turns into a basic political right to justification. And here the answer is that it is the context of a particular, "domestic" society and its basic structure – a context into which (in the normal case) persons are born as citizens, that is, where they find themselves situated as members of a historically situated political community and order. In this context, they are the subjects of immediate legal and political authority and power, and as citizens, they have a right to demand that this authority is justifiable given their basic interests and claims. It is then their common "project," so to speak, to establish and maintain a just(ifiable) basic structure. At the core of such a basic structure lies the basic right to justification which then is being exercised, interpreted, and institutionalized in light of the particular self-understanding of the members of the political community, so that the "construction" of a basic structure deserves to be called their joint undertaking. Whereas on the abstract moral level it is possible to construct a list of human rights that are to be accepted and realized in every legitimate basic structure, it is only in particular political contexts that they are concretely interpreted, institutionalized, and guaranteed (see Forst 1999a, parts II and III). The abstract right to justification, therefore, makes substantive demands on a justified basic structure, but as concrete demands these are the claims of the citizens themselves, thus making political autonomy the central aim of this structure.

This aim calls for a distinction between *minimal* and *maximal justice*. The former entails the basic rights and institutions necessary for the exercise of the right to political justification, including rights to personal liberty, rights to political participation, and rights to an effective use of these rights. These establish a minimally just discursive basic structure. Maximal justice is the result of the justificatory discourses made possible by that structure, discourses about the details of economic production and distribution, of the legal system, the educational system, and so forth. Not all of this is covered by minimal justice, for this only establishes a threshold of political and social equality, making justificatory discourses possible in the first place.[20] Minimal justice calls for a *basic structure of justification*, maximal justice for a *fully justified basic structure*. The former is the necessary condition for the latter.

The emphasis on the politically autonomous establishment of a just basic structure in a particular context of justice responds to the worries mentioned above (II.b and II.e) that a globalist perspective disregards those contexts of citizens' political self-determination, concrete justice, and particular obligations to fellow citizens. It is true that the primary political context of justice is the domestic one, and neglecting it is a potential source of injustice. Justice thus starts "from within," from within a political and social context of struggles for a better society, a context of mutual obligations and of solidarities. Based on the general right to justification, this normative perspective thus allows for a plurality of concrete "projects" of justice among citizens – which, in reality, amounts to a plurality of concrete settings of struggles for justice. The culture-neutrality of the starting point of the right to justification thus turns into a culture-sensitive argument for political plurality and autonomy.

---

[20] Even though he does not make this distinction, I take Habermas's (1996a, 122f.) abstract list of rights to be essential for minimal justice as I understand it. Going beyond Habermas, I would stress that part of minimal justice is a (qualified) "veto right" of citizens in matters of justice that affect the realization of that minimum. The important formulation of a "veto" of the "worst off" appears in Rawls (1999b, 131).

VIII

This is not the whole story, however. For two reasons a domestic project of justice cannot be conceived of without a conception of transnational justice. First, regarding a domestic context of justice as exclusive and as having absolute priority could lead to injustice, for example, in cases where the state in question benefits from unjust relations towards other states, be it relations of direct political or even military domination, or of economic domination and exploitation. Globalists are right in stressing the proviso that internal justice cannot be established on the basis of external injustice (III.b). Hence the need for principles of justice which range from the classical principles of international justice[21] to principles of global distributive justice.

Second, seen from the perspective of disadvantaged societies, the establishment of internal justice may not be possible in an international regime that obstructs these attempts and struggles for internal justice. If external factors (1) lead to a situation of unfair economic relations and economic failure and even to a lack of basic means for subsistence, and if these same factors (2) stabilize a system of internal political domination and repression, this needs to be addressed by a conception of transnational justice. As Pogge (2001) explicates in his discussion of the "international borrowing principle" and the "international resource principle," there are a number of points at which the contemporary international system leads not merely to a domination of economically weak states, but also to relations of domination within those states. For the elites of such states (typically, but not always, dictators) use their position to cooperate with powerful global players (Western governments, banks, companies) and to exploit their own countries' natural and human resources in order to increase their power and to enrich themselves.[22] Here again there is a case where internal and external justice do presuppose one another, but in a different way: internal justice is made impossible by external influence.

To break the vicious circle of multiple, internal and external domination and to establish *political autonomy both within particular states and within the international system*, a principle of *minimal transnational justice* is called for. According to this principle, members of societies of multiple domination have a legitimate claim to the resources necessary to establish a (minimally) justified democratic order within their political community *and* that this community be a participant of (roughly) equal standing in the global economic and political system. And the citizens of the societies benefiting from the present global system do have a collective

---

[21] See, for example, Rawls's (1999a, 37) list of the principles of the law of peoples, with the peculiarity of the "duty of assistance," which I address below.

[22] See, for example, reports on how German banks, companies, and the government cooperated with the Nigerian dictator Abacha and the former Indonesian president Suharto (Balzli and Herbermann 2000; Altemeier and Schumann 2000).

"duty of assistance," to use Rawls's term, to provide those necessary resources (ranging from food, housing, and medical care to a basic education, information, the possibility of effective participation, and so on) to attain self-government. On the one hand, this argument for minimal transnational justice and a duty of assistance agrees with Rawls's (1999a, 118) claim that it should be the aim of justice to "to assist burdened societies to become full members of the Society of Peoples and to be able to determine the path of their own future for themselves." On the other hand, it does not accept a clear separation between internal and external factors of economic and political failures, for these are related in complex ways. Thus, as far as the question of the sources of poverty and underdevelopment is concerned (II.f), it is right to argue both that there are often internal political failures responsible for extreme forms of a lack of basic goods and that these are not simply "homemade" problems. Hence, societies that benefit from the present global system (and thereby also from internal domination in disadvantaged societies) have concrete duties of justice to establish minimally fair transnational terms of discourse and of cooperation.

Transnational minimal justice aims at the establishment of a basic structure of justification both *within* domestic societies and *between* them: this is the only way in which both interrelated forms of domination, internal and external, can be overcome. The duty to establish minimal justice contains a number of measures to be taken that I cannot even begin to discuss here. They have the goal of changing the present political and economic global system to create conditions of equal influence of states in (more or less institutionalized) procedures of decision-making that are powerful enough to affect the global economic system[23] and to end the support for dictatorial regimes. Furthermore, basic human rights, especially minimum social standards, have to be realized and guaranteed (possibly by supranational institutions) in all societies in order to make sure that the influence of states in such procedures is also the influence of their citizens and not just of powerful elites in such countries. Internal and external democratization have to be realized together; both will require a redistribution of resources and a change of the existing global order to a substantial degree.[24]

IX

But this is still only a step towards the establishment of a fully justified transnational basic structure, that is to say, towards *maximal* justice. For

---

[23] See Bohman's (1999) important argument for cosmopolitan democracy "as the equal access to influence and institutionalization."

[24] It will, of course, also require a change of attitudes and what Habermas (1998, 168) calls a "sense of cosmopolitan forced solidarity." How such a change can come about is a difficult question, but the idea of "forced solidarity" indicates that it has to be accompanied, if not triggered, by a problem consciousness and sense of crisis that calls for drastic changes in the existing order, be they economic or ecological crises.

minimal justice establishes only minimally fair conditions of reciprocal justification: that is, conditions for a discourse about fair economic and social cooperation, the use and distribution of resources, the establishment of transnational institutions that are to control transnational actors, and so on. And in those justificatory discourses a number of considerations of justice will come into play: considerations of historical justice between, for example, former colonies and colonial states, principles of justice regarding the distribution of natural resources, and questions of ecological justice towards future generations, to name just a few. There is thus no single or simple overarching principle (beyond that of justification) to be applied here, but a plurality of considerations relevant to the issue at hand. And since these discourses are based on a standard of minimal justice and (roughly) equal participatory power, they will not be conducted – as they are at present – under conditions of inequality and domination, leaving the weak states hardly any chance of influence. Based on such a minimum of fairness, a picture of complex justice may emerge that contains various principles and considerations. A variation on Rawls's Difference Principle, then, does reappear as a transformed democratic principle of justice: in matters of basic justice which touch the participatory minimum, there is a (qualified) "veto right"[25] of the worst off, such that no decision can be made that is reciprocally and generally rejectable by those in the weakest position.

Whether the institutionalization of minimal justice and the results of justificatory discourses on that basis will lead to a federation of states in a subsidiary "world republic" (Höffe 1999, part 2; Lutz-Bachmann 1996 and 1999) or to something like a "world state" is hard to predict and not to be predetermined; it is a matter of the kind of institutions that are seen to be necessary to fulfill the demands of justice. Still, the realization of the minimum already presupposes a much higher degree of institutionalization than the present one, both for safeguarding the social minimum within states and for establishing (roughly) equal standing between states. This, no doubt, would already be an enormous achievement.

X

In conclusion, my claim is that the critical theory of transnational justice sketched above tries to capture the strongest arguments of both sides of the debate between statists and globalists. It starts from a critical view of the relevant contexts of justice without disregarding either the domestic ones or the global one or reducing one to the other; it contains a clear diagnosis of the injustice that is to be addressed by principles of transnational justice; it rests on a "thin" but strong normative foundation that can plausibly claim to be both culture-neutral and culture-sensitive; it contains a plurality of considerations of justice; and it stresses the autonomy of the members of political

[25] See note 20 above.

communities both as an internal and an external principle: self-government in a justified basic structure remains the central aim of the theory. Without autonomy of this sort, justice cannot be established, for justice in political contexts demands that there are no social relations "beyond justification."

Acknowledgments

I thank the participants of the conference on global justice in Bielefeld for their helpful questions and remarks concerning my argument. And I owe special thanks to Joel Anderson for his critical reading of this text and his important suggestions.

References

Altemeier, Inge, and Harald Schumann. (2000). "Der überflüssige Strom." *Der Spiegel*, 22 (29 May), 204f.

Altvater, Elmar, and Birgit Mahnkopf. (1999). *Grenzen der Globalisierung: Ökonomie, Ökologie und Politik in der Weltgesellschaft.* Münster: Verlag Westfälisches Dampfboot.

Balzli, Beat, and Jan Dirk Herbermann. (2000). "Berüchtigte Kundschaft." *Der Spiegel*, 22 (29 May), 102.

Barry, Brian. (1991). "Humanity and Justice in Global Perspective." In *Liberty and Justice: Essays in Political Theory 2*, 182–210. Oxford: Clarendon Press.

Beitz, Charles. (1983). "Cosmopolitan Ideals and National Sentiment." *Journal of Philosophy*, 80, 591–600.

———. (1999a). *Political Theory and International Relations.* New edition with an afterword. Princeton: Princeton University Press. First edition published 1979.

———. (1999b). "Social and Cosmopolitan Liberalism." *International Affairs*, 75, 515–29.

Bohman, James. (1999) "International Regimes and Democratic Governance: Political Equality and Influence in Global Institutions." *International Affairs*, 75, 499–513.

Chwaszcza, Christine. (1996). "Politische Ethik II: Ethik der internationalen Beziehungen." In *Angewandte Ethik: Die Bereichsethiken und ihre theoretische Fundierung*, edited by Julian Nida-Rümelin, 154–98. Stuttgart: Kröner.

Forst, Rainer. (1994). *Kontexte der Gerechtigkeit: Politische Philosophie jenseits von Liberalismus und Kommunitarismus.* Frankfurt am Main: Suhrkamp. English translation: *Contexts of Justice* (Berkeley and Los Angeles: University of California Press, 2001).

———. (1999a). "The Basic Right to Justification: Toward a Constructivist Conception of Human Rights." *Constellations*, 6, 35–60.

———. (1999b). "Die Rechtfertigung der Gerechtigkeit: Rawls' Politischer

Liberalismus und Habermas' Diskurstheorie in der Diskussion." In *Das Recht der Republik*, edited by Hauke Brunkhorst and Peter Niesen, 105–68. Frankfurt am Main: Suhrkamp.

———. (1999c). "Praktische Vernunft und rechtfertigende Gründe: Zur Begründung der Moral." In *Motive, Gründe, Zwecke: Theorien praktischer Rationalität*, edited by Stefan Gosepath, 168–205. Frankfurt am Main: Fischer.

Foucault, Michel. (1990). *The History of Sexuality*. Vol. 1. New York: Vintage.

Habermas, Jürgen. (1984 and 1987). *The Theory of Communicative Action*. 2 vols. Trans. T. McCarthy. Boston: Beacon Press.

———. (1996a). *Between Facts and Norms: Contributions to a Discourse Theory of Law and Democracy*. Trans. W. Rehg. Cambridge, Mass.: MIT Press.

———. (1996b). "Kants Idee des ewigen Friedens – aus dem historischen Abstand von zweihundert Jahren." In *Frieden durch Recht: Kants Friedensidee und das Problem einer neuen Weltordnung*, edited by Matthias Lutz-Bachmann and James Bohman, 7–24. Frankfurt am Main: Suhrkamp.

———. (1998). "Die postnationale Konstellation und die Zukunft der Demokratie." In *Die postnationale Konstellation*. Frankfurt am Main: Suhrkamp.

Held, David, Anthony McGrew, David Goldblatt, and Jonathan Perraton. (1999). *Global Transformations: Politics, Economics and Culture*. Oxford: Polity Press.

Höffe, Otfried. (1999). *Demokratie im Zeitalter der Globalisierung*. München: C. H. Beck.

Honneth, Axel. (1994). "The Social Dynamics of Disrespect: On the Location of Critical Theory Today." *Constellations*, 1, 255–69.

Hume, David. (1978). *A Treatise of Human Nature*. Ed. L. A. Selby-Bigge. 2nd ed. Oxford: Clarendon Press.

Hurrell, Andrew. (2001). "Global Inequality and International Institutions." *Metaphilosophy*, 32:1/2.

Kant, Immanuel. (1968). "Zum ewigen Frieden: Ein philosophischer Entwurf." In *Kants Werke*, Akademie-Textausgabe. Vol. 8. Berlin: de Gruyter.

Kersting, Wolfgang. (1996). "Weltfriedensordnung und globale Verteilungsgerechtigkeit: Kants Konzeption eines vollständigen Rechtsfriedens und die gegenwärtige politische Philosophie der internationalen Beziehungen." In "Zum ewigen Frieden," *Grundlagen, Aktualität und Aussichten einer Idee von Immanuel Kant*, edited by Reinhard Merkel and Roland Wittmann, 172–212. Frankfurt am Main: Suhrkamp.

Kratochwil, Friedrich V. (1998). "Vergeßt Kant! Reflexionen zur Debatte über Ethik und internationale Politik." In *Politische Philosophie der internationalen Beziehungen*, edited by Christine Chwaszcza and Wolfgang Kersting, 96–149. Frankfurt am Main: Suhrkamp.

Lutz-Bachmann, Matthias. (1996). "Kants Friedensidee und das rechts-philosophische Konzept einer Weltrepublik." In *Frieden durch Recht*, edited by Matthias Lutz-Bachmann and James Bohman, 25–44. Frankfurt am Main: Suhrkamp.

———. (1999). "'Weltstaatlichkeit' und Menschenrechte nach dem Ende des überlieferten 'Nationalstaats.'" In *Recht auf Menschenrechte*, edited by Hauke Brunkhorst, Wolfgang Köhler, and Matthias Lutz-Bachmann, 199–215. Frankfurt am Main: Suhrkamp.

Maus, Ingeborg. (1999). "Menschenrechte als Ermächtigungsnormen internationaler Politik oder: der zerstörte Zusammenhang von Menschenrechten und Demokratie." In *Recht auf Menschenrechte*, edited by Hauke Brunkhorst, Wolfgang Köhler, and Matthias Lutz-Bachmann, 276–92. Frankfurt am Main: Suhrkamp.

Miller, David. (1995). *On Nationality*. Oxford: Clarendon Press.

Nielsen, Kai. (1983). "Global Justice and the Imperatives of Capitalism." *Journal of Philosophy*, 80, 608–10.

Nussbaum, Martha. (1990). "Aristotelian Social Democracy." In *Liberalism and the Good*, edited by R. Bruce Douglass, Gerald M. Mara, and Henry S. Richardson, 203–52. New York: Routledge.

O'Neill, Onora. (1986). *Faces of Hunger: An Essay on Poverty, Justice and Development*. London: Allen & Unwin.

———. (1991). "Transnational Justice." In *Political Theory Today*, edited by David Held, 276–304. Stanford: Stanford University Press.

———. (1998). "Justice and Boundaries." In *Politische Philosophie der internationalen Beziehungen*, edited by Christine Chwaszcza and Wolfgang Kersting, 502–22. Frankfurt am Main: Suhrkamp.

Pogge, Thomas. (1989). *Realizing Rawls*. Ithaca: Cornell University Press.

———. (1992). "Cosmopolitanism and Sovereignty." *Ethics*, 103, 48–75.

———. (1999). "Human Flourishing and Universal Justice." *Social Philosophy and Policy*, 16, 333–61.

———. (2001). "Priorities of Global Justice." *Metaphilosophy*, 32:1/2.

Rawls, John. (1999a). *The Law of Peoples*. Cambridge, Mass.: Harvard University Press.

———. (1999b). *A Theory of Justice*. 2nd ed. Cambridge, Mass.: Harvard University Press. First edition published 1971.

Scanlon, Thomas. (1998). *What We Owe to Each Other*. Cambridge, Mass.: Harvard University Press.

Shue, Henry. (1983). "The Burdens of Justice." *Journal of Philosophy*, 80, 600–608.

———. (1996). *Basic Rights*. 2nd ed. Princeton: Princeton University Press. First edition published 1980.

Thompson, Janna. (1992). *Justice and World Order*. London: Routledge.

Walzer, Michael. (1994). *Thick and Thin: Moral Argument at Home and Abroad*. Notre Dame: University of Notre Dame Press.

12

AGENTS OF JUSTICE

ONORA O'NEILL

Cosmopolitan Principles and State Institutions

Many of the best-known conceptions of justice are avowedly cosmopolitan.[1] They propose basic principles of justice that are to hold without restriction. Whether we look back to Stoic cosmopolitanism, to medieval Natural Law theory, to Kantian world citizenship, or to twentieth-century theory and practice – Rawls and the U.N. Universal Declaration of Human Rights of 1948, for example – the scope of *principles* of justice is said to be universal or cosmopolitan, encompassing all humans. As is well known, such principles have been compromised in various ways, for example, by the exclusion or partial exclusion of slaves, women, labourers, or the heathen from the scope of justice; these exclusions have been a focus of much debate, and recent cosmopolitan conceptions of justice have condemned them.

However, there are other, less evident exclusions created by the commonplace assumption that cosmopolitan principles are to be instituted in and through a system of states. Many recent challenges have argued that the exclusions that borders create are further injustices, and that they should be addressed by abolishing borders, or at least by reducing the obstacles they present to movements of people, goods, or capital. Some conclude that justice requires the construction of a world state;[2] others, that borders should be (more) open to the movement of peoples (Carens 1987); others, that powerful regional and global institutions can mitigate or redress inequalities that states and borders create (Pogge 1994; Held 2000). I am at least partly sceptical about those attempts to realise cosmopolitan principles through cosmopolitan or global institutions that

---

[1] Some relativists, communitarians, and nationalists are avowedly anticosmopolitan, but often with less startling conclusions than the conceptual resources of their starting points might permit.

[2] There are many versions of the thought that supra-statal or global governance should replace states, often and perhaps inaccurately seen as a Kantian position (Lutz-Bachmann 1997; Habermas 1995; Mertens 1996).

do not show what is to prevent global governance from degenerating into global tyranny and global injustice. Big may not always be beautiful, and institutional cosmopolitanism may not always be the best route to universal justice. In this chapter I begin to explore a more realistic, and also (I hope) a more robust, view of the plurality of agents of justice that might play some part in institutionalising cosmopolitan principles of justice.

A plausible initial view of agents of justice might distinguish *primary agents of justice*, with capacities to determine how principles of justice are to be institutionalised within a certain domain, from other, *secondary agents of justice*. Primary agents of justice may construct other agents or agencies with specific competencies: they may assign powers to and build capacities in individual agents, or they may build institutions – agencies – with certain powers and capacities to act. Sometimes they may, so to speak, build from scratch; more often they reassign or adjust tasks and responsibilities among existing agents and agencies, and control and limit the ways in which they may act without incurring sanctions. Primary agents of justice typically have some means of coercion, by which they at least partially control the action of other agents and agencies, which can therefore at most be secondary agents of justice. Typically, secondary agents of justice are thought to contribute to justice mainly by meeting the demands of primary agents, most evidently by conforming to any legal requirements they establish.

There is no fundamental reason why a primary agent of justice should not be an individual, for example, a prince or leader; and in some traditional societies that has been the case. Equally, there is no fundamental reason why a primary agent of justice should not be a group with little formal structure, for example, a group of elders or chieftains, or even a constitutional convention; and in other instances this has been the case. However, in modern societies institutions with a considerable measure of formal structure, and preeminently among them states, have been seen as the primary agents of justice. All too often they have also been agents of injustice.

A low-key view of the matter might be simply this: it is hard to institutionalise principles of justice, and although states quite often do not do very well as primary agents of justice, they are the best primary agents available and so are indispensable for justice. Institutions with a monopoly of the legitimate use of coercion within a given, bounded territory often behave unjustly, both to those who inhabit the territory and to outsiders, but we have not found a better way of institutionalising justice. On such a view the remedy for state injustice is not the dismantling of states and of the exclusions their borders create, but a degree of reform and democratisation coupled with international (that is, interstatal) agreements.

This very general response seems to me to take no account of the fact that states may fail as primary agents of justice for a number of different reasons. Sometimes they have the power to act as primary agents of justice, but use that power not to achieve justice, but for other ends. When these ends include a great deal of injustice, we may speak of *rogue states*; and these are common enough. But on other occasions states fail because they are too weak to act as primary agents of justice: although they are spoken of as states, even as sovereign states, this is no more than a courtesy title for structures that are often no more than *dependent states* or *quasi states.*[3]

These two types of failure pose quite different problems for other agents of justice. Powerful rogue states confront all other agents and agencies with terrible problems. Compliance with their requirements contributes to injustice rather than to justice; noncompliance leads to danger and destruction. These problems and conflicts formed a staple of twentieth-century political philosophy, in which discussions of the circumstances that justify or require revolution and resistance against established states, or noncompliance with and conscientious objection to state requirements, have been major themes. But when failure of supposed primary agents of justice arises not from abuse but from lack of state power, the problems faced by other agents and agencies are quite different. In such cases it is often left indeterminate what the law requires, and the costs of complying with such laws as exist are increased, if only because others do not even aim to comply. Unsurprisingly, many of the stratagems to which agents and agencies turn when states are weak are themselves unjust. Where agents and agencies cannot rely on an impartially enforced legal code, they may find that in order to go about their daily business they are drawn into bribery and nepotism, into buying protection and making corrupt deals, and so ride roughshod over requirements of justice. If the agents and agencies that could in better circumstances be secondary agents of justice are reduced to these sorts of action in weak states, why should we even continue to think of them as agents of justice?

Cosmopolitan Rhetoric and State Action: The Universal Declaration

These issues are often obscured because much of the cosmopolitan rhetoric of contemporary discussions of justice says little about the agents and agencies on which the burdens of justice are to fall. Nowhere is this more evident than in the text of the Universal Declaration of Human Rights of 1948. In this brief and celebrated text, nations, peoples, states, societies, and countries are variously gestured to as agents against whom individuals may have rights. Little is said about any differences between

---

[3] There is considerable disagreement about whether states *in general* have become weaker as globalisation has progressed. Strange (1996) thinks that they have; Mann (1997) and Held (2000) think that the picture is mixed. However, there is little doubt that many of the member states of the United Nations are weak by almost any standard, and that some are no more than quasi states (see Migdal 1988 and Jackson 1990).

these varying types of agents, or about their capacities and vulnerabilities, and there is no systematic allocation of obligations of different sorts to agents and agencies of specific types. If we inhabited a world in which all states were strictly nation-states, and in which no nation spread across more than one state or formed more than one society, the failure to distinguish these terms and the entities to which these terms refer might matter rather less. But that is not our world. Few states are nation-states; many nations spread across a number of states; the individuation of societies, peoples, and countries is notoriously complex. It may seem a scandal that the Universal Declaration is so cavalier about identifying agents of justice.[4]

Even if it is cavalier, I think that it is fairly easy to understand why the framers of the Universal Declaration felt no need for precision. The Declaration approaches justice by proclaiming rights. It proclaims what is to be received, what entitlements everyone is to have; but it says very little about which agents and agencies must do what if these rights are to be secured. Like other charters and declarations of rights, the Universal Declaration looks at justice from a recipient's perspective: its focus is on recipience and rights rather than on action and obligations. Hence it is about rights and rights holders that the Declaration is forthrightly cosmopolitan. It identifies the relevant recipients clearly: rights are ascribed to "all human beings" (Art. 1), and more explicitly, to "everyone . . . without distinction of any kind, such as race, colour, sex, language, religion, political or other opinion, national or social origin, property, birth or other status" (Art. 2). Rights are explicitly to be independent of an individual's political status: "no distinction shall be made on the basis of the political, jurisdictional or international status of the country or territory to which a person belongs, whether it be independent, trust, non-self-governing – or under any other limitation of sovereignty" (Art. 2). Human rights are to reach into all jurisdictions, however diverse.

So far, so cosmopolitan: the universalist aspirations are unequivocal. However, since nothing is said about the allocation of obligations to meet these aspirations, we do not yet know whether these universal rights are matched and secured by universal obligations, or by obligations held by some but not by all agents and agencies. This is a more complex matter than may appear. Whereas traditional liberty rights for all have to be matched by universal obligations to respect those rights (if any agent or agency is exempt from that obligation, the right is compromised), other universal rights cannot be secured by assigning identical obligations to all agents and agencies. Universal rights to goods and services, to status and participation, cannot be delivered by universal action. For these rights the allocation of obligations

---

[4] I suspect that in the middle of the twentieth century it was usual to assume that all *states* were *nation-states*, and then to refer to them simply as *nations* (Morgenthau 1948; for the influence of this book, see Vasquez 1983 and 1988).

matters, and some means of designing and enforcing effective allocations is required if any ascription of rights is to have practical import.

The Universal Declaration in fact resolves this problem by taking a nonuniversalist view of the allocation of obligations. For example, Articles 13–15 reveal clearly that the primary agents of justice are to be states (referred to in several different ways). In these articles the Declaration obliquely acknowledges that different agents are to be responsible for securing a given right for different persons, depending on the state of which they are members. The import of these articles is probably clearest if they are taken in reverse order.

The two clauses of Article 15 read as follows:

1. Everyone has the right to a nationality.
2. No one shall be arbitrarily deprived of his nationality nor denied the right to change his nationality.

Evidently the term "nationality" is not here being used in the sense that is more common today, to indicate a specific ethnic or cultural identity. If the Declaration used "having a nationality" to mean "having an ethnic or cultural identity," it would not need to prohibit deprivation of nationality, or assert rights to change one's nationality; it would need rather to speak of rights to express, foster, or maintain one's nationality. "Having a nationality" as it is understood in the Declaration is a matter of being a member of one or another state:[5] such membership is indeed something of which people may be deprived, and which they can change, and which some people – stateless people – lack.

A right to a nationality, in the sense of being a member of some state, is pivotal to the Declaration's implicit conception of the agents of justice. It is by this move that a plurality of bounded states – explicitly anticosmopolitan institutions – are installed as the primary agents of justice, who are to deliver universal rights. This becomes explicit in Articles 13 and 14, which make the following contrasting claims:

Article 13
1. Everyone has the right to freedom of movement and residence within the borders of each state.
2. Everyone has the right to leave any country, including his own, and to return to his country.

---

[5] Evidently the framers of the Declaration could not speak of "citizenship," since they were working in a world in which there were numerous colonies, trust territories, and dependent territories whose inhabitants were not all of them citizens. Even today, when there are fewer such territories, the term "citizenship" would be inappropriate, since there are many members of states who do not enjoy full citizenship status, including minors and resident aliens, whose rights are nevertheless important.

Article 14
1. Everyone has the right to seek and to enjoy in other countries asylum from persecution.
2. This right may not be invoked in the case of prosecutions genuinely arising from non-political crimes or from acts contrary to the purposes and principles of the United Nations.

The rights proclaimed in Articles 13 and 14 make it clear that the Declaration assumes a plurality of bounded states and exclusive citizenship. It is only in a world with this structure that it makes sense to distinguish the rights of freedom of movement, of exit and of reentry, that an individual is to enjoy in whichever state recognises him or her as a member, from the quite different right to asylum which a persecuted individual may have in states of which he or she is not a member. Rights, it appears, may legitimately be differentiated at boundaries: my rights in my own state will not and need not be the same as my rights in another state. In a world without bounded states, these distinctions would make no sense. Here it becomes quite explicit that the Declaration views states as the primary agents of justice: a cosmopolitan view of rights is to be spliced with a statist view of obligations.

The statism of the Declaration should not surprise us. Its preamble addresses member states who "have pledged themselves to achieve, in co-operation with the United Nations, the promotion of universal respect for and observance of human rights and fundamental freedoms." Yet since states cannot implement justice, let alone global justice, without constructing and coordinating many other agents and agencies, it is a matter for deep regret that the Declaration is so opaque about allocating the obligations of justice. The reason for regret is that in the end obligations rather than rights are the active aspects of justice: a proclamation of rights will be indeterminate and ineffective unless obligations to respect and secure those rights are assigned to specific, identifiable agents and agencies which are able to discharge those obligations (O'Neill 1996, 1999).

If the significant obligations that secure rights and justice are to be assigned primarily to states, much would have been gained by making this wholly explicit. In particular, it would have exposed the problems created by rogue states and weak states, and the predicaments created for other agents and agencies when states fail to support justice. Such explicitness might also have forestalled the emergence of the free-floating rhetoric of rights that now dominates much public discussion of justice, focuses on recipience, and blandly overlooks the need for a robust and realistic account of agents of justice who are to carry the counterpart obligations. This rhetoric has (in my view) become a prominent and persistently damaging feature of discussions of justice since the promulgation of the Universal Declaration.

Cosmopolitan Rhetoric and State Action: Rawls's Conception of Justice

It is not only in the Universal Declaration of Human Rights and the attendant culture of the human rights movement that we find cosmopolitan
thinking about justice linked to statist accounts of the primary agents of
justice. This combination is also standard in more theoretical and philosophical writing that assigns priority to universal rights: as in declarations
of rights, so in theories of rights, giving priority to the perspective of recipience distracts attention from the need to determine which agents of justice
are assigned which tasks. More surprisingly, statist views of the primary
agents of justice can also be found in theoretical and philosophical writing
on justice that does *not* prioritise rights.

A notable example of hidden statism without an exclusive focus on
rights is John Rawls's political philosophy. This is the more surprising
because Rawls hardly ever refers to states, and then often with some hostil-
ity. He claims throughout his writings that the context of justice is a
"bounded society," a perpetually continuing scheme of cooperation which
persons enter only by birth and leave only by death, and which is self-sufficient.[6] In his later writing he increasingly relies on a *political* conception
of bounded societies, seeing them as domains within which citizens
engage in public reason, which he defines as "citizens' reasoning in the
public forum about constitutional essentials and basic questions of justice"
(Rawls 1993, 10, cf. 212ff.; 1999, 132–33). He consequently views
peoples rather than states as the primary agents of justice. Yet his account
of peoples is surprisingly state-like: "Liberal peoples do, however, have
their fundamental interests as permitted by their conceptions of right and
justice. They seek to protect their territory, to ensure the security and safety
of their citizens, and to preserve their free political institutions and the
liberties and free culture of their civil society" (1999, 29).[7] Rawls,
however, maintains that in speaking of a bounded society and its citizens
he is *not* speaking of a territorial state. This is surely puzzling: if nobody
is to enter except by birth or leave except by death, the boundaries of the
polity must be policed; the use of force must be coordinated, indeed
monopolised, in the territory in question. If there is a monopoly of the use
of legitimate force for a bounded territory, we are surely talking of entities
which fit the classical Weberian definition of a state.

---

[6] This formulation is to be found from the first pages of John Rawls, *A Theory of Justice*
(1971). In later work his emphasis on bounded societies continues, but their liberal democracy and the citizenship of their members are increasingly emphasised; these shifts are corol-
laries of his shift to "political" justification. For some further textual details, see O'Neill
1998.

[7] Note also the following passage: "The point of the institution of property is that, unless
a definite agent is given responsibility for maintaining an asset . . . that asset tends to deteriorate. In this case the asset is the people's territory and its capacity to support them in
perpetuity; and the agent is the people themselves as politically organised" (Rawls 1999,
39).

The reason why Rawls so emphatically denies that states are the primary agents of justice appears to me to be that he has in mind one specific and highly contentious conception of the state. In *The Law of Peoples* he explicitly rejects the realist conception of state that has been of great influence in international relations. He sees states as "anxiously concerned with their power – their capacity (military, economic, diplomatic) – to influence others and always guided by their basic interests" (Rawls 1999, 28). He points out: "What distinguishes peoples from states – and this is crucial – is that just peoples are fully prepared to grant the very same proper respect and recognition to other peoples as equal" (Rawls 1999, 35). In Rawls's view states cannot be adequate agents of justice because they necessarily act out of self-interest; they are rational but cannot be reasonable.

However, this supposedly realist conception of the state is only one among various possibilities. Rawls's choice of peoples rather than states as the agents whose deliberations are basic to justice beyond boundaries is, I think, motivated in large part by an inaccurate assumption that states *must* fit the "realist" paradigm and hence are unfit to be primary (or other) agents of justice. Yet states *as we have actually known them* do not fit that paradigm.[8] The conception of states and governments as having limited powers, and as bound by numerous fundamental principles in addition to rational self-interest, is part and parcel of the liberal tradition of political philosophy and is central to contemporary international politics. States as they have really existed and still exist never had and never have unlimited sovereignty, internal or external, and have never been exclusively motivated by self-interest.[9] States as they actually exist today are committed by numerous treaty obligations to a limited conception of sovereignty, to restrictions on the ways in which they may treat other states, and by demands that they respect human rights. Peoples as they lived *before* the emergence of state structures probably did not have bounded territories; those peoples who developed the means to negotiate with other peoples, to keep outsiders out and to make agreements, did so by forming states and governments by which to secure bounded territories.

---

[8] Theorists of international relations acknowledge that many of the states we see around us fall far short of the realist paradigm of statehood: they speak of quasi states and dependent states. Rawls acknowledges that realism provides a poor account of state action – yet leaves realists in possession of the concept of the state (Rawls 1999, 46).

[9] A recent comment runs: "From the days of E. H. Carr . . . on, realists have claimed that their theories are empirically accurate, robust and fruitful, empirically sound guides to practice, and explanatorily powerful. . . . But what has been found is that the realist paradigm has not done well on any of these criteria" (Vasquez 1988, 372). Although a "revealed" (ascriptive, interpretive) view of self-interest may seemingly rescue the claim that states act only out of self-interest from this and other empirical defects, this is a Pyrrhic victory. As with analogous moves in discussions of individual motivation, a "realist" insistence that state action *must* be self-interested survives only by offering a trivialising and unfalsifiable interpretation of motivation.

The motive of self-interest ascribed to states or other agencies in would-be realist thinking is so open to multiple interpretations that I do not believe that we are likely to get far in trying to determine whether agents or agencies – whether states or companies or individuals – are or are not always motivated by self-interest, or *necessarily* motivated by self-interest, however interpreted. I suspect that ascriptions of self-interest often have a plausible ring only because they are open both to a tautologous and to an empirical interpretation. If the empirical interpretation of self-interested motivation fails for agents and agencies of any sort (as, according to Vasquez, it fails for states), the tautologous interpretation lingers in the background, sustaining an unfalsifiable version of "realism" by which the action of states (or companies, or individuals) is taken to define and reveal their motivation and their interests.

Once we have shed the assumption that all states (or other agents and agencies) must conform to this "realist" model, we can turn in a more open-minded way to consider the capacities for action that agents and agencies of various sorts, including states, actually have. In particular, we may then be in a position to say something about predicaments that arise when some states are too weak to act as primary agents of justice.

States as Agents of Justice: Motivation and Capabilities

Once we set aside the "realist" paradigm of state agency, many questions open up. Perhaps states are agents of a more versatile sort than "realists" assert, and are capable of a wider range of motivation than self-interest (as has been argued by various "idealist" theorists of international relations). Perhaps states are not the only agents of significance in building justice: various nonstate actors may also contribute significantly to the construction of justice. Perhaps a system of states can develop capacities for action which individual states lack.

These are very large questions, and the literature on international relations has dealt in part with many of them. However, for the present I want to take a quite restricted focus, with the thought that it may be useful to work towards an account of agents of justice by attending specifically to their powers rather than to their supposed motives.

A focus on the powers of states may seem to return us to classical discussions of sovereignty. That is not my intention. An analysis of *state power* is not an account of *state powers*; nor is an analysis of the *power* of other agents and agencies an account of their *powers*. The powers of all agents and agencies, including states, are multiple, varied, and often highly specific. These specificities are worth attending to, since it is these capacities that are constitutive of agency, and without agency any account of obligations (and hence any account of rights or of justice) will be no more than gesture.

Amartya Sen has introduced the useful notion of a *capability* into development economics; it can also be helpful in discussing the powers of states, and of other agents and agencies.[10] Agents' capabilities are not to be identified with their individual capacities or with their aggregate power. An agent or agency, considered in the abstract, may have various capacities or abilities to act. For example, a person may have the capacity to work as an agricultural labourer or an ability to organise family resources to last from harvest to harvest; a development agency may have the capacity to distribute resources to the needy in a given area. However, when a social and economic structure provides no work for agricultural labourers or no resources for a given family to subsist on or for an agency to distribute, these capacities lie barren. From the point of view of achieving justice – however we conceptualise it – agents and agencies must dispose not only of capacities which they could deploy if circumstances were favourable, but of capabilities, that is to say, of *specific, effectively resourced capacities which they can deploy in actual circumstances*. Capabilities are to capacities or abilities as effective demand is to demand: it is the specific capabilities of agents and agencies in specific situations, rather than their abstract capacities or their aggregate power, that are relevant to determining which obligations of justice they can hold and discharge – and which they will be unable to discharge (Sen 1999, 18–19, 38–39, 72–76, 288). The value of focusing on capabilities is that this foregrounds an explicit concern with the action and with the results that agents or agencies can achieve in actual circumstances, and so provides a *seriously realistic starting point for normative reasoning*, including normative claims about rights.

A focus on capabilities quickly reveals how defective weak states may be as agents of justice, and makes vivid why it is important also to think about other possible agents of justice in weak states. Weak states may simply lack the resources, human, material, and organisational, to do very much to secure or improve justice within their boundaries. They may lack capabilities to regulate or influence the action of certain other agents or agencies, or to affect what goes on in certain regions of the state, or to achieve greater justice. They may fail to represent the interests of their citizens adequately in international fora and may agree to damaging or unsupportable treaties or loans. They may lack the capabilities to end or prevent rebellions and forms of feudalism, insurgency and secession, banditry and lawlessness, or to levy taxes or enforce such laws as they enact in the face of powerful clans or corrupt factions. Often when we speak of such entities as "states," the term is used in a merely formal sense, as a largely

---

[10] For present purposes I do not intend to discuss the links which Sen draws between capabilities and their actualisation in an agent's functionings, or his arguments to identify which functionings, hence which capabilities, are valuable (Sen 1993, 1999; Nussbaum 2000). The usefulness of a focus on capabilities does not depend on basing it on one rather than another theory of value, or on one rather than another account of justice, rights, or obligations.

honorific appellation, and it is widely acknowledged that they lack capabilities that would be indispensable in any primary agent of justice.

Sometimes the lack of capabilities of states arises because other agents and agencies within or beyond the state have usurped those capabilities. The weakness of the Colombian state reflects the military and enforcement capabilities acquired by Colombian drug cartels; the weakness of a number of African states reflects the military capabilities achieved by secessionist and insurgent groups and movements within those states. However, even in cases where certain nonstate agents have acquired selected state-like capabilities, which they use to wreak injustice, they do not enjoy the range of capabilities held by states that succeed in being primary agents of justice. When weak states lack capabilities to be primary agents of justice, there is usually no other agent or agency that has acquired these missing capabilities. The fact that a state is incapable of securing the rule of law, or the collection of taxes, or the provision of welfare within its terrain is no guarantee that any other agent or agency has gathered together these missing capabilities. An unpropitious bundling or dispersal of capabilities may simply leave both a weak state and all those agencies that are active within and around it incapable of securing (a greater measure of) justice.

When states fail as agents of justice, the problem is not, therefore, simply a general lack of power. It is rather a lack of a specific range of capabilities that are needed for the delivery of justice – and specifically for the coordination, let alone enforcement, of action and obligations by other agents and agencies. Unfortunately, weak states often retain considerable capabilities for injustice even when wholly unable to advance justice. In these circumstances other agents and agencies may become important agents of justice.

Nonstate Actors as Agents of Justice

The odd phrase "nonstate actor" as currently used in international relations is revealing. It identifies certain types of agents and agencies *by reference to what they are not*. In an area of inquiry in which states have classically been thought of as the primary agents (not only of justice), the phrase "nonstate actor" has been invented to refer to a range of agencies that are neither states nor the creations of states (Risse-Kappen 1995). Etymology might suggest that all agents and agencies other than states – from individual human agents to international bodies, companies, and nongovernmental institutions – should count as nonstate actors. In fact, the term is usually used more selectively, to refer to institutions that are neither states, nor international in the sense of being interstatal or intergovernmental, nor directly subordinate to individual states or governments, *but that interact across borders with states or state institutions*. Some nonstate actors may acquire capabilities that make them significant agents of justice – and of injustice.

Examples of nonstate actors in this relatively restricted sense include (at least) those international nongovernmental organisations that operate across borders (INGOs), transnational or multinational companies or corporations (TNCs/MNCs), and numerous transnational social, political, and epistemic movements that operate across borders (sometimes known as "global social movements" or GSMs).[11] Here I shall refer to a few features of INGOs and TNCs, but say nothing about other types of nonstate actors.

Nobody would doubt that some nonstate actors aspire to be, and sometimes become, agents of justice; others may become agents of injustice. However, their mode of operation in weak states is quite different from the standard activities of secondary agents of justice. Nonstate actors do not generally contribute to justice by complying with state requirements: in weak states those requirements may be ill defined, and where they are adequately defined, compliance may contribute to injustice. Sometimes INGOs seek to contribute to justice in weak states by helping or badgering them into instituting aspects of justice which a state with more capabilities might have instituted without such assistance or goading. INGOs may do this by mobilising external powers (other states, international bodies, public opinion, GSMs), by doing advocacy work that assists weak states in negotiations with others, by mobilising First World consumer power, or by campaigning for and funding specific reforms that contribute to justice in a weak or unjust state. The typical mission and raison d'être of INGOs is to contribute to specific transformations of states, governments, and polities – quite often to a single issue or objective. Although INGOs cannot themselves become primary agents of justice, they can contribute to justice in specific ways in specific domains. Even when they cannot do much to make states more just, they may be able to help prevent weak states from becoming wholly dysfunctional or more radically unjust. Their difficulties and successes in doing so are not different in kind from the long and distinguished tradition of reform movements and lobbies within states whose ambitions for justice do not extend beyond improvements within (certain aspects of) that particular polity or state.

Some nonstate actors, in particular INGOs, may contribute to justice precisely because the states in which they operate are relatively weak, because they can act opportunistically and secure an unusual degree of access to some key players, and because they are not restricted by some of the constraints that might face nonstate actors in states with greater and better-coordinated capabilities. Their successes and failures as agents of justice are therefore analogous neither to the achievements and failures of stronger states with the capabilities to be primary agents of justice, nor to those of secondary agents of justice within stronger states.

---

[11] For discussion of ways in which global social movements may act transnationally, see O'Brien et al. 2000.

Other nonstate actors are not defined by their reforming aims, and it may seem that they are less likely to be able to contribute to justice in weak states. For example, TNCs are often thought of as having constitutive aims that prevent them from being agents of justice at all, except insofar as they are secondary agents of justice in states that have enacted reasonably just laws. If this were correct, TNCs could not contribute to justice in weak states where laws are ill defined or ill enforced, and the very notion of compliance with law may be indeterminate in many respects. Companies, we are often reminded, have shareholders; their constitutive aim is to improve the bottom line. How then could they be concerned about justice, except insofar as justice requires conformity to law?

This view of TNCs seems to me sociologically simplistic. Major TNCs are economically and socially complex institutions of considerable power; their specific capabilities and constitutive aims are typically diverse and multiple. To be sure, they have to worry about their shareholders (even institutions that lack shareholders still need to balance their books and worry about the bottom line). Yet a supposition that companies must be concerned *only* about maximising profits seems to me on a par with the "realist" supposition that states can act *only* out of self-interest. The notion of the *responsible company* or *responsible corporation* is no more incoherent than the notion of the liberal state; equally, the notion of the *rogue company* or *rogue corporation* is no more incoherent than that of the rogue state. If these notions seem incoherent, it may be because claims that some company pursues only economic self-interest (understood as shareholder interest) are shielded from empirical refutation by inferring interest from whatever is done: whatever corporate behaviour actually takes place is defined as pursuit of perceived shareholder interest.

Much popular and professional literature on TNCs wholly disavows this trivialising conception of the pursuit of self-interest, and accepts that TNC action can be judged for its contribution to justice – or to injustice. For example, TNCs have often been criticised for using their considerable ranges of capabilities to get away with injustice: for dumping hazardous wastes in states too weak to achieve effective environmental protection; for avoiding taxation by placing headquarters in banana republics; for avoiding safety legislation by registering vessels under "flags of convenience" or by placing dangerous production processes in areas without effective worker protection legislation. If the critics who point to these failings really believed that TNCs cannot but maximise profits, these objections would be pointless; in fact, they assume (more accurately) that major TNCs can choose among a range of policies and actions. Yet surprisingly little is said – outside corporate promotional literature – about the action of companies that insist on decent environmental standards although no law requires them to do so, or on decent standards of employment practice or of safety at work even where they could get away with less. In some cases TNCs operating in weak states with endemic corruption may go further to advance justice, for example, by refusing complicity with certain sorts of corruption or by insisting on widening the benefits of investment and production in ways that local legislation does not require and that local elites resist.

These commonplace facts suggest to me that it is more important to consider the capabilities rather than the (supposed) motivation of TNCs. Many TNCs are evidently capable of throwing their considerable weight in the direction either of greater justice, or of the status quo, or of greater injustice. In many cases it may be a moot point whether their motivation in supporting greater justice is a concern for justice, a concern to avoid the reputational disadvantages of condoning or inflicting injustice, or a concern for the bottom line *simpliciter*. However, unclarity about the motivation of TNCs does not matter much, given that we have few practical reasons for trying to assess the quality of TNC motivation. What does matter is what TNCs can and cannot do, the capabilities that they can and cannot develop.

If these thoughts are plausible, it is plain that TNCs can have and can develop ranges of capabilities to contribute both to greater justice and to greater injustice. Shareholder interests are, of course, important to all TNCs, but they underdetermine both what a given TNC can and what it will do. Fostering justice in specific ways is an entirely possible corporate aim; so, unfortunately, is contributing to injustice. Although TNCs may be ill constructed to substitute for the full range of contributions that states can (but often fail to) make to justice, there are many contributions that they can make, especially when states are weak. Corporate power can be great enough to provide the constellation of individuals and groups with influence in weaker states with powerful, even compelling, reasons to show greater respect for human rights, to improve environmental and employment standards, to accept more-open patterns of public discourse, or to reduce forms of social and religious discrimination. Corporate power can be used to support and strengthen reasonably just states. Equally, TNCs can accept the status quo, fall in with local elites and with patterns of injustice, and use their powers to keep things as they are – or indeed to make them more unjust.

In the end, it seems to me, any firm distinction between primary and secondary agents has a place only where there are powerful and relatively just states, which successfully discipline and regulate other agents and agencies within their boundaries. But once we look at the realities of life where states are weak, any simple division between primary and secondary agents of justice blurs. Justice has to be built by a diversity of agents and agencies that possess and lack varying ranges of capabilities, and that can contribute to justice – or to injustice – in more diverse ways than is generally acknowledged in those approaches that have built on supposedly realist, but in fact highly ideologised, views of the supposed motivation of potential agents of justice.

References

Carens, Joseph. (1987). "Aliens and Citizens: The Case for Open Borders." *The Review of Politics*, 49, 251–73.

Habermas, Jürgen. (1995). "Kants Idee des ewigen Frieden aus dem historischen Abstand." *Kritische Justiz*, 28, 293–318. Translated into English as "Kant's Idea of Perpetual Peace, with the Benefit of Two Hundred Years' Hindsight," in *Perpetual Peace: Essays on Kant's Cosmopolitan Ideal*, edited by James Bohman and Matthias Lutz-Bachmann, 113–53 (Cambridge: MIT Press, 1997).

Held, David. (2000). "Regulating Globalisation? The Reinvention of Politics." *International Sociology*, 15, 394–408.

Jackson, Robert H. (1990). *Quasi States: Sovereignty, International Relations, and the Third World*. Cambridge: Cambridge University Press.

Lutz-Bachmann, Matthias. (1997). "Kant's Idea of Peace and a World Republic." In *Perpetual Peace: Essays on Kant's Cosmopolitan Ideal*, edited by James Bohman and Matthias Lutz-Bachmann, 59–76. Cambridge: MIT Press.

Mann, Michael. (1997). "Has Globalisation Ended the Rise and Rise of the Nation-State?" *Review of International Political Economy*, 4, 472–96.

Mertens, Thomas. (1996). "Cosmopolitanism and Citizenship: Kant against Habermas." *European Journal of Philosophy*, 4, 328–47.

Migdal, Joel S. (1988). *Strong Societies and Weak States: State–Society Relations and State Capabilities in the Third World*. Princeton, N.J.: Princeton University Press.

Morgenthau, Hans J. (1948). *Politics among Nations: The Struggle for Power and Peace*. New York: Knopf. Revised edition published 1978.

Nussbaum, Martha C. (2000). *Women and Human Development: The Capabilities Approach*. Cambridge: Cambridge University Press.

O'Brien, Robert, et al. (2000). *Contesting Global Governance: Multilateral Economic Institutions and Global Social Movements*. Cambridge: Cambridge University Press.

O'Neill, Onora. (1996). *Towards Justice and Virtue: A Constructive Account of Practical Reasoning*. Cambridge: Cambridge University Press.

———. (1998). "Political Liberalism and Public Reason: A Critical Notice of John Rawls, *Political Liberalism*." *Philosophical Review*, 106, 411–28.

———. (1999). "Women's Rights: Whose Obligations?" In *Women's Voices, Women's Rights: Oxford Amnesty Lectures, 1996*, edited by Alison Jeffries. Reprinted in *Bounds of Justice*, by Onora O'Neill (Cambridge: Cambridge University Press, 2000).

Pogge, Thomas. (1994). "An Egalitarian Law of Peoples." *Philosophy and Public Affairs*, 23, 195–224.

Rawls, John. (1971). *A Theory of Justice*. Cambridge: Harvard University Press.

———. (1993). *Political Liberalism*. New York: Columbia University Press.

———. (1999). *The Law of Peoples*. Cambridge: Harvard University Press.

Risse-Kappen, Thomas, ed. (1995). *Bringing Transnational Relations Back In: Non-State Actors, Domestic Structures, and International Institutions*. Cambridge: Cambridge University Press.

Sen, Amartya. (1993). "Capability and Well Being." In *The Quality of Life*, by Martha C. Nussbaum and Amartya Sen, 30–53. Oxford: Clarendon Press.

———. (1999). *Development as Freedom*. Oxford: Oxford University Press.

Strange, Susan. (1996). *The Retreat of the State: The Diffusion of Power in the World Economy*. Cambridge: Cambridge University Press.

Vasquez, John A. (1983). *The Power of Power Politics: A Critique*. New Brunswick, N.J.: Rutgers University Press.

———. (1988). *The Power of Power Politics: From Classical Realism to Neo-Traditionalism*. Cambridge: Cambridge University Press. Revised version of *The Power of Power Politics: A Critique*, by John A. Vasquez.

13

GLOBAL JUSTICE: IS INTERVENTIONISM DESIRABLE?

VÉRONIQUE ZANETTI

I

On 20 April 1994, the European Parliament published a "Resolution on the right of humanitarian intervention," a decision concerning the right of humanitarian intervention for a state or a group of states in cases of important violations of human rights. The parliament defines *humanitarian intervention* "as the protection, including the threat or use of force, by a state or group of states of the basic human rights of persons who are subjects of and/or residents in another state."[1]

This document is interesting in several respects. First, it confirms an important move in international law towards an internationally acknowledged expansion of human rights. Through their codification in numerous international documents, basic rights can no longer be regarded as simply an internal matter for the states; consequently, the international community presents an increasing readiness to officially sanction acts of violation committed by a government against its people. Moreover, the European Parliament's declaration not only underlines the moral evolution which materializes in the codification of human rights; it even asserts that the confirmed evolution of customary law leads to the codification of a "right of humanitarian intervention." Last but not least, the declaration maintains that such intervention is not in contradiction with international law, although it formulates the concept of right in a way that is translatable into the vocabulary of individual rights.[2] Indeed, by speaking of a right of intervention, the resolution leaves open a crucial question: Who is the subject of the right? This can be understood, in the classical sense, as a right for states to intervene when peace is threatened. But it can also be understood as stipulating that individuals have a right to intervention in their favor in cases of important violations. In this second sense, the state is no longer

---

[1] *Official Journal of the European Communities*, Nr C 128/225, Wednesday, 20 April 1994.

[2] The European Parliament "considers that current international law does not necessarily represent an obstacle to the recognition of the right of humanitarian intervention" (ibid.).

the holder of the right, and thus it becomes possible to speak of an individual right for intervention.

This second reading carries significant consequences. According to the rhetoric of rights which attributes to them a corresponding duty, one sees that the normative consequences of the application of the right require from the states a completely different commitment in cases of a right *to* intervene than in cases of a right *of* intervention. The first refers to state B's right to intervene in state A, and the second to the right of state A's citizens to have state B intervene in state A on their behalf. As long as the state is the holder of the right, the corresponding duty prohibits the addressee from infringing upon the intervention. The right-holder is granted a legal capacity that it is free to perform or not. This allowance represents an exception to the general principle of nonintervention. This means that the principle acts as the legal rule and the intervention represents a permissible or tolerated exception. By contrast, if the victims possess a "right of humanitarian intervention," the corresponding duty implies that other countries have the (inevitably positive) duty to intervene when the circumstances correspond to those agreed on. Theoretically at least, each individual has a right, according to the international documents, that his existence be protected by an institution; consequently, this institution therefore has an obligation towards him. The protection is provided in the first instance by the government to which the individual belongs. When the government itself is at the origin of the violation or when it is incapable of offering its citizens a reasonable guarantee of protection, the responsibility lies with the supranational institution to which authority has been delegated.[3] Consequently, humanitarian intervention no longer constitutes a tolerated exception to the general rule, but rather a duty inscribed in the logic of the universality of basic human rights.

II

The central question, however, still remains: Which kinds of violations of fundamental rights legitimate an intervention? Both the state practice and the literature on the subject agree in general that only massive violations of the rights of life and security legitimate an intervention. The violations in question belong almost exclusively to the catalogue of physical violence: genocide, ethnic cleansing, deportation. But, as Thomas Pogge points out in his chapter in this volume, "[d]eaths and harms from direct violence around the world . . . are vastly outnumbered by deaths and harms due to poverty. In 1998, some 588,000 deaths were due to war. . . . Starvation and preventable diseases, by contrast, claimed about 18 million human lives, thus causing about one-third of all human deaths" (2001, 9).

---

[3] I have explored this thought in more detail in my 1999.

If the number of victims of violation counts as a decisive factor for legitimizing an intervention, it is undeniable that the right to humanitarian intervention should also extend to the victims of extreme poverty.

Along these lines, Henry Shue has convincingly shown that the right to subsistence belongs to a corpus of basic rights because it is in several respects more fundamental than political and civil rights. First, it offers individuals the material conditions necessary for the realization of their other rights. Second, without the creation of material conditions, the legal freedom to do or not to do something is a pure delusion. Finally, we can show that basic rights not only invest individuals with a dignity essential to the flourishing of their personality, but that they are also intrinsically linked to the principle of equal respect owed to individuals (see Gosepath 1998). Basic rights are not, therefore, only a means towards the realization of other rights, but they also have a content which is essential enough to be guaranteed by the constitution (see Alexy 1994).

We see, then, that the theory of international relations faces totally new difficulties if it admits that the innumerable victims of misery are victims of a violation of their basic rights as well, and thus are entitled to expect that the international community intervene in their favor if their country does not sufficiently guarantee their rights. The problems are first empirical in nature: While it is relatively easy to establish who are the authors and who are the victims of a genocide, an ethnic cleansing, a massacre, or officially condoned acts of torture, it is infinitely more difficult to establish that minimal social rights have been violated – apart from cases where a government purposely starves part of its population or when a government is so corrupt that an exploiting elite literally deprives the majority of the population of the means to survive. The problems are also theoretical in nature because it must be shown that below a certain grade of social inequality or a certain grade of injustice in the institutional structures, we must consider not only whether the fundamental individual rights have not been adequately met, but also whether a violation has even taken place.

Undeniably, the view that individuals have more than a moral right to international institutions that protect and adequately guarantee their fundamental rights (including a corpus of minimal social rights) leads ultimately to a radical change in the conception of the world order, the relations between states, the responsibility of the international community towards the world's citizens – and, consequently, to a change in the principle of intervention.

III

We now need to ask: What are the consequences for the mutual duties of states when the right to subsistence is included within the core of minimal fundamental rights? In addressing this question, I will concentrate on two main strategies. The first establishes a division of moral labor between the domestic and the international levels, and thus sees governments as having a primary obligation towards their own people, while the international community serves primarily to establish background conditions necessary for the maintenance of peace and the flourishing of domestic societies. I will take up Rawls's idea of a duty of assistance among the principles of international law. Such assistance constitutes an important first step towards concretizing social individual rights. I will show, however, that Rawls's principle of assistance is not up to the consequences of his cosmopolitan premises. Moreover, inscribed within a structurally deficient construction of international relations, the principle has little chance of reaching the expected aims.

The second strategy, that of the theoreticians of global justice, abolishes the separation between nationals and foreign citizens, and grounds social justice in the right of each individual, as a citizen of the world, to access to social primary goods. This theory offers a greater chance of attaining the desired social rights. The theoreticians of global justice are nearly the only ones who have taken seriously the fact that all individuals have a legitimate claim, independent of their citizenship, to a minimum standard allowing them to lead a decent life. Moreover, unlike Rawls, they have drawn the logical and moral consequences of their requirement into the realm of international relations. In the next section I will argue, however, that their proposal for reforming global institutions remains nonetheless insufficient to attain their goals.

In *The Law of Peoples* Rawls attempts to provide "a particular political conception of right and justice that applies to principles and norms of international law and practice" (Rawls 1999, 3; hereafter cited as LP). These should be obtained by running a second session of the original position, in which states rather than persons are to be represented. Rawls's second original position, which brings together the representatives of liberal societies, adopts eight principles that he says well-ordered societies accept as constitutive principles of the rights of peoples. The eighth principle stipulates that "peoples have a duty to assist other peoples living under unfavorable conditions that prevent their having a just or decent political and social regime" (LP 37).

It is important here to underline that the principle clearly speaks of a duty. In this sense, the assistance is not merely a charitable act dependent upon the good will of the donor countries. The duty of assistance has a target: "it seeks to raise the world's poor until they are either free and equal citizens of a reasonable liberal society or members of a decent hierarchical society." But it also has a cutoff point, since the principle ceases to apply once the target is reached (LP 119). The principle of assistance is, thus, only a principle of transition in that it applies only as long as societies desiring to achieve liberal or decent basic institutions are too burdened to be able to do so. We can, therefore, imagine that, given the fulfillment of certain required political conditions (nonaggressive external politics and an absence of corruption), a threshold of poverty is considered a sufficient base for receiving aid. In this case, the criteria would specify a commonly fixed and accepted list of duties.

Although the above-mentioned points represent an improvement in comparison to the existing situation, one must, nonetheless, question whether the duty of assistance, besides the other principles of the Law of Peoples, truly offers an adequate instrument for the implementation of the basic rights of individuals throughout the world. First, the concept of duty remains surprisingly indefinite, situated in a gray zone which provides little information about its status and its mode of realization. Does, for example, the obligation of assistance generate a moral or a legal obligation? We are entitled to think that, being one of the eight constitutive principles of the Law of Peoples, the duty of assistance thereby generates a legal obligation. However, Rawls gives no precise information about the structure of the supranational institutions which are entitled to fix the amount of assistance, or any clear criteria for being a beneficiary, nor does he make any mention of the coercive measures to be used against peoples who do not meet their obligations or who use the assistance for unacceptable purposes. Moreover, not only does Rawls remain silent on these significant points, but he denies the main potential beneficiaries a voice in establishing the terms of assistance: The societies burdened by unfavorable conditions are deprived of a place in the original position because they do not belong to the circle of "decent" peoples. The burdened societies are those which, while not expansive or aggressive, "lack the political and cultural traditions, the human capital and know-how, and, often, the material and technological resources needed to be well-ordered" (LP 106).

In spite of reiterated critiques from the cosmopolitans, Rawls persists in refusing to include the principle of distributive justice within the corpus of the Law of Peoples. According to him, its adoption, at the second level, would be unreasonable in several respects:

1. It would contradict the liberal principle of toleration in expecting all people to have the equal liberal rights of citizens in a constitutional democracy (LP 82).
2. It would require more than is necessary to maintain peaceful international relations: a certain level of resources is not required for the creation of decent political institutions.
3. It would create relations of dependency which depart from the pursued goals. Rawls sees the principle of assistance as only a principle of transition that applies as long as societies wishing to achieve liberal or decent basic institutions are too burdened to be able to do so.
4. It would possibly give rise to injustice by penalizing some economic choices – for example, a country which decides to industrialize and to increase its rate of savings would be taxed more than another country that had the same level of wealth initially but which made no effort to limit its expenses.

5. Finally, since justice is interpreted in terms of the reciprocity of benefits among persons placed under a scheme of mutual cooperation,
   obligations of justice need not be as equally developed in the international sphere as they are in the state-domain; the world is not a cooperative partnership in the same sense that the nation-state is.

The crucial aim of the duty of assistance is to bring burdened peoples
into the sphere of liberal or decent peoples. However, because, for Rawls,
a country's political culture rather than its wealth is the central element
needed for creating decent political institutions, the arbitrariness of the
distribution of natural resources does not constitute a matter of justice.
Consequently, priority of assistance goes to peoples likely to concur with
the aims of well-ordered societies. As a result, by exempting nonliberal
peoples from the principle of distributive justice, the so-called principle of
toleration exempts them from having any entry into a structure which has
already excluded them. They never have the chance to decide if they desire
the principle of toleration and, therefore, whether they desire that the principle of distributive justice apply to them or not. Moreover, a well-ordered
society whose economic situation dangerously threatens the maintenance
of its democratic institutions is not regarded as an automatic beneficiary of
assistance because it belongs to a zone circumscribed by the second original position. At most, it may benefit from charitable assistance.

In reality, the idea of toleration masks a rather conservative principle of
autonomy of states inherited from classical international law: "the representatives of peoples will want to preserve the independence of their own
society and its equality in relation to others. In the working of organizations and loose confederations of peoples, inequalities are designed to
serve the many ends that peoples share" (LP 115). In Rawls's view (as in
Kant's), the choice of the international structure falls on a confederation of
states/peoples which are articulated around mainly negative obligations;
however, there exists no supranational institution entitled to the monopoly
of power and to the attribution of jurisdictions. International relations are
governed by law; however, states/peoples are not forced to join the society
of peoples. Some common aims nonetheless are set – such as security and
peace – but states/peoples have no obligation concerning the means necessary to realize these aims. Nothing, for example, forces states/peoples to
sign and ratify conventions on disarmament. Aside from these structural
defects, Rawls constructs an international model which right from the
beginning accommodates societies which do not completely fulfill his
universal requirement of equal treatment of individuals within religious,
ethnic, or social groups. Admittedly, these concessions are made in the
(Kantian) hope of progress by way of the influence of example. However,
they erode the pursued aims and weaken the already precarious stability of
this loose confederation of states/peoples.

Finally, as I said before, the principle of assistance, being a duty – and probably a legal one – obliging wealthy societies towards those which are too burdened to have just institutions, offers a clear advantage in comparison to the arbitrary and precarious current situation concerning help for developing countries. But it is regrettable that such an important principle for the establishment of peaceful relations between states serves mostly a classical conception of international relations and is not supported by the instruments necessary for its implementation. Indeed, this loose confederation of peoples is a form of organization that is insufficient to realize the desired goals, and the establishment of the principle of nonintervention is an unsuitable tool. The Rawlsian construction grants states a certain sovereignty over their own people, and thus leaves only serious violations of rights as objects of sanctions or intervention. This means that intervention or sanctions become legitimate only in cases where a state's practice aims at deliberately depriving part of the population access to subsistence goods. Moreover, without a monopoly of power, intervention becomes open to a unilateral use of coercive measures that depend on the availability of military forces by allied governments. However, no mention is even made of the obligation of these governments to join the military forces. Neither is any penalty envisioned against the countries which might refuse to cooperate in the application of the sanctions against a third party, or which might be unwilling to contribute to the creation of an intervening force. Furthermore, the proposal is not only unsatisfactory regarding the structure in place, but also quite problematic regarding the pursued aims. Indeed, because the principle of nonintervention prevails except in cases of massive violations, many situations of gross underfulfillment of basic rights remain unrecognized. Thus, the individuals have no chance for the international community to intervene in their favor.

IV

In contrast to Rawls's strategy, the cosmopolitans' globalist premises promise better results for realizing individuals' basic rights. Everyone, they say, is entitled to institutions that satisfy minimum standards of humanity and justice. And, importantly, the boundaries between states are no excuse for the perpetuation of inequality.

For Charles R. Beitz, as for Brian Barry and for Thomas Pogge, a global individualist contract is the only logical answer to Rawlsian liberal premises. Furthermore, they continue, such a contract, in applying maximum criteria to the original situation, would inevitably lead to the integration of the principle of distributive justice in the list of chosen principles. Moreover, cosmopolitans contend that it is morally unacceptable that some people, just because they have been born in the "wrong" part of the world, have nearly no access to necessary goods.

A fundamental question still remains: What kind of political structure should be responsible for guaranteeing individuals the exercise of their rights? Towards whom do individuals have rights if states, the traditional holders of sovereignty, are divested of their legitimacy and become increasingly deprived of their power to act?

Because, for the cosmopolitan, each individual is potentially the addressee of the right, each is under the obligation to institutionalize a legal structure capable of protecting as well as implementing these rights. The global validity of human rights is consequently activated only through the emergence of a global scheme of social institutions. One has, therefore, good reason to expect that the cosmopolitan position desires the creation of a global sovereign institution. Indeed, already within the concepts of objective liberty and of justice, subjects must be considered to be "mit-Bürger," coauthors of the jurisdiction under which they obtain the mutual recognition of their rights. The recognition of these rights implies reciprocity and universality right from the beginning. It would, therefore, seem to be within the logic of cosmopolitanism to wish for the formation of something equivalent to a world state. On this point, I completely agree with Kersting: "If we choose a traditional contractualist beginning and work with an individualistic original situation, the theory of global justice must adopt the form of the foundation of a world state. If we try to evade a world state even though we are interested in a theory of a just international order, we have to construct a theory of international relations based on the order of law and peace" (Kersting 1997, 292).

However, the representatives of cosmopolitanism deny the necessity of this conclusion: "As I have suggested at various points," Beitz remarks, "a cosmopolitan conception of international morality is not equivalent to, nor does it necessarily imply, a political program like those often identified with political universalism, world federalism, or 'world order.' It is important to distinguish moral structures from political ones, and to recognize that global normative principles might be implemented otherwise than by global institutions conceived on the analogy of the state" (1979, 182–83). The question still remains of how these institutions are to be implemented.

V

The recognition of a severe inequality of opportunities between persons living in wealthy countries and those living in poor countries can give rise to two different moral interpretations. First, it can be translated into a global individual egalitarianism which recognizes each person as having an equal right to a share of the available resources. The world's resources should be owned and controlled by all its inhabitants as equals. Because adequate access to resources is a prerequisite for successful domestic institutions, and because inequality in the distribution of natural resources is arbitrary, there is a moral requirement to compensate for the injustice of the effects of the distribution (Beitz and Barry).

The second interpretation emphasizes a noticeably different meaning of injustice: What is unjust is not so much the unequal distribution of natural resources as the fact that this inequality actually results from acts of violence which the international institutions endorse by giving themselves an institutional legitimization allowing them to resist reforms. This is the reason why, ideally, it would be desirable that the social contract be a cosmopolitan contract right from the outset. It should not reside in institutional models which have not been approved by, or even submitted to, the individuals' representatives. A fairer distribution of natural resources (through the global resources dividend, for example [see Pogge 1998]) is not an aim in itself derived from an egalitarian premise, but a possible means of compensating for injustice and of partially repairing its damages (Pogge 1992b). As Pogge states, this second option requires less than the moral interactionism which imposes duties towards persons in need without taking account of personal relationships between individuals or of the causal link to suffering: "We are asked to be concerned about human-rights violations not simply insofar as they exist at all, but only insofar as they are produced by social institutions in which we are significant participants" (1992b, 93). Individuals have, above all, the duty to know about the repercussions of the rules of the institutions which they have chosen or to which they belong, and they should either withdraw from those generating injustice or attempt reform.

The two theories have totally different consequences for international politics. By insisting on the requirement of redistribution, the first theory (and its institutional form) leads inevitably to the creation of a central supranational, strongly interventionist structure. Barry admits this: It is within the logic of cosmopolitan morality that individuals should be the units of the redistribution and that a global income tax should be levied on individuals according to a uniform progressive tariff regardless of their country of residence. The concession to reality that recommends a redistribution from rich countries to poor ones cannot be the whole story, because it cannot be indifferent to the way in which the benefits of the transfer are distributed within the recipient country. Consequently, there exists in the cosmopolitan morality "a strong *prima facie* case for international intervention" (Barry 1996, 16).

Indeed, at least two dangers threaten a global redistributive practice: a form of anarchy in the application of the rule and a misappropriation of the help. The functioning of the rule is threatened when some countries comply and others do so only partially or not at all. It is also to be feared that redistribution could be for some states an incentive to keep their gross national product sufficiently low in order to be a beneficiary and to take advantage of the help without even attempting to realize the required aims. For the redistribution to bear the expected fruits, it is essential (1) that all countries comply with the payment of taxes; (2) that the criteria which determine the beneficiaries be acknowledged by all and that the demands be treated according to a transparent procedure open to all and reviewable on demand if there is ground for protest; (3) that funds from taxation be used in favor of persons who are most in need; and (4) that countries which refuse to discharge their payments or that use them for unjust aims be subject to previously fixed sanctions.

As I stated previously, Barry draws the moral conclusion that the state practice must become strongly interventionist. Since the individual should be the real beneficiary of redistribution, it is essential that the funds be used to improve his living conditions and to provide him easier access to primary goods. In Barry's model, states are in a global scheme in which they are deprived of their moral legitimacy and denied the power to act without a clearly defined transfer of capacities enabling global institutions to perform a function of replacement or subsidiarity vis-à-vis national institutions. We should, however, ask which institution has the authority and the coercive means to impose the aims of justice and democracy. How should we interpret the "strong *prima facie* case for international intervention"? Who is authorized and entitled to intervene? With which means? And in which cases? How can we avoid a situation in which a main donor demands the right to control the use the beneficiaries make of the funds, while in turn refusing to submit to an equivalent external inspection?

Pogge admits that his proposal to redistribute dividends from natural resources is feasible only if "backed by sanctions." He denies, however, that this leads to a centralization of the power monopoly: All countries are required to impose sanctions (see Pogge 1994, 219). We can, though, easily imagine that a country would have no interest in exercising sanctions against another country with which it keeps a dense commercial exchange. In order to prevent the former from bargaining its noncompliance, it is necessary to have an institution entitled with exclusive power and legitimacy to control the states, to compel them to apply the imposed sanctions, and to compensate the countries strongly penalized by applying them. In other words, a regulatory force is needed whose legal authority is acknowledged by the states and which, in cases of conflict, holds the means to impose its decisions with the help of force if necessary.

By insisting on the role of nongovernmental actors in the globalization of rights and on individual responsibility for the effects of global institutions, Pogge corrects the centralizing consequences of the redistributive strategy by diffusing the intervening power. Indeed, all institutions should be evaluated according to their consequences for the rights of the individuals they concern. These individuals are expected not only to withdraw their support of an unjust institution but also to reform it. In this way, the cosmopolitan model entrusts civil society with the task of interfering in the domestic affairs of other states.

Under this point of view at least, the notion of intervention is modified in the direction of a global interventionism which is in favor of human rights and of democracy. As this view switches from a negative connotation

– the interdiction to intervene – to a positive connotation,[4] the modification, in comparison to the classical conception, works on at least three levels: on the level of the actors, on the level of the definition, and on the level of political practice.

1. On the level of the actors: Traditionally, only states are subject to the nonintervention principle. By scattering the notion of sovereignty, the cosmopolitan theory broadens the circle of intervening parties to include international organizations, multinational companies, and nongovernmental organizations, as well as other forms of private organizations.

2. On the level of the definition: In the classical sense, the intervention is characterized by the coercive measures against the sanctioned state and by the threat of resort to violence in cases of a lack of cooperation. Coercive measures are defined as physical constraint extending to the use of military force. Implicitly, therefore, intervention can be carried out only by a state or a group of states or by an international institution in possession of the monopoly of force. In contrast, it is clear that private actors are not in possession of such a monopoly and that the threat they represent is of quite another nature. It is directed primarily towards the manipulation of public image by exerting psychological pressures which can have significant economic repercussions. Exemplary is Greenpeace's capacity to mobilize support to pressure France to cease nuclear testing in the South Pacific by gathering more than 7 million signatures from people in some thirty countries ("Protests" 1995).

Would we consider these pressures as forms of coercive measures? The U.N. Charter gives no precise definition of "coercive measures," although these terms occur in several articles. One usually considers military actions and economic embargoes as coercive in the sense of Article 53. Nothing prevents us, however, from understanding this term in a much larger sense. By insisting upon the military character of the coercive action, international law facilitates its task by using semantic instruments which, at first glance, are quite clear: Humanitarian intervention is a military intervention. International law deprives itself, however, of the possibility of questioning the legitimacy of other interventionist measures which would be less dangerous or less expensive and which, especially when used preventively, would have positive effects. One must, however, be conscious that expanding the concept in such a way inevitably opens a Pandora's box of all sorts of pressures and influences which could lead to an undesired change in a government's political or economic behavior. And such forms of pressures or influence are almost without limit, especially when extended into the realm of all potential actors.

---

[4] Cf. the opposition between the classical position of J. Isensee and the largely interventionist conception of Czempiel (1995).

3. On the level of political practice: In its classical definition, the principle governing the intervention is clearly a negative principle, linked to the prohibition of the usage of violence against a sovereign authority. On the contrary, the cosmopolitan theory confers upon it a positive connotation by viewing it as an instrument for imposing human rights and democracy on a global scale.[5]

The cosmopolitan approach, however, is not without disadvantages. The concept of "institution" is a protean term; international organizations, churches, trade unions, universities, voluntary associations, and families are all institutions. And when these institutions enter the international scene, they are intermingled with no clear hierarchy or definite political influence. Regarding the result of this process, Anne-Marie Slaughter is ironic: One would have a "world order in which global networks of governance link Microsoft, the Roman Catholic Church, and Amnesty International to the European Union, the United Nations and Catalonia" (1997, 184). This wide distribution of power not only lacks the legitimizing authority necessary for democracy but it also leads to an uncontrolled – and uncontrollable – use of interventionist measures. The question I wish to address is: If we emancipate the actors and broaden indefinitely the extension of the concept of coercive measures, is it still possible to distinguish between interventions that are morally and legally required and those that are not?

VI

The representatives of global justice are perfectly correct when they denounce the blindness of political scientists who attribute deficiencies in the systems of rights to essentially local factors; without the more or less active participation of wealthy states or of multinational companies, corrupted governments would not long remain in power. The catalogue of human rights must be implemented on the global scale. And there are very few chances for this implementation as long as there is an ever-widening gulf between the gross national product of the poorer countries and that of the wealthier ones. Extreme poverty, indeed, not only contributes significantly to the underfulfillment of political rights needed to carry out necessary political reforms; it also makes poor people easy prey for bargaining, and fragile pawns in a game of power in which they have no influence. The cosmopolitan conception is, therefore, entirely correct in recentering the imperative of justice within the realm of international relations.

---

[5] The title of an article by Ernst-Otto Czempiel (1987) is very revealing of this change: "Gewaltfreie Intervention zugunsten von Demokratisierungsprozessen" (Nonviolent intervention in favor of democratization).

216 VÉRONIQUE ZANETTI

There now remains the question of which institutions we desire in order to obtain more justice in the world. In my opinion, Rawls's view and the cosmopolitan argument share a common structural deficiency regarding the global institutions which should secure the implementation of individuals' rights. For if one proclaims that all individuals have equal rights to goods and services, it is essential to establish global institutions towards which these rights can be claimed. Without a legislative, judicial, and executive central system, the world legal order is condemned to remain a provisional – not a peremptory – legal order, to recall the Kantian vocabulary. What is therefore required is a structure equivalent to that of a world government.

The model of a vertically dispersed sovereignty which would substitute for a world government confuses the normative level concerning the establishment of legitimate sovereignty with the political level of the exercise of power.[6] If the world government is to be compatible with political pluralism, it is certainly an essential condition that the exercise of power be dispersed and attributed according to the principle of subsidiarity. Nevertheless, if the world government should ensure the implementation of global legislation concerning the protection of rights, justice, security, and ecology, it has to be endowed with the corresponding legal and executive powers. When the authority on these questions is assigned to a global government, the government becomes sovereign and the institutions placed under its control lose the right to decide on these subjects by their own authority. Otherwise, the normative function of a global institution, which is to reduce the other institutions' capacity for bargaining power, completely loses its relevance. Granted, one may maintain – as Kant does and as Rawls seems to want to – that a loose confederation of states presents advantages similar to those of a world government without involving its dangers. Indeed, according to this view, the withdrawal from the confederation would entail for a country so many risks and inconveniences that sanction mechanisms would be unnecessary. However, if the confederation gives each member the full liberty to decide whether or not to apply the legal norms that the representatives of the states have demo-cratically chosen, it deprives itself of the authority to transform the decisions into law. Pogge recognizes this himself when he speaks about the problem of weapon control: "it is not feasible to reduce and eliminate national control over weapons of mass destruction through a program that depends upon the voluntary cooperation of each and every national government. What is needed, therefore, is the centrally enforced reduction and elimination of such weapons" (1992a, 62). If so, however, the sovereignty on that question – as on the question of global economic justice or ecology – is not vertically spread, but is in the hands of the global institution and in its hands alone.

---

[6] On this point I share entirely the position defended by Christoph Horn (1996, 227–51).

When applied to the question of intervention, this means, in my opinion, that the decision to use coercion and its employment must be part of the sovereignty of a global institution which, in its turn, can delegate its authority. Such a centralization is not incompatible with the maintenance of the positive aspects discussed above which are entailed in the revised version of the intervention. The sphere of coercive means should, for example, be enlarged so as to include numerous peaceful means as well. Above all, the concept of preventive intervention should be analyzed and integrated within the catalogue of official measures at the disposal of the international community when it is active in places of the world where the political situation is particularly under pressure. Preventive intervention could be initiated, according to documents established by nongovernmental organizations, commissions of inquiry, or diplomats in service that denounce systematic violations of rights, ideologically supported violations by the government, or violations due to outbursts of anarchy.

Such intervention, taking place before conflicts escalate, would allow many lives to be spared (on both sides), would be better adapted to the country and its needs, would be less expensive for the international community, and might, finally, not be perceived by the country in which the intervention takes place as a humiliating form of guardianship or as a media-driven act of charity. I therefore agree that civil society should be given a decisive role in the implementation of human rights; it is, for example, undeniable that nongovernmental organizations play an essential role at the level of observing, gathering, and broadcasting information. We must, however, emphasize that they do not have – and should not have – the acknowledged power to sanction. Humanitarian intervention must be a legal act. This means that the criteria which legitimate intervention should be codified and that sanctions should follow rules that apply to all situations which satisfy the criteria. Only in this way will it be possible to prevent the arbitrary treatment of persons in need and to assure that intervention does not serve the particular interests of powerful institutions.

Acknowledgments

I am grateful to Klaus-Gerd Giesen, Jean-Christophe Merle, and Alessandro Pinzani for their many fruitful comments on this chapter. I would also like to thank Heidi White and Gayle Wurst for their gracious help with the translation.

References

Alexy, Robert. (1994). *Theorie der Grundrechte*. Frankfurt am Main: Suhrkamp.

Barry, Brian. (1996). "Nationalism, Intervention, and Redistribution." Working chapter no. 3. Institut für Interkulturelle und Internationale Studien.

Beitz, Charles. (1979). *Political Theory and International Relations.* Princeton: Princeton University Press.

Czempiel, Ernst-Otto. (1987). "Gewaltfreie Intervention zugunsten von Demokratisierungsprozessen." In *Internationale Politik und der Wandel von Regimen,* edited by Gesine Schwan, 55–75. Köln: Heymann.

———. (1995). "Die Intervention: Politische Notwendigkeit und strategische Möglichkeit." In *Ist das Prinzip der Nichteinmischung überholt?,* edited by Hartmut Jäckel, 49–74. Baden-Baden: Nomos.

Gosepath, Stefan. (1998). "Zu Begründungen sozialer Menschenrechte." In *Philosophie der Menschenrechte,* edited by S. Gosepath and G. Lohmann. Frankfurt am Main: Suhrkamp.

Horn, Christoph. (1996). "Philosophische Argumente für einen Weltstaat." *Allgemeine Zeitschrift für Philosophie,* 21, 227–51.

Kersting, Wolfgang. (1997). *Recht, Gerechtigkeit und demokratische Tugend.* Frankfurt am Main: Suhrkamp.

Pogge, Thomas. (1992a). "Cosmopolitanism and Sovereignty." *Ethics,* 103:1, 48–75. Reprinted in *Political Restructuring in Europe,* edited by Chris Brown, 89–122 (London: Routledge, 1994).

———. (1992b). "An Institutional Approach to Humanitarian Intervention." *Public Affairs Quarterly,* 6:1, 89–103.

———. (1994). "An Egalitarian Law of Peoples." *Philosophy and Public Affairs,* 23:3, 195–224.

———. (1998). "A Global Resources Dividend." In *Ethics of Consumption: The Good Life, Justice, and Global Stewardship,* edited by David A. Crocker and Toby Linden, 501–36. Lanham, MD: Rowman and Littlefield.

———. (2001). "Priorities of Global Justice." *Metaphilosophy,* 32:1/2.

"Protests Swamp Paris Post Office." (1995). *Washington Post* (29 Oct.), A34.

Rawls, John. (1999). *The Law of Peoples.* Cambridge: Harvard University Press.

Slaughter, Anne-Marie. (1997). "The Real New World Order." *Foreign Affairs,* 78:5, 183–97.

Zanetti, Véronique. (1999). "Die Verrechtlichung der humanitären Intervention: Eine Chance oder eine Bedrohung?" In *Ein Ethos für eine Welt? Globalisierung als ethische Herausforderung,* edited by Karl-Josef Kuschel et al., 200–223. Frankfurt: Campus.

14

THE NEW INTERVENTIONISM

MICHAEL W. DOYLE

The forcible separation of Kosovo from Serbia de facto and East Timor from Indonesia de jure are the latest of the new interventions, but in recent years they were preceded by armed interventions to protect Kurds and rescue the Somali people from starvation, the ouster by invasion of a military coup in Haiti, and a series of heavily induced mediations that brought to an end civil wars in Cambodia, El Salvador, Croatia, and Bosnia. Interventions once aroused the condemnation of international moralists. Now failures to intervene or to intervene adequately in places such as Rwanda or Sierra Leone do (see, e.g., Walzer 1977 and 1995).

This volume focuses on global economic justice. But global political justice, including the rights and wrongs of intervention, and global economic justice are intimately linked by how the international community interprets and enforces sovereignty. First, as Thomas Pogge notes in his chapter, "Our global order is disadvantageous to the global poor by sustaining oppression and corruption, and hence poverty, in the developing world" (2001, 22). Current sovereignty rules allow governments legal legitimacy without sufficient discrimination between just and unjust regimes. Any recognized government, even repressive ones, can sell domestic assets and have access to the World Bank, International Monetary Fund (IMF), and other sources of international borrowing that the countries' populations then become bound to repay, irrespective of how wise or unwise, corrupt or honest, the policy choices were. Second, international political institutions allocate scarce goods at the international level, as do the World Bank, the IMF, and the World Trade Organization (WTO), and the rules that govern their decisions are generally not politically fair or neutral.[1] Third, some forms of economic deprivation reach to the level of life-taking in a way so direct that they constitute political oppression as well.[2] Systematic starvation targeted

---

[1] These issues are discussed in this volume by Andrew Hurrell (2001) and, in passing, by others.

[2] Related points to these are raised in Véronique Zanetti's paper (2001) and Onora O'Neill (1986).

against specific social groups constitutes genocide. Governments that direct such crimes are as guilty as those who turn their guns on their own people, and governments so weak that they cannot prevent starvation have a consequent duty to accept and assist international assistance. But, fourth, sovereignty rules also protect governments in the developing world from many of the traditional forms of exploitative imperialism that were practiced in the nineteenth century. And, fifth, while global economic justice may require the wealthy states to assist the poor and require the poor states to distribute their national income in a fair manner, global political justice stands aside, treating states that meet minimum protection conditions for their own populations as sovereign. Traditionally these legal and ethical barriers to infringement on sovereignty have been high, designed to protect national autonomy from external interference.

This chapter focuses on the boundaries of political sovereignty, one key aspect of global political justice and an important background condition to the issues treated in the other chapters of this volume. I first present an interpretive summary of the traditional arguments against and for intervention, stressing, to a greater extent than is usual, the consequentialist character of the ethics of intervention. It makes a difference whether we think that an intervention will do more good than harm, and some of the factors that determine the outcome are matters of strategy and institutional choice. I then explore the significance of a key factor that makes for much of what is new in the new interventionism: the role of multilateral and particularly U.N. authorization and implementation. Should the more salient role of the United Nations lead us to a more expansive tolerance of international intervention? Should global standards of justice, political and economic, therefore be more widely enforced against claims to national autonomy?

Principles of Nonintervention and Intervention

Principles of nonintervention and intervention have been justified in various ways. In international law, "intervention" is dictatorial interference in the political independence and territorial integrity of a sovereign state. Although the principles underlying this prohibition never have been formally ratified as a single treaty according to a set of philosophical precepts, they nonetheless, throughout time, have been justified by scholars, by politicians, and by citizens who have sought to provide good reasons why one should abide by these conventional principles of classic international law and good reasons why one should, on some occasions, override them.[3]

Nonintervention has been a particularly important and occasionally

---

[3] Insightful studies of the historical context on the doctrine of nonintervention are Vincent (1974) and Graham (1987).

disturbing principle for liberal political philosophers.[4] On the one hand, liberals have provided some of the very strongest reasons to abide by a strict form of the nonintervention doctrine. It was only with a security of national borders that liberals such as Immanuel Kant and John Stuart Mill thought that peoples could work out the capacity to govern themselves as free citizens. On the other hand, those very same principles of universal human dignity when applied in different contexts have provided justifications for overriding the principle of nonintervention.

John Stuart Mill developed the core of a modern understanding of human dignity and its implications for hard political choices. He saw human beings as being fundamentally equal, sentient beings capable of experiencing pleasure and pain. Our natural sympathy should thus lead us to choose acts and rules that maximize the greatest pleasure and minimize pain for the greatest number. But, as an important feature of the proper understanding of long-run utility, he wanted to ensure that utility maximization included both the freedom to lead unrestricted lives that did not harm others and the realization that not all pleasures and pains were equal. Some were higher, some lower; some expressed human creativity, others did not: poetry was better than pushpin (a nineteenth-century version of "gameboy").

Politically, two principles followed from his application of utilitarian ethics. The first was maximum equal liberty, allowing each adult to develop his or her own potentiality on the view that each individual was the best judge of what was and was not in his or her interest, so long, however, as no one interfered with the equal liberty of others. The second was representative government. To maximize the utility value of collective decisions it would be best to give decisive weight to the preferences of the majority, as represented by knowledgeable politicians.

Internationally, one might think that these principles would give rise to a commitment to an international version of the U.S. Constitution's "Guarantee Clause" (Art. 4, sec. 4), in which each state is guaranteed (required to have) a republican form of government, and the Fourteenth Amendment, in which all states are required to provide equal protection of the laws to all citizens. But for Mill this was not so. Instead, he argues against that kind of a global guarantee, drawing thereby an important line between domestic and international justice.

---

[4] Although liberal principles of human rights and support for democratic institutions provide the most clearly articulated principles of intervention and nonintervention, other schools of international ethics have addressed the issue. In many respects the principles of nonintervention can be seen as a code or summary of the sort of principles that a cautious realist would most want to have govern the international system. But with frequent justifications for preventive war, principles of nonintervention seem to have a thin foundation in realist ethics, which finds them valuable only to the extent they are useful from a national point of view.

Nonintervention
Arguments against intervention have taken the form of both direct principles and indirect, or procedural, considerations. Like many liberals, Mill
dismissed without much attention realist arguments in favor of intervention to promote national security, prestige, or profits. However prevalent
those motives have been in history, they lack moral significance, as for that
matter would justifications associated with intervening to promote an idea
or ideology.

First, the most important *direct* consideration for the liberals was that
nonintervention reflected and protected human dignity (or rights, though
Mill disliked the word). Nonintervention could enable citizens to determine their own way of life without outside interference. If democratic
rights and liberal freedoms were to mean something, they had to be
worked out among those who shared them and were making them through
their own participation. Kant's "Perpetual Peace" (1970, written in 1795)
had earlier made a strong case for respecting the right of nonintervention
because it afforded a polity the necessary territorial space and political
independence in which free and equal citizens could work out what their
own way of life would be.[5] For Mill, intervention undermined the authenticity of domestic struggles for liberty. A free government achieved by
means of intervention would not be authentic or self-determining but
determined by others and not one that local citizens had themselves
defined through their own actions. (Good governance was more like poetry
than pushpin.)

John Stuart Mill provided a second powerful direct argument for nonintervention, one focusing on likely consequences, when he explained in his
famous 1859 essay on nonintervention that it would be a great mistake to
export freedom to a foreign people that was not in a position to win it on
its own (Mill 1973). A people given freedom by a foreign intervention
would not, he argued, be able to hold on to it. It is only by winning and
holding on to freedom through local effort that one acquired a true sense
of its value. Moreover, it was only by winning freedom that one acquired
the political capacities to defend it adequately against threats both at home
and abroad. The struggle mobilized citizens into what could become a
national army and mobilized as well a capacity and willingness to tax
themselves for public purposes.

If, however, a liberal government were to be introduced into a foreign
society, in the "knapsack," so to speak, of a conquering liberal army, the
local liberals placed in power would find themselves immediately in a
difficult situation. Not having been able to win political power on their

---

[5] See Immanuel Kant, "Perpetual Peace" (1970), particularly the preliminary articles of
a perpetual peace in which he spells out the rights of nonintervention that he hopes will hold
among all states even in the state of war. These rights take on an absolute character within
the pacific union of republican states.

own, they would have few domestic supporters and many nonliberal domestic enemies. One of three different things would then occur:

1. The liberals would begin to rule as did previous governments, that is, to repress their opposition. The intervention would have done no good; it simply would have created another oppressive government.
2. The society would simply collapse in an ensuing civil war. Intervention, therefore, would have produced not freedom and progress, but a civil war with all its attendant violence.
3. The intervenors would continually have to send in foreign support. Rather than having set up a free government, one that reflected the participation of the citizens of the state, the intervention would have set up a puppet government, one that reflected the will and interests of the intervening, the truly sovereign state.[6]

A third argument against intervention was difficulties of transparency. Historically, it has proven difficult to identify authentic "freedom fighters." Particular national regimes of liberty and oppression are difficult for foreigners to "unpack," reflecting, sometimes, complicated historical compromises and contracts of a Burkean sort among the dead, the living, and the yet to be born. Michael Walzer, as did Mill, acknowledges that sovereignty and nonintervention ultimately depend upon consent. If the people welcome an intervention or refuse to resist, something less than aggression has occurred (Walzer 1985, 221 n. 7). But we cannot make those judgments reliably in advance. We should assume, he suggests, that foreigners will be resisted, that nationals will protect their state from foreign aggression. For even if the state is not just, it is their state, not ours. We have no standing to decide what their state should be. We do not happen to be engaged full time, as they are, in the national historical project of creating it. All the injustices, therefore, which do justify a domestic revolution do not always justify a foreign intervention. Following Mill, Walzer says that domestic revolutions need to be left to domestic citizens. Foreign interventions to achieve a domestic revolution are likely over the long run to be ineffective and cause more harm than they eliminate. It is for these reasons that we should want to respect locally negotiated amnesties even when perpetrators of crimes are known, as in South Africa or El Salvador. The amnesty can represent the price of peace or the difficulty of finding local clean hands.

Fourth, the necessary "dirty hands" of violent means often become "dangerous hands" in international interventions. International history is rife with interventions justified by high-sounding principles – ending the slave trade or suttee or introducing law and order and civilized behavior – turning into self-serving, imperialist "rescues" in which the intervenor

---

[6] A good discussion of consequentialist issues can be found in Ellis (1992).

stays to profit and control. Requiring that the intervenor be impartial, looking for something more than a unilateral decision, and respecting the multilateral processes of international law are thus important procedural considerations in weighing the justice of an intervention.

Fifth, interventions can violate the principles of proportionality and last resort. Villages should not be destroyed in order to be saved and negotiations should be tried before dictatorial means are adopted.

Indirect reasons for nonintervention, those bearing on other valued ends, have also been important constraints. Interventions foster militarism and expend resources needed for other national and international goals. But key among the indirect considerations are the rules of international law among sovereign civilized states which prohibit intervention and embody the value of coordination and consensual legitimacy. Rules, any rules, have a value in themselves by helping to avoid unintended clashes and their consequences to human life. They serve as focal points for coordination – rules of the road, such as "drive on the right." Without some rule, unsought strife would ensue. International laws, moreover, were painstakingly achieved by compromises among diverse moralities. The mere process of achieving consent made them legitimate. They were agreed upon and *pacta sunt servanda* (Nardin 1983; Franck 1995).

Intervention
Liberal arguments supporting intervention fall into various camps. Some liberals, strong cosmopolitans, hold that the rights of cosmopolitan freedom are valuable everywhere for all people. Any violation of them should be resisted whenever and wherever it occurs, provided that we can do so proportionally – without causing more harm than we seek to avoid (Arkes 1986, chaps. 11–13; Luban 1980).[7] But others take more seriously the full range of Kantian and Millian grounds for nonintervention and think that they must be respected or addressed. Some give reasons to override the nonintervention principle; others, to disregard the principle. In the first, the principles in favor of nonintervention still hold, but other considerations seem more important. In the second, the principles do not apply to the particular case.

In "A Few Words on Nonintervention" J. S. Mill argued that there were three good reasons to *override* what should be the usual prohibition against intervention. In these arguments the considerations against intervention are present, but other more important values trump them. Although interventions usually do more harm than good, Mill noted three, now unusual exceptions.

In a system-wide, internationalized civil war such as that waged

---

[7] Transformed in a political and expediential way, these views relate to those adopted by the Reagan administration in its defense of global "freedom fighters." See a valuable discussion of this by Charles Beitz (1988).

between Protestantism and Catholicism in the sixteenth century, or liberalism and despotism in Mill's own time, nonintervention can neglect vital transnational sources of national security. If all of each group truly aligns with its fellows overseas irrespective of interstate borders, and if others are intervening in support of their faction, then not intervening in support of yours is dangerous. While this argument is logical on its face, its historical accuracy is questionable. Even in the polarizing religious wars of the sixteenth and seventeenth centuries, Elizabeth the Great's best admiral was a Catholic, and France, under Cardinal Richelieu, wisely aligned with the Protestant principalities that would support her.

Second, following a just war, the victor, rather than halting his armed forces at the restored border, can intervene to remove a "perpetual" or a standing "menace" to peace, whether a person or a regime. Mill's reference was sending Napoleon to Elba (and then, as if to prove the point, further away, to St. Helena). Reconstruction in the U.S. South drew inspiration from these considerations. In our time, the reference is de-Nazification in Germany following World War Two and the breaking up of the *zaibatsu* in Japan. Some hoped that drawing Saddam Hussein's chemical, biological, and nuclear fangs would have a similar effect.

Most pertinently for today's debates on intervention, Mill argues that some civil wars become so protracted and so seemingly irresolvable by local struggle that a common sense of humanity and sympathy for the suffering of the noncombatant population calls for an outside intervention to halt the fighting in order to see if some negotiated solution might be achieved under the aegis of foreign arms. Mill here cites the at least partial success of outsiders in calling a halt to and helping settle the protracted mid-century Portuguese civil war and the Greek-Turkish conflict. Outsiders can call for separation or reconciliation in these circumstances. Greece was thus separated from Turkey and Belgium from Holland in 1830 following the forceful mediation of two liberal statesmen, Palmerston and Guizot. Later, impartial mediation imposed power-sharing reconciliation on Portugal in the 1850s, which produced two generations of peace among the contesting factions under the rule of King Pedro.

There are other injustices that justify us in *disregarding* the prohibition against intervention, for sometimes the national self-determination that nonintervention is designed to protect and the harms that nonintervention tries to avoid are so clearly undermined by the domestic oppression and suffering that borders permit that nonintervention is not relevant. In these circumstances, the local government in effect loses its claim to singular national authenticity. Together with, and building on, John Stuart Mill's classic essay, Michael Walzer offers us three cases where an intervention serves the underlying purposes that nonintervention was designed to uphold (Walzer 1977, 106–8, 339–42).

The first is when too many nations contest one piece of territory. When an imperial government opposes the independence of a subordinate nation or when there are two distinct peoples, one attempting to crush the other, then national self-determination cannot be a reason to shun intervention. What is missing is the "one" nation. Here foreigners can intervene to help the liberation of the oppressed people, once that people has demonstrated through its own "arduous struggle" that it truly is another nation. Then decolonization is the principle that should rule, allowing a people to form its own destiny. One model of this might be the American Revolution against Britain; another in Mill's time was the 1848–1849 Hungarian rebellion against Austria; and in our time the many anticolonial movements in Africa and Asia that quickly won recognition and, in a few cases, support from the international community.

The second instance in which the principle against intervention should be disregarded is counterintervention in a civil war. A civil war should be left to the combatants. When conflicting factions of one people are struggling to define what sort of society and government should rule, only that struggle should decide the outcomes – not foreigners. But when an external power intervenes on behalf of one of the participants in a civil war, then another foreign power can counterintervene to balance the first intervention. This second intervention serves the purposes of self-determination, which the first intervention sought to undermine. Even if, Mill argued, the Hungarian rebellion were not clearly a national rebellion against "a foreign yoke," it was clearly the case that Russia should not have intervened to assist Austria in its suppression. By doing so, St. Petersburg gave others a right to counterintervene.

Third, one can intervene for humanitarian purposes – to halt what appears to be a gross violation of the rights to survival of a population. When we see a pattern of massacres, the development of a campaign of genocide, the institutionalization of slavery – violations that are so horrendous that in the classical phrase they "shock the conscience of mankind" – one has good ground to question whether there is any national connection between the population and the state that is so brutally oppressing it. Under those circumstances, outsiders can intervene. But the intervenor should have a morally defensible motive and share the purpose of ending the slaughter and establishing a self-determining people. (Self-serving interventions promote imperialism.) Furthermore, intervenors should act only as a "last resort," after exploring peaceful resolution. They should then act only when it is clear that they will save more lives than the intervention itself will almost inevitably wind up costing, and even then with minimum necessary force. It makes no moral sense to rescue a village and start World War Three or destroy a village in order to save it. Thus, even though one often finds humanitarian intervention abused, Michael Walzer has suggested that a reasonable case can be made that the Indian invasion of East Pakistan in 1971, designed to save the people of what became

Bangladesh from the massacre that was being inflicted upon them by their own government (headquartered in West Pakistan), is a case of legitimate humanitarian intervention. It allowed the people of East Pakistan to survive and form their own state.

Today, Mill's most controversial case would be benign colonialism. His principles of nonintervention only hold among "civilized" nations. "Uncivilized" peoples, among whom Mill dumps most of Africa, Asia, and Latin America, are not fit for the principle of nonintervention. Like Oude (in India), they suffer four debilitating infirmities – despotism, anarchy, amoral presentism, and familism – that make them incapable of self-determination. The people are imposed upon by a "despot . . . so oppressive and extortionate as to devastate the country." Despotism long endured has produced "such a state of nerveless imbecility that everyone subject to their will, who had not the means of defending himself by his own armed followers, was the prey of anybody who had a band of ruffians in his pay." The people, as a result, deteriorate into amoral relations in which the present overwhelms the future and no contracts can be relied upon. Moral duties extend no further than the family; national or civic identity is altogether absent.

In these circumstances the best that can happen for the population is a benign colonialism. Normal relations cannot be maintained in such an anarchic and lawless environment. The most a well-intentioned foreigner owes these peoples is paternal education. For like children or lunatics, they can benefit from nothing else.

It is important to note that Mill advocates neither exploitation nor racialist domination. He applies the same reasoning to once primitive northern Europeans who benefited from the imperial rule imposed by civilized Romans. The duties of paternal care, moreover, are real, precluding oppression and exploitation and requiring care and education designed to one day fit the colonized people for independent national existence. Nonetheless, the argument also rests on wild (wildly perverse?) readings of the history and culture of Africa and Asia and Latin America. Anarchy and despotic oppression did afflict many of the peoples in these regions, but ancient cultures embodying deep senses of social obligation made nonsense of presentism and familism.

Shorn of its cultural "Orientalism," Mill's argument for trusteeship addresses one serious gap in our strategies of humanitarian assistance: the devastations that cannot be readily redressed by a quick intervention designed to liberate an oppressed people from the clutches of foreign oppression or a domestic despot. But how does one prevent benign trusteeship from becoming malign imperialism, particularly when one recalls the flowery words and humanitarian intentions that accompanied the conquerors of Africa? How far is it from the Anti-Slavery Campaign and the Aborigine Rights Protection Society to King Leopold's Congo and Joseph Conrad's "Heart of Darkness"?

The New Interventionism

Two developments in the 1990s have contributed to a new sense of when and how to intervene. The first is a revived role for international multilateral authorization, and the second is a new set of peacekeeping strategies that mix consent and coercion. The two are connected. The second would not be seen as legitimate or in fact be effective without genuine multilateral engagement; the new authorization for multilateral intervention would not be tolerated as legitimate unless it could be done less intrusively than direct intervention.

Multilateral Revival

In the early 1990s, with the end of the Cold War, the U.N. agenda for peace and security rapidly expanded. At the request of the U.N. Security Council Summit of January 1992, Secretary-General Boutros Boutros-Ghali prepared the conceptual foundations of an ambitious U.N. role in peace and security for both international and domestic disputes in his seminal report, *An Agenda for Peace* (1992).[8]

At the same time, the Security Council expanded the operational meaning of the U.N. Charter Article 2(7) authority to override domestic sovereignty when (Article 39) "threats to peace, breaches of the peace, acts of aggression" arose. The new interpretation of U.N. jurisdiction soon appeared to include a wide range of what were once seen as infringements of traditional sovereignty. Indeed, the phrase beginning "threats to peace" came to mean severe domestic violations of human rights, civil wars, humanitarian emergencies, and almost whatever a Security Council majority (absent a Permanent Member veto) said it was.[9]

These two developments had roots in the striking changes in the international system that emerged at the end of the Cold War. A new spirit of multilateral cooperation from the U.S.S.R., beginning with President Gorbachev's reforms and continuing under President Yeltsin's rule of Russia, met a new spirit of tolerance from the United States. Together the two former adversaries broke the forty-year gridlock in the U.N. Security Council. Post–Cold War cooperation meant that the Security Council was now functioning as the global guardian of peace and security. The Security Council had now become what it was supposed to have been since 1945 – the continuation, incorporated in the design of the U.N. Charter, of the

---

[8] Between 1987 and 1994, the Security Council quadrupled the number of resolutions it issued, tripled the peacekeeping operations it authorized, and increased from one to seven per year the number of economic sanctions it imposed. Military forces deployed in peacekeeping operations increased from fewer than 10,000 to more than 70,000. The annual peacekeeping budget accordingly skyrocketed from $230 million to $3.6 billion in the same period, thus reaching about three times the regular U.N. operating budget of $1.2 billion. See United Nations (1995, 4).

[9] For a discussion of the traditional Cold War interpretations of the phrase, see Goodrich, Hambro, and Simons (1969, 293–300).

World War Two Grand Alliance. At the same time, there also emerged an ideological community of democratic values that gave specific content to the cooperative initiatives of these years. The Vienna Conference on Human Rights (1993) and President Gorbachev's plea before the General Assembly for "Global Human Values" (A/43/PV72) signified that human rights were no longer merely a Western, but rather a global, principle of good governance (United Nations 1993).

The international legal prohibitions against intervention were more relevant than ever given the demands for national dignity made by the newly independent states of both the Third World and the former Second World. But the rules as to what constitutes intervention and what constitutes international protection of basic human rights shifted as well. Sovereignty was redefined to incorporate a global interest in human rights protection. A newly functioning United Nations, moreover, was seen to be a legitimate agent to decide when sovereignty was and was not violated.

The revival of the U.N. Security Council led to a reaffirmation after years of Cold War neglect of the U.N. Charter's Article 2(7) affirming nonintervention, except as mandated by the Security Council under Chapter VII. The United Nations then claimed a "cleaner hands" monopoly on legitimate intervention. Although the letter of the charter prohibited U.N. authorizations of force other than as a response to threats or breaches of "international" peace, the Genocide Convention and the record of condemnation of colonialism and apartheid opened an informally legitimate basis for involvement in domestic conflict. The Security Council's practice thus broadened the traditional reasons for intervention, including aspects of domestic political oppression short of massacre and human suffering associated with economic misfeasance – the so-called "failed states" and the *droit d'ingerence* (Damrosch 1993; Helman and Ratner 1992–93). Building on new interpretations advanced during the Cold War that made, for example, apartheid a matter for international sanction, the United Nations addressed the starvation of the Somali people when it became clear that its government was incapable of doing so. (In this case, however, the traditional criterion of "international" threats was also invoked – Somali refugees spreading across international borders – in order to justify forcible intervention under Chapter VII.) The Security Council also demanded international humanitarian access to vulnerable populations, insisting, for example, that humanitarian assistance be allowed to reach the people affected in Yugoslavia and in Iraq.

Regions differed on the first dimension of operational sovereignty. The Association of Southeast Asian Nations (ASEAN) remained a bastion of strict sovereignty, and nonintervention is the norm. Although Cambodia's and Burma's acceptances into ASEAN were delayed by their human rights record and instability, they were both eventually accepted. The Organization of African Unity (OAU), on the other hand, has defined standards of (1990) "Good Governance" that included democracy and declared

(3 July 1993) that internal disputes are matters of regional concern. And, more strikingly, the Organization of American States, or OAS (in Res. 1080 and in the "Santiago Commitment of 1991") has declared coups against democracy illegitimate and has adopted economic sanctions against coups in Haiti and Peru. The European Union makes democracy an element in the criteria it demands for consideration in membership.

It was also important that the "international community" had a newly legitimate means of expressing its collective will on an internationally impartial basis. The Security Council lays claim to being the equivalent of a "global jury" (Farer 1993) representing not merely the individual states of which it was composed but also a collective will and voice of the "international community." The Security Council included five permanent members (the United States, Russia, France, the United Kingdom, and the People's Republic of China) and ten nonpermanent members, always including members from Asia, Africa, and Latin America. Its authorization for an intervention required the affirmative vote of nine states, including no negative votes from the five permanent members and four positive votes from the smaller countries. Such a vote would have to represent all major ethnic groups and religions, large and small countries, capitalist and socialist economies, and democratic and nondemocratic polities. If the mandated operation is directed by the United Nations, and if troops and funding are required, many other troop-contributing states will be needed and they can say no in practice. The combination makes for a genuinely international impartial intervention – "cleaner hands."

Multidimensional Peace Operations

Increasingly, legitimate authorization would have little moral significance were it not able to take advantage of considerably better strategy. One important reason for rejecting intervention was that it did harm. It failed to support self-determination and it either caused or failed to correct devastation. New developments in multidimensional peacekeeping suggest that U.N. involvement has a better record, particularly when it mixes consent with coercion and exploits new strategies for enhancing consent and establishing a sustainable, self-determining peace.

The United Nations has not been successful in classical armed interventions authorized under Chapter VII of the U.N. Charter, as in Somalia or as in parts of the UNPROFOR mandate in the former Yugoslavia. There the United Nations, as have unilateral interventions when seizing sovereignty, met with resistance and either inflicted excess casualties (Somalia) or failed to provide adequate protection (Bosnia). Elsewhere the record has been much better. Taking a substantial step beyond "first generation" operations in which the United Nations monitored a truce (Cyprus), and keeping a significant step short of the third generation "peace enforcing" operations in which the United Nations used force to impose a peace

(Somalia), "second generation" *multidimensional operations* have been based on consent of the parties. But the nature of and purposes for which consent has been granted are qualitatively different from those of traditional peacekeeping. In these operations, the United Nations is typically involved in implementing peace agreements that go to the roots of the conflict, helping to build a long-term foundation for stable, legitimate government. As Secretary-General Boutros-Ghali observed in *An Agenda for Peace*, "peace-making and peace-keeping operations, to be truly successful, must come to include comprehensive efforts to identify and support structures which will tend to consolidate peace. . . . [T]hese may include disarming the previously warring parties and the restoration of order, the custody and possible destruction of weapons, repatriating refugees, advisory and training support for security personnel, monitoring elections, advancing efforts to protect human rights, reforming or strengthening governmental institutions and promoting formal and informal processes of political participation" (1992, p. 32, para. 55).

UNTAC in Cambodia, for example, was based on the consent of the parties, as expressed in the Paris Agreements, but it induced (that is, intervened in) key aspects of that consent and moved beyond monitoring the actions of the parties to the establishment of a Transitional Authority that actually implemented directly crucial components of the mandate and substituted for Cambodian sovereignty in key areas. Moreover, its scale was vastly larger than all but the enforcement mandates and it found itself operating without the continuous (in the case of the Khmer Rouge) or complete (in the case of the other factions) cooperation of the factions.

The United Nations has a commendable record of success in second generation, multidimensional peace operations as diverse as those in Namibia (UNTAG), El Salvador (ONUSAL), Cambodia (UNTAC),[10] Mozambique (ONUMOZ), and Eastern Slavonia, Croatia (UNTAES). The U.N. role in helping settle those conflicts has been fourfold. It served as a *peacemaker* facilitating a peace treaty among the parties; as a *peacekeeper* monitoring the cantonment and demobilization of military forces, resettling refugees, and supervising transitional civilian authorities; as a *peace-builder* monitoring and, in some cases, organizing the implementation of human rights, national democratic elections, and economic rehabilitation; and in the last resort and in a discrete, carefully constrained, and impartial manner as a *peace-enforcer*.

Though nonenforcing and consent-based, these operations are far from harmonious and noninterventionary. Consent is not a simple "bright line"

---

[10] Before the United Nations became involved, during the Cold War when action by the Security Council was stymied by the lack of consensus among its five permanent members, the international community allowed Cambodia to suffer an auto-genocide and El Salvador a brutal civil war. Indeed the great powers were involved in supporting factions who inflicted some of the worst aspects of the violence the two countries suffered. We should keep this in mind when we consider the United Nations' difficulties in Somalia and Bosnia.

demarcating the safe and acceptable from the dangerous and illegitimate. Each function has required an enhanced form of interventionist consent to authorize the United Nations to help make a peace in the contentious environment of civil strife.

Peacemaking. Achieving a peace treaty has often required heavy persuasion (again a form of intervention) by outside actors. In Cambodia, the U.S.S.R. and China are said to have let their respective clients in Phnom Penh and the Khmer Rouge know that ongoing levels of financial and military support would not be forthcoming if they resisted the terms of a peace treaty that their patrons found acceptable. Peace treaties may themselves depend on prior sanctions, threats of sanctions, or loss of aid, imposed by the international community.[11]

The construction of an agreed peace is more than worth the effort. The process of negotiation among the contending factions can discover the acceptable parameters of peace that are particular to the conflict. Going beyond an agreed truce or disarmament, a comprehensive peace treaty addresses grievances and establishes new institutions that test the true willingness of the parties to reconcile. Peace negotiations, furthermore, can mobilize the support of local factions and of the international community in support of implementing the peace. And a negotiated peace treaty can establish new entities committed to furthering peacekeeping and peace-building.[12]

In the 1990s, the United Nations developed a set of crucially important innovations that help manage the making of peace on a consensual basis. First among them is the diplomatic device that has come to be called the "friends of the secretary-general." This brings together multinational leverage for U.N. diplomacy to help make and manage peace. Composed of ad hoc, informal, multilateral diplomatic mechanisms that join together states in support of initiatives of the secretary-general, it legitimates with the stamp of U.N. approval and supervision the pressures interested states can bring to bear to further the purposes of peace and the United Nations.

Playing a crucial role in the secretary-general's peacemaking and preventive diplomacy functions, these groupings serve four key functions. First, the limited influence of the secretary-general can be leveraged, multiplied and complemented, by the "friends." The United Nations'

[11] The Governor's Island Accord, which produced the first (ineffective) settlement of the Haitian conflict, resulted from economic sanctions on arms and oil imposed by the United Nations and OAS on Haiti as a whole. Sanctions targeted on the perpetrators (the military elite and their supporters) might have been much more effective (and were later imposed in the summer of 1994). Restrictions on the overseas private bank accounts and air travel of the ruling elite would both have been more just and perhaps more effective than general economic sanctions whose impact was most severe on the most vulnerable and from which the elite may actually have benefited.

[12] For a wide-ranging collection of recent experience in U.N. and other peacemaking, see Crocker, Hampson, and Aall (1999).

scarce attention and even scarcer resources can be supplemented by the diplomacy, finances, and clout of powerful, interested actors. The second value is legitimization. The very act of constituting themselves as a group, with the formal support of the secretary-general, lends legitimacy to the diplomatic activities of interested states that they might not otherwise have.[13] It allows for constructive diplomacy when accusations of special and particular national interest could taint bilateral efforts. The third value is coordination. The friends mechanism provides transparency among the interested external parties, assuring them that they are all working for the same purposes, and when they are doing so, allowing them to pursue a division of labor that enhances their joint effort. It ensures that diplomats are not working at cross purposes because they regularly meet and inform each other of their activities and encourage each other to undertake special tasks. And fourth, the friends mechanism provides a politically balanced approach to the resolution of civil wars through negotiation. It often turns out that one particular "friend" can associate with one faction just as another associates with a second. In the Cambodian peace process, China back-stopped the Khmer Rouge, just as France did Prince Sihanouk and Russia (with Vietnam) did the State of Cambodia. The friends open more flexible channels of communication than a single U.N. mediator can provide. They also advise and guide the U.N. intermediaries in the peace-keeping and peacebuilding discussed below, although the process tends to work best when they support rather than move out in front of the United Nations.

Peacekeeping. Even consent-based peace agreements fall apart. In the circumstances of partisan violence and "failed states," agreements tend to be fluid. In the new civil conflicts, parties cannot force policy on their followers and often lack the capacity or will to maintain a difficult process of reconciliation leading to a reestablishment of national sovereignty (Roberts 1993; Durch 1993a; Berdal 1993; Weiss 1993; Hampson 1996).

The United Nations thus developed a flexible political strategy to win and keep popular support and create (not just enjoy) the support of local forces of order. In a failed state, as was the case in a society subject to colonial rule, what is most often missing is modern organization. This was what colonial metropoles supplied, in their own self-interest, as they mobilized local resources to combat local opposition. Over the longer run, indigenous forces such as the political Zamindars and the King's Own African Rifles and other locally recruited military battalions (not metropolitan troops) were the forces that made imperial rule effective, that preserved a balance of local power in favor of metropolitan influence – and

---

[13] For a good discussion of the United Nations', and especially the secretary-general's, potential strength as a diplomatic legitimater, see Picco (1994). The "friends" mechanism seems to answer many of the objections to U.N. mediation expressed by Touval (1994).

that kept it cheap. Drawing on the history of imperial institution building (while avoiding imperial exploitation and coercion), an effective and affordable strategy for U.N. peace operations faced a greater challenge. It needed to discover ways to generate *voluntary* cooperation from divided local political actors and mobilize existing local resources for *locally legitimate*, collective purposes.[14] And it had to do so *rapidly*.

Recent peacekeeping experience has suggested a second peacekeeping innovation: an ad hoc, semisovereign mechanism designed to address those new challenges by dynamically managing a peace process and mobilizing local cooperation. Examples of these ad hoc semisovereign mechanisms include the Supreme National Council (SNC) in Cambodia and the Commission on the Peace (COPAZ) in El Salvador.

It has often been remarked that Chapter VI presents the United Nations with too little authority and Chapter VII offers too much; and that Chapter VI is associated with too little use of force and Chapter VII with too much. The value of these ad hoc, semisovereign artificial bodies is that they provide a potentially powerful, political means of encouraging and influencing the shape of consent. Indeed, these semisovereign artificial bodies can help contain the erosion of consent and even manufacture it where it is missing. Created by a peace treaty, they permit the temporary consensus of the parties to be formally incorporated in an institution with regular consultation and even, as in the Cambodian Supreme National Council, a semiautonomous sovereign will. These mechanisms have proven crucial in a number of recent U.N. missions. They can represent the once warring parties and act in the name of a preponderance of the "nation" without the continuous or complete consent of all the factions. They can both build political support and adjust – in a legitimate way, with the consent of the parties – the mandate in order to respond to unanticipated changes in local circumstances.

In Cambodia, the SNC, constructed by the Paris Peace Agreements, "enshrined" Cambodian sovereignty. The council, composed of the four factions and chaired by Prince Sihanouk, offered a chance for these parties to consult together on a regular basis and endorse the peace process. It also lent special authority to Prince Sihanouk, who was authorized to act if the SNC failed to achieve a consensus. Beyond that, it empowered the United Nations, represented by Special Representative Yasushi Akashi, to act in the

---

[14] It is interesting in this light to note that some key, early U.N. experts in peacekeeping were eminent decolonization experts, deeply familiar with the politics of colonial rule, as was Ralph Bunche from the U.N. Trusteeship Division. See Urquhart (1993, chapter 5) and, for a discussion of imperial strategy, Doyle (1986, chapter 12). But there are key differences. Empires were governed primarily in the interests of the metropole; U.N. peace operations explicitly promote the interests of the host country. And what made imperial strategy work was the possibility of coercive violence, the over-the-horizon gunboats that could be and often were offshore. That, for good and bad, is what the United Nations usually lacks, unless it calls in the enforcement capacity of the major powers. Rehabilitation assistance is sometimes an effective carrot, but not the equivalent of the Royal Navy.

interests of the peace process, if Sihanouk failed to do so. Artificially created, the SNC thus established a semisovereign legal personality designed to be responsive to the general interests of Cambodia (even when a complete consensus was lacking among all the factions) *and* to the authority of the U.N. special representative. Acting in the name of Cambodia – as a step in the implementation of the Paris Agreements – the SNC acceded to all the major human rights conventions (including the first and second Covenants on Human Rights) and it authorized the trade embargo against illegal exports of logs and gems. The SNC was the forum that endorsed the protracted and sensitive negotiations over the franchise. It legitimated the enforcement of certain elements of the peace, absent the unanimous consent of the parties and without the necessity of a contentious debate at the Security Council. It could have exercised greater authority, perhaps even designing an acceptable scheme for rehabilitation, if Prince Sihanouk or Mr. Akashi had been both willing and able to lead it in that direction.

COPAZ, in El Salvador, played a related, although much less authoritative, role in the Salvadoran peace process, serving as a forum for consultation among the Frabundo Marti National Liberation Front (FMLN), the government, and the other political parties. Designed to monitor and establish a forum for the participation of civilian society in the peace process, it was the only political institution that embodied the full scope of Salvadoran politics, the only institution that could legitimately speak for "El Salvador." That its role in the peace process proved to be minimal was unfortunate. And in Somalia, the "Transitional National Council" was designed to perform a similar function, but its failure to obtain support from the leading actors was perhaps the single most disturbing problem in the peacekeeping process, one that seriously eroded the attempt to create a peace.

Peacebuilding. Multidimensional, second generation peacekeeping pierces the shell of national autonomy by bringing international involvement to areas long thought to be the exclusive domain of domestic jurisdiction. If a peacekeeping operation is to leave behind a legitimate and independently viable political sovereign, it must help transform the political landscape by building a new basis for domestic peace.

Traditional strategies of conflict resolution, when successful, were designed to resolve a dispute between conflicting parties. Successful resolution could be measured by (1) the stated reconciliation of the parties; (2) the duration of the reconciliation; and (3) changes in the way parties behaved toward each other.[15] But successful contemporary peacebuilding does not merely change behavior; more importantly, it transforms identities and institutional context. More than reforming play in an old game, it changes the game.

---

[15] For a good account of traditional views of reconciliation, see A. B. Fetherston (1994, 11), discussing a paper by Marc Ross.

This is the grand strategy General Sanderson invoked when he spoke of forging an alliance with the Cambodian people, bypassing the factions. Reginald Austin, electoral chief of UNTAC, probed the same issue when he asked what the "true objectives" of UNTAC are: "Is it a political operation seeking a solution to the immediate problem of an armed conflict by all means possible? Or does it have a wider objective: to implant democracy, change values and establish a new pattern of governance based on multi-partism and free and fair elections?" (Austin 1993).

UNTAC helped create new actors on the Cambodian political scene: the electors, a fledgling civil society, a free press, a continuing international and transnational presence. The Cambodian voters gave Prince Ranariddh institutional power, and the Khmer Rouge was transformed from an internationally recognized claimant on Cambodian sovereignty to a domestic guerrilla insurgency. The peacebuilding process, particularly the election, became the politically tolerable *substitute* for the inability of the factions to reconcile their conflicts.

The U.N. role, mandated by these complex agreements rather than Chapter VII, included monitoring, substituting for, renovating, and, in some cases, helping to build the basic structures of the state. The United Nations has been called in to demobilize and sometimes to restructure and reform once warring armies; to monitor or to organize national elections; to promote human rights; to supervise public security and help create a new civilian police force; to control civil administration in order to establish a transitional politically neutral environment; to begin the economic rehabilitation of devastated countries; and, as in the case of Cambodia, to address directly the values of the citizens, with a view to promoting democratic education.

The parties to these agreements, in effect, consent to limitation of their sovereignty for the life of the U.N.-sponsored peace process. They do so because they need the help of the international community to achieve peace. But acceptance of U.N. involvement in implementing these agreements is less straightforward than, for example, consenting to observance of a cease-fire. Even when genuine consent is achieved, it is impossible to provide for every contingency in complex peace accords. Problems of interpretation arise, unforeseen gaps in the accords materialize, and circumstances change. The original consent, as the Salvadoran peace process suggests, can become open-ended and, in part, a gesture of faith that later problems can be worked out on a consensual basis. In the process, the international community, represented by the United Nations, exercises a monitoring pressure to encourage progress on the reform of the judiciary, the expansion of the electoral rolls, and the operation of a free press.

But authentic and firm consent in the aftermath of severe civil strife, such as that which Cambodia endured, is rare. The first clear implication has been the consequent importance of risk-spreading multidimensionality. When successful, the United Nations has designed in as many routes to peace – institutional reform, elections, international monitoring, economic rehabilitation – as the parties would tolerate.

Second, the international negotiators of a peace treaty and the U.N. designers of a mandate attempted to design in bargaining advantages for the U.N. authority. Even seemingly extraneous bargaining chips become useful as the spirit of cooperation erodes under the pressure of misunderstandings and separating interests. The United Nations counted upon the financial needs of the Cambodian factions to ensure their cooperation and designed an extensive rehabilitation component to guarantee steady rewards for cooperative behavior.[16] But the Khmer Rouge's access to illicit trade (with the apparent connivance of elements of the Thai military along the western border) eliminated this bargaining chip. And the suspicion of the dominant faction's (SOC, the "State of Cambodia") rivals prevented a full implementation of rehabilitation in the 80 percent of the country it controlled.

Third, the architects of the U.N. operation therefore also designed into the mandate as much independent implementation as the parties will agree to in the peace treaty. In Cambodia, the electoral component and refugee repatriation succeeded simply because they did not depend on the steady and continuous positive support of the four factions. Each component had an independent sphere of authority and organizational capacity that allowed it to proceed against everything short of the active military opposition of the factions. Civil administrative control and the cantonment of the factions failed because they relied on the continuous direct and positive cooperation of each of the factions. Each of the factions, at one time or another, had reason to expect that the balance of advantages was tilting against itself, and so refused to cooperate. A significant source of the success of the election was Radio UNTAC's ability to speak directly to the potential Cambodian voters, bypassing the propaganda of the four factions and invoking a new Cambodian actor, the voting citizen. But voters are only powerful for the five minutes it takes them to vote, if there is not an institutional mechanism to transfer democratic authority to bureaucratic practice.

In these circumstances, the United Nations tried to create new institutions to assure that votes in U.N.-sponsored elections "counted" more. The United Nations sought to leave behind a larger institutional legacy, drawing, for example, upon the existing personnel of domestic factions, adding

---

[16] This link was drawn explicitly by Deputy Secretary Lawrence Eagleburger at the Conference on the Reconstruction of Cambodia, on June 22, 1992, in Tokyo, where he proposed that assistance to Cambodia be "through the SNC – to areas controlled by those Cambodian parties cooperating with UNTAC in implementing the peace accords – and only to those parties which are so cooperating" (Press Release USUN-44-92, June 23, 1992). Disbursing the aid through the SNC, however, gave the Khmer Rouge a voice, as a member of the SNC, in the potential disbursement of the aid.

to them a portion of authentic independents, and training a new army, a new civil service, a new police force, and a new judiciary. These are the institutions that can be decisive in ensuring that the voices of the people, as represented by their elected representatives, shape the future.

Peace-enforcing. In this active process of consent-based intervention, the United Nations seeks to avoid the trade-offs between too much force and too little. The dangers of Chapter VII enforcement operations, whether in Somalia or Bosnia, leave many observers to think that it is extremely unlikely that troop-contributing countries will actually sign up for such operations. The risks are far more costly than the member states are willing to bear for humanitarian purposes. But when we look at Chapter VI operations, we see that consent by parties easily dissolves under the difficult processes of peace. U.N. operations in the midst of civil strife have often been rescued by the *discrete, impartial, but nonneutral use of force* by the United Nations, as were the operations in the Congo, when Katanga's secession was forcibly halted, and as was the operation in Namibia, when the Southwest Africa People's Organization's violation of the peace agreement was countered with the aid of South African forces.[17] But both nearly derailed the peace process by eroding local, regional, or global support. Given those options, the semisovereign artificial bodies offer the possibility of midcourse adjustments and "nationally" legitimated enforcement (should it be needed). It is important to stress that the U.N. use of force must have an impartial dimension. In Cambodia, for example, UNTAC – operating in full accord with the Paris Agreements – appealed to *all* the factions to protect the election.[18] The appeal was impartial and based upon the peace treaty to which all the parties had consented. (This is now called "strategic" as opposed to "tactical" consent in U.N. circles.) The result was distinctly not neutral among the parties as the armies (most effectively, SOC's army) that were cooperating with the peace plan pushed the Khmer Rouge back from the population centers. This subcontracted use of force permitted a safer vote with a larger – hence more legitimate – turnout in the last week of May 1993.[19] In 1996, in Eastern Slavonia, relying firmly on the consent of both President Milosevic and President Tudjman,

---

[17] For an account of the episode, see Durch (1993b).

[18] The People's Republic of China did not want to see the Khmer Rouge destroyed; the U.S.S.R. did not want to destroy SOC; and France and the United States did not want to destroy FUNCINPEC (the royalist party). Each of the great powers is a permanent member of the Security Council and has veto on U.N. activity. Similar diversity applies with regard to the aims of troop-contributing countries. The gamble is as noted above: an impartial intervention will elicit enough support from international actors and from the parties that multilateral assistance will be sufficient to establish a peace, especially when supplemented by impartial use of force as described in the paragraphs above.

[19] Conversation with Lt. Gen. John Sanderson (UNTAC Force Commander) at the Vienna Seminar, March 5, 1995. On May 28, 1993, I observed this in process around the small town of Stoung, which was surrounded by the Khmer Rouge. The Indonesian battal-

UNTAES successfully exercised its "executive authority" and employed overwhelming coercive force against the paramilitary gangs controlling the Djeletovici oil fields. Ad hoc semisovereign entities systematize and artificially (but usefully) enhance the process of consent in the direction of the promotion of peace while avoiding the dangers associated with attempts to implement an externally forced peace.

Conclusions

U.N. peacemaking strategies will not eliminate the formidable practical challenges of making, keeping, and building peace in the midst of protracted civil wars. Some crises will not find their solution. Nor does Security Council authorization solve the moral dilemmas of when and why intervention should be allowed. The best line between national autonomy and international responsibility is subject to continuous moral and political adjustment. But today as the United Nations is under attack in the United States and elsewhere, we should not neglect its authentic peacemaking potential. Employing strategies of enhanced consent, the United Nations can play a constructive role in the forging of peace and reconstruction in those areas of the world in need of assistance. Recent practice, moreover, has established jurisdiction over economic injustices when strong states set out to deliberately starve their own populations or where very weak states fail to meet minimum standards of human sustenance. Decent poor states need only the material and technical assistance of the international community to improve the welfare of their populations and thereby promote global economic justice. The United Nations has developed the interventionary tools to deal with indecent oppressive states and weak incapable states. The experience of the 1990s shows that it can offer a better prospect of effectively intervening against the first (as in Bosnia [after 1995] and Kosovo and East Timor) and assisting the second with long-term peacebuilding (as in Mozambique and Cambodia).

Reliance on the United Nations can help us avoid the dangerous and often counterproductive effects of unilateral armed imposition and the equally dangerous effects of untrammeled national autonomy in the midst of gross abuses of human rights. Fortunately, in the right circumstances, the United Nations can be the legitimating broker in the making, keeping, and building of a stable peace that takes the first steps toward the opening of political space for human rights, participatory communal self-expression, and basic human welfare.

Acknowledgments

I am grateful to the participants at the Bielefeld conference on global justice

ion established an inner perimeter around the town. The CPAF (SOC army) created an outer perimeter and trucked in voters from outlying villages.

240 MICHAEL W. DOYLE

and to Thomas Pogge, Andrew Hurrell, and Peter Singer for their comments on this chapter. I also extend my thanks to the Christian Johnson Endeavour Foundation, and to the Hewlett Foundation for a fellowship at the Center for Advanced Study in the Behavioral Sciences.

References

Arkes, Hadley. (1986). *First Things*. Princeton: Princeton University Press.
Austin, Reginald. (1993). "Electoral Report." Phnom Penh: UNTAC.
Beitz, Charles. (1988). "The Reagan Doctrine in Nicaragua." In *Problems of International Justice*, edited by Steven Luper-Foy, 182–95. Boulder: Westview.
Berdal, Mats. (1993). *Whither UN Peacekeeping?* Adelphi Paper 281. London: International Institute for Security Studies.
Boutros-Ghali, Boutros. (1992). *An Agenda for Peace*. New York: United Nations.
Crocker, Chester, Fen Hampson, and Pamela Aall, eds. (1999). *Herding Cats: Multiparty Mediation in a Complex World*. Washington: U.S. Institute of Peace.
Damrosch, Lori. (1993). "Introduction." In *Enforcing Restraint: Collective Intervention and Internal Conflicts*, edited by Lori Damrosch, 1–26. New York: Council on Foreign Relations Press.
Doyle, Michael. (1986). *Empires*. Ithaca: Cornell University Press.
Durch, William, ed. (1993a). *The Evolution of UN Peacekeeping*. New York: St. Martin's Press.
Durch, William. (1993b). "The UN Operation in the Congo." Chapter 19 of *The Evolution of UN Peacekeeping*, edited by William Durch. New York: St. Martin's Press.
Ellis, Anthony. (1992). "Utilitarianism and International Ethics." In *Traditions of International Ethics*, edited by Terry Nardin and David Mapel, 158–79. Cambridge: Cambridge University Press.
Farer, Thomas. (1993). "A Paradigm of Legitimate Intervention." In *Enforcing Restraint: Collective Intervention and Internal Conflicts*, edited by Lori Damrosch, 316–47. New York: Council on Foreign Relations Press.
Fetherston, A. B. (1994). "Putting the Peace Back into Peacekeeping." *International Peacekeeping*, 1:2, spring.
Franck, Thomas. (1995). *Fairness in International Law and Institutions*. Oxford: Clarendon Press.
Goodrich, Leland M., E. Hambro, and Anne Simons. (1969). *Charter of the United Nations*. New York: Columbia University Press.
Graham, Gerald. (1987). "The Justice of Intervention." *Review of International Studies*, 13, 133–46.
Hampson, Fen. (1996). *Nurturing Peace*. Washington: U.S. Institute of Peace.

Helman, Gerald, and Steve Ratner. (1992–93). "Saving Failed States."
    Foreign Policy, 89, 3–20.
Hurrell, Andrew. (2001). "Global Inequality and International
    Institutions." *Metaphilosophy*, 32:1/2.
Kant, Immanuel. (1970). "Perpetual Peace." (Written in 1795.) In *Kant's
    Political Writings*, edited by Hans Reiss and translated by H. B. Nisbet.
    Cambridge: Cambridge University Press.
Luban, David. (1980). "Just War and Human Rights." *Philosophy and
    Public Affairs*, 9:2, winter. Reprinted in *International Ethics*, edited by
    Charles Beitz (Princeton: Princeton University Press, 1985), 195–216.
Mill, John S. (1973). "A Few Words on Nonintervention." (Written in
    1859.) In *Essays on Politics and Culture*, edited by Gertrude
    Himmelfarb, 368–84. Gloucester: Peter Smith.
Nardin, Terry. (1983). *Law, Morality and the Relations of States*.
    Princeton: Princeton University Press.
O'Neill, Onora. (1986). *Faces of Hunger: An Essay on Poverty,
    Development and Justice*. London: Allen and Unwin.
Picco, Giandommenico. (1994). "The U.N. and the Use of Force." *Foreign
    Affairs*, 73:5, 14–18.
Pogge, Thomas. (2001). "Priorities of Global Justice." *Metaphilosophy*,
    32:1/2.
Roberts, Adam. (1993). "The United Nations and International Security."
    Survival, 35:2, summer.
Touval, Saadia. (1994). "Why the UN Fails." *Foreign Affairs*, 73:5, 44–57.
United Nations. (1993). *Vienna Declaration and Program of Action*.
    A/CONF. 157/23.
——. (1995). *Supplement to "An Agenda for Peace": Position Paper of
    the Secretary-General on the Occasion of the Fiftieth Anniversary of the
    United Nations*. A/50/60;S/1995/1, 3 January 1995.
Urquhart, Brian. (1993). *Ralph Bunche, An American Life*. New York:
    Norton.
Vincent, John. (1974). *Nonintervention and International Order*.
    Princeton: Princeton University Press.
Walzer, Michael. (1977). *Just and Unjust Wars*. New York: Basic Books.
——. (1985). "The Moral Standing of States: A Response to Four Critics."
    In *International Ethics*, edited by Charles Beitz. Princeton: Princeton
    University Press.
——. (1995). "The Politics of Rescue." *Dissent*, winter, 35–41.
Weiss, Thomas. (1993). "New Challenges for UN Military Operations."
    The Washington Quarterly, 16:1, winter.
Zanetti, Véronique. (2001). "Global Justice: Is Interventionism
    Desirable?" *Metaphilosophy*, 32:1/2.

15

FEDERAL INEQUALITY AMONG EQUALS:
A CONTRACTUALIST DEFENSE

ANDREAS FØLLESDAL

1. Introductory Remarks

Federal political orders often exhibit a conflict between the ideals of equality and political autonomy. Individuals in different subunits often enjoy systematically different standards of living conditions, partly as a result of the political powers enjoyed by these subunits. This chapter concerns the legitimacy of such federal inequality.

Federal arrangements may seem an attractive possibility for cosmopolitan political theorists criticized for requiring a world state. A typical response is that moral or normative cosmopolitanism – equal respect owed every affected person – does not entail institutional or legal cosmopolitanism in the form of a risky and unstable unitary world state (Beitz 1994; Pogge 1992a). Indeed, at least since Immanuel Kant, federal arrangements have been favored as being less prone to despotism, yet compatible with cosmopolitan principles of justice (Kant 1970). Still, much recent political philosophy has focused on principles for unitary states with a central sovereign (symptomatically, cf. Rawls 1993, xxii).

The federations of concern here are nonunitary political orders. The central and multiple regional loci of government enjoy final legislative or executive authority with regard to some functions, often by way of constitutionally enumerated powers (Riker 1993, 509).

While federal arrangements may be appealed to in theory, egalitarian cosmopolitans may not permit them in practice. Strictly egalitarian distributive requirements, for instance in the form of a global difference principle, would seem to require highly centralized legislative and executive powers to regulate all interaction with distributive implications. Indeed, one of James Madison's arguments for a federation of states was that it would prevent "an equal division of property, or for any improper or wicked project" (Madison 1961a). Hence we must ask whether cosmopolitan political theories can allow political autonomy of subunits to such an extent as to allow substantial economic and social inequality among citizens of different subunits. The question of concern to us is not whether some inegalitarian federal arrangements might be a second-best improvement within reach. For instance, some political autonomy over certain policy sectors is often accorded as part of political bargains among sovereign states in forming a federation. The issue is instead whether federal arrangements with substantial inequality may be normatively legitimate.

This question is of practical relevance for work on global justice, given the recent normative defenses of global egalitarianism in the form of a global difference principle (Beitz 1979, 152; Barry 1989, 187–89; Scanlon 1974, 202–3). Such standards may appear so counterintuitive to the voting populations of rich states that all appeals to global justice are dismissed as a slippery slope best avoided. The fear of what ideal justice requires may prevent smaller steps to alleviate the abysmal conditions of our nonideal world, be it in the form of transfers of goods and services or support for domestic and international institutional redesign. If principles of justice for federations impose less stringent demands, this reaction may be avoided, and powerful rich states may legitimately opt for federal responses.[1]

Similarly, fears of such egalitarian conclusions may keep richer states from institutionalized cooperation with poor states. Thus the club of rich states in the European Union (EU) is currently committed to regional funds and agricultural subsidies, thereby "demonstrating consistency and solidarity . . . between the Member States and between their peoples" (*Treaty on European Union* 1997, art. 1). These criteria and policies are subject to intense reformulation in preparation of the envisioned ascension of poor applicant states. An unmodified commitment to equalize living standards would entail politically unacceptable costs, since the applicant states' gross national product per capita is only 20 to 11 percent of the EU average. Admission of the applicant states and their citizens as equals would therefore create tensions unless economic inequality can be defended within the European political order.

This chapter explores how the claims individuals may have against institutions may legitimately depend on whether these are unitary or federal institutions. I shall defend the view that federal arrangements can legitimately engender somewhat unequal shares of benefits and burdens among citizens of different subunits. Individuals' interest in equal shares of income and wealth may be weighed against their interest in political control enjoyed by their subunit.

The remaining part of this introduction provides a brief sketch of some elements of liberal contractualism. Section 2 considers some answers to the question, Why equality? Section 3 explores, only to dismiss, a defense for inequality within federations on the basis that these arguments for

[1] It might be argued, for example, by extending Pogge's arguments concerning moral loopholes, that these conclusions provide illegitimate incentives for rich states to create federal solutions and maintain their unjust privileges (Pogge 1989, 253; Pogge 1992b). The issue addressed here concerns whether somewhat inegalitarian federal orders are illegitimate, not whether all attempts at creating federations are legitimate.

equality fail to apply. Section 4 considers liberal contractualist reasons for subunit autonomy. Section 5 identifies three reasons why the subunit poor may benefit from such subunit autonomy even at some economic cost. I argue that such reasons permit some deviations from the egalitarianism defended in section 2. The discussion also highlights the precarious role of states as the subunits of normatively defensible federal political orders.

First, I want to discuss some elements of liberal contractualism used as the normative bases for this exploration of federal inequality.

Many normative political theories have a normative egalitarian premise that all affected parties are worthy of equal concern and respect. This commitment to equal respect is cosmopolitan, in the sense of being universal: those on the inside of state and subunit borders have fundamentally the same moral standing as outsiders.

This is taken to mean that every affected individual's interests, suitably delineated, must be secured and furthered by the social institutions as a whole (Dworkin 1978). Contractualist theories hone this vague commitment by invoking the notion of hypothetical consent (O'Neill 1989; Habermas 1991, 235). The principles of legitimacy we should hold institutions to are those that the affected persons would unanimously consent to under conditions that secure and recognize their status as appropriately free and equal, thus manifesting "our respect for the reasonableness of others" (Macedo 1990). Such principles allow each of us to "justify one's actions to others on grounds they could not reasonably reject" (Scanlon 1982, 116; cf. Barry 1989, 8). The specific conditions, and the significance of consent, vary among these theories in ways that need not concern us here.

Among the interests of individuals that can command general agreement for purposes of such arguments about legitimate social orders are the satisfaction of basic needs and all-purpose means for pursuing one's conception of the good life. Furthermore, individuals must be acknowledged to have an interest in procedural control over the social institutions that shape values, goals, options, and expectations.

The topic of concern here is principles for assessing the rules of institutions that have a pervasive impact on us. Institutions are rule-governed practices established and maintained through the threat of force. They provide the backdrop for the distribution of important goods, powers, burdens, and obligations necessary for a variety of interests. Institutions also shape our expectations and values, and changes in institutions challenge our ability to maintain coherence and continuity in our lives. These considerations give us good reasons to claim a share in the political authority to make and change these rules.

The contractualist approach leads us to search for principles for institutions, against which no reasonable objections can be made. Three features are relevant for the following arguments. Such principles of justice, or particular institutions, are not generated by the process of checking whether equal respect is secured. Instead, the procedure of hypothetical consent provides checks drawn from interests at stake, but does not aim for a deduction of principles or institutions. Second, the process allows for several alternative principles. Thus the set of principles may be underdetermined, in the sense that alternative principles may all be unobjectionable. Third, a set of principles may allow a variety of sets of institutional arrangements, each of which satisfies the distributive requirements of liberal contractualism.

This tradition might thus allow that several different institutional arrangements are just. The unity provided by such a theory is hence not one of deduction – blueprints of institutional design are not on the agenda. Instead, the normative assessment of institutions shows that they are consistent with, and can be regarded as an expression of, a view of individuals as enjoying equal respect. For instance, the role of the state is underdetermined. It remains an open question whether universal basic income at some level is appropriate, or whether the state should be less directly involved in the form of transfers.[2] This is partly a matter of the long-term effects of moral hazard and incentive effects on the recipients, but also legitimately a question of historical fit and decision by democratic fiat. Similarly, consider the variety of institutional arrangements in European states concerning such important topics as old-age pensions and health insurance. Careful assessment of their consequences may show that reasonable objections can be made against some such arrangements, but it is by no means clear that only one of them is best by standards of distributive justice. One important task in the EU is thus to reform roughly just domestic institutions as required by increased interdependence, while respecting individuals' legitimate expectations.

2. Why Equality?

Some liberal theories appear to take for granted that equal respect for all entails equal shares – be it of goods, opportunities, resources, or initially un-owned things (Cohen 1989; Dworkin 1981a; Dworkin 1981b; Dworkin 1987; Sen 1980; Steiner 1994). Others, such as Rawls's theory of justice as fairness, give a similar impression, since the principles famously require equal shares of economic and social goods, except insofar as inequalities benefit all (Rawls 1971).

I here explore the room contractualism allows for inequalities – that is, when substantive inequality survives reasonable objections. Whether substantive inequality constitutes a violation of the commitment to normative equality, and hence gives rise to justifiable feelings of inferiority and second-rate citizenship, can best be determined by considering normative

[2] For basic income, cf. Jordan (1998) and van Parijs (1995).

arguments for equal treatment. Such analysis of arguments for equality is particularly important when our intuitions about equality appear to conflict with other intuitions, and where an intuitive "weighing" of these intuitions is controversial or unsatisfactory. The task in this section is precisely to determine what reasons can be offered for equal shares of benefits. Four grounds for lamenting inequalities can be identified on the basis of the interests at stake.[3]

a. Prevent Misery

If we seek to avoid reasonable objections to normative principles, surely acceptable institutions must engender and distribute benefits so as to meet the basic vital needs of all, to secure their survival. Human rights can be interpreted and defended as a requirement on domestic and international regimes to secure the satisfaction of such needs (Føllesdal 1991). The current world order fails dismally on this point: those with nothing to sell in markets cannot buy food, and large economic inequalities can even prevent wage earners from acquiring sufficient food. Differences in relative political power perpetuate abysmal prenatal health care for the poor, and international regimes fail to include obligations of international support as final resorts when domestic resources run out or when government powers are grossly abused.

But this argument from basic needs and human rights does not require equality of condition (Raz 1986; Miller 1995, 191). Rather, this consideration only prohibits drastic inequality regarding certain specific goods, insofar as these inequalities engender misery.

b. Prevent Domination

A social order is objectionable if some individuals can drastically restrict the attractive options of others, prevent deliberation, or otherwise leave them at the mercy of the powerful. The reason is that individuals have an interest in maintaining control over the social factors that shape their own lives – particularly if the alternative is that others wield such control. One important strand of recently resuscitated republicanism has focused on this interest in avoiding subjection to the arbitrary will of others (Pettit 1997; Skinner 1998). Large inequalities of wealth or income opportunities can prevent the less privileged from exercising control over their lives and subject them to the arbitrary bargaining power of the powerful in various spheres of life.

Again, this argument does not support equal distribution *tout court*. The prevention of domination prohibits only those inequalities that impact objectionably on the distribution of control over individuals' lives.

---

[3] For details, cf. Føllesdal (2000a) and Beitz (2001). I draw on Scanlon (1997) and Temkin (1993 and 1995).

c. Ensure Fair Procedures

A further ground for equality also stems from our interest in controlling the social factors that shape our lives. Many social procedures and mechanisms require for their fairness a roughly equal distribution of procedural input levers. Some adversarial procedures illustrate this: If legal trials are to regularly identify the guilty, competent counsel must represent both parties. Democratic arrangements likewise require a broad dispersal not only of formal political power, but also of education and income and wealth, since relative shares of these levers often matter for the real value of formal political power (Dahl 1985, 55). Similarly, markets provide an efficient allocation of goods relative to a base line – but only under conditions that include information about alternative buyers and sellers, the likely consequences, inability to create oligarchies, and so forth. Certain forms of inequalities in information or organizational resources may therefore prevent efficiency.

Note that such arguments primarily apply when we have independent standards for determining what outputs the procedure should generate. Moreover, such considerations may sometimes favor unequal distribution of formal levers such as voting powers. Consider, for example, that citizens of differently populated member states of the EU enjoy different representation in the political bodies. Small populations enjoy more formal power than the principle "one person, one vote" would allow. (These biases will diminish but not disappear with the forthcoming expansion of the EU.) Germany, with more than 80 million citizens, has ninety-nine members in the European Parliament and ten votes in the Council of the European Union. So each member of the European Parliament (MEP) from Germany represents more than 820,000 Germans, and each German vote in the council represents more than 8 million Germans. In contrast, each MEP from Ireland represents 240,000 Irish citizens (out of a total of 3.4 million), and each Irish vote in the council represents 1.2 million Irish. The Luxembourgians, in all 400,000, enjoy even more formal political power: each of their six MEPs represents 70,000 people, and each of their two votes in the council represents 200,000.

Such outcomes are typical of the bargain between small and large states joining in federal arrangements. Yet this formal inequality has not been perceived as disrespectful, presumably because citizens have assumed that there are good reasons for the skewed power. For instance, arguments can be made that smaller political units need such overrepresentation to reduce the risk of being permanently outvoted in political decisions (Føllesdal 1998a).

d. Provide Equal Shares of Products of Cooperation

Individuals may claim equal shares of certain goods when they have contributed equally to the production of the benefits, and when no one can be said to have prior claims to the benefits – for instance, when there is no prior agreement regarding distribution and each party's contribution cannot be determined.[4] When several individuals jointly labor to produce goods, they have equal claims regarding these goods.[5]

We may think of social institutions as the social practices that are maintained by the use of legal powers. Sanctions enforce the public rules and provide public assurance of general compliance, and authoritative interpretations apply the rules to new or difficult cases.

Legal rights in a broad sense are aspects of such social institutions. Within a state, Hohfeldian legal claims, powers, privileges, and immunities are constituted by the rules of rights of practices (Hohfeld 1964). These rights include political power, property rights, and even income. Take money as an example: it exists only as part of a social practice regulated by rules defining legal tender, where it is common knowledge that all accept the currency in return for goods and services (cf. Coleman 1990, 119). And an individual who owns something has acquired it according to public rules regulating entitlements. Insofar as she has complied with these rules, the object is clearly hers, and not anybody else's. But her claim of ownership is only true – and can only be made sense of – because these rules of ownership are publicly known and generally complied with by those participating in that practice. While her entitlements are hers, the entitlements are entitlements only because others regulate their actions according to public rules.

Legal rights are thus goods that are products of cooperation. These rights are aspects of social institutions, and they only exist insofar as these practices are maintained, as they are by all law-abiding citizens. Someone enjoys these claim-rights and immunities only when the participants in the practice generally recognize and act according to the rules specifying these rights. The general compliance with these rules constitutes these legal rights.

Those who participate in this sense are not only those who are producing material goods with the expectation that their expectations of reward will be honored. Rather, those who produce the legal rights are all those participants who regulate their actions according to the rules of the practice, for instance, by refraining from taking the material goods identified as the property of others. They thereby cooperate in maintaining the practices defining property.

The argument for equal shares of products applies to this account of the nature of legal rights. Citizens have equal moral claims on how social institutions should regulate the legal distribution of political power, income, and other legal rights, where there are no prior claims on such

---

[4] Steiner (1994) focuses on the latter; in the following I pursue the former premise.

[5] Scanlon notes (1988, 12) that this argument is weak: "the force of appeals . . . depends on a prior claim that as participants in a cooperative scheme the individuals in question have equal claim to the fruits of this cooperation. This is an appealing moral idea, but a controversial one to serve as the starting point for an argument in support of a particular conception of justice." My account in the following seeks to make the premise more acceptable.

goods. This is not an argument for a policy of providing each person with an equal amount of money per year, but rather a condition on the institutions when operating dynamically, creating and honoring expectations among those choosing employment, and selecting places of work. This is precisely the issue concerning how institutions should affect the distribution of these goods, for example, through rules of acquisition and transfer that shape individuals' preferences and aspirations, and the incentives and expectations of desert. Since these legal rights exist only through the cooperation of all, all participants in social institutions have a prima facie equal moral claim to the legal rights that arise within such institutions.[6]

I submit that this account provides an argument in favor of Rawls's egalitarian principles for social primary goods – that is, political and civil rights, and equality of opportunity and income and wealth (Rawls 1999). These goods are legal rights, rights-clusters specified by rules governing the practices maintained by citizens.

To summarize, the arguments surveyed only apply to a limited subject, namely, the distributive impact of institutions and policies. Moreover, the arguments regarding equality are limited in scope: they do not support claims to equality of quality of life generally. Rather, the arguments are addressed to institutions, and require that they prevent *certain* inequalities, namely, those that are instrumental in maintaining misery, domination, or skewed procedures. And the institutions should engender equal shares of *certain* goods, namely, income, wealth, educational and employment opportunities for talents, and political and civil rights – what Rawls calls social primary goods. These arguments may leave some room for inequality in the distribution of other goods.

3. Domestic Equality, Global Inequality?

A defense of federal inequality may argue that these arguments for equality fail to hold within federal arrangements, regarded as cooperation among sovereign states. I shall suggest that this strategy is not satisfactory.

On the standard view of the states system, these reasons for equality fail to hold across state borders. Sovereign states enjoy broad formal powers of external sovereignty, in the sense that there are few if any decision-making bodies above them, and states enjoy immunity from forcible intervention in determining the social institutions which shape citizens' lives.

---

[6] One might think that equal impact on capabilities, rather than equal shares, would be another plausible principle. Problems of interpersonal interval comparability of capabilities count against this standard once basic functionings are satisfied, or so I argue in Føllesdal 1991. I am grateful to Andrew Kuper for reminding me of this. The concern is not that capability sets cannot be ranked – which they presumably can, even beyond basic functionings, within some ranges. The comparability problems of equality are stronger since we must compare intervals between capability sets.

Several of the arguments sketched above apply to international inequalities of income and wealth. Natural facts and the actions of other powerful agents often restrict the range of alternatives open to governments. Market competition, oligarchic transnational corporations, structural adjustment policies, and international human rights norms affect a state's ability to determine its international and domestic policies. However, in a system of sovereign states, international inequalities in income do not fully determine the domestic distribution of control over nonmaterial goods. A claim to international equality of income and wealth is not obvious on the basis of the concern to avoid misery or domination, or to secure fair processes, as long as states enjoy some de facto external sovereignty. Government policies can buffer the impact of international economic inequalities, and they may seek to insulate the domestic population from the impact of international economic inequality.

In addition, foreigners in poor states cannot obviously claim that they participate in shared institutions with individuals in rich states. The "constitutive" argument for equal shares of products of cooperation thus does not apply across state borders as traditionally conceived.

This sketch indicates how liberal contractualism might in principle allow inequality across state borders within a system of sovereign states – though only within limits concerning misery, domination, and fair procedures. However, the premises do not match our present world order. Citizens of different states participate in a wide range of shared practices and regimes across state borders. The global economic interdependence wrought by trade and finance makes individuals more vulnerable to cross-border effects of misery, domination, and unfair procedures – and makes it less plausible to regard domestic economies as constituted solely by cooperation among compatriots.[7]

The level of interdependence is clearly very high in several federations. In the EU, member states have pooled sovereignty to such an extent that it seems plausible that similar distributive principles must apply as within a state (Føllesdal 2000a). Shared institutions-including freedom of movement for capital, workers, goods, and services, and, for some states, monetary union with a common currency – render citizens vulnerable to shocks otherwise buffered by government intervention. The political units of the region are very closely intertwined. It seems implausible to claim that citizens of one European state maintain domestic social institutions that are separable from those of neighboring states and of the union.

The upshot of this is that it seems difficult to defend economic inequality within federal arrangements, since the arguments for equal shares, and against inequality, apply among individuals who share social institutions, as is the case in federal political orders. Yet there are other arguments for

[7] Several other authors on global justice make similar points – Beitz (1979); Pogge (1994); Lichtenberg (1981); O'Neill (1996); and cf. Miller (1995, 104–5).

permitting inequality, namely, for the sake of subunit autonomy in federal arrangements.

4. Why Subunit Autonomy?

Split Legislative and Executive Competence
Federal arrangements have been presented as solutions to a wide range of perceived problems suffered by unitary governments, in order to secure peace, institutional innovation, efficiency, liberty, and the like. Many forms of local autonomy will allow inequality across subunits, in apparent conflict with normative egalitarianism.

According to the account presented above, legal autonomy is a cluster of legal powers in Hohfeld's sense. It is a product of cooperation that should be shared equally among citizens. The question of concern here is how to allocate such powers between the central and the subunit level. We do that by comparing the likely effects – benefits and burdens, risks and opportunities – of alternate allocations of authority. For our purposes, the interesting versions of local autonomy are those where some final legislative or executive authority is permanently allocated to the subunits of a political order, rather than placed with a central unit. Delegation of administrative authority to subunits is not at issue.

The legitimacy of such split authority can be assessed by a hypothetical contract between representatives of joining nations or states, deciding on the terms of their federation without knowing which nation or people they represent (Norman 1994). These approaches can easily be suspected of reifying social groups and being committed to normative communitarianism instead of maintaining normative individualism, unless firmly based on arguments appealing exclusively to the interests of individuals. Several reasons may be offered for why individuals can reasonably seek protection and furtherance of some of their interests within such a nonunitary political order.

Protection against Domination
One of the historical arguments for nonunitary political orders is that they protect against unjust domination. In a federal system "the parts are so distant and remote that it is very difficult, either by intrigue, prejudice, or passion, to hurry them into any measures against the public interest" (Hume 1793, 514–15; cf. Madison 1961a, b; Beer 1993, 266; Sunstein 1994, 323). Two arguments can be discerned. First, the federal level of deliberation and legislation provides a second chance to protect against abuse by local majorities. Second, larger units provide better checks on tyranny since majority coalitions in larger polities are less likely to actively harm a local minority.

Protection against abusive power is surely valuable. However, the added deliberation provided by two-stage decisions is not a feature of the split authority we address. This benefit stems from the political authority enjoyed jointly by subunits, in what is sometimes called interlocking federalism (Scharpf 1985). It primarily holds where enhanced ability to block decisions is important. This argument is weaker under other circumstances, for instance, when the status quo is drastically unjust, or when interests other than avoiding domination are more important – such as the need for joint action to secure basic needs and fair distributions. The second argument begs a central question of the political orders we consider. If larger units indeed provide better checks against tyranny, it remains unclear why subunits should have powers at all.

Immunity from Larger Unit

Consider a political order where individuals' interests and preferences vary according to parameters such as geography and resources, or tastes and values. At least four reasons can be discerned for placing some decisions with subunits.

a. Avoid Domination Historically, one important argument stems from the "republican" concern to avoid subjection to others, in this case the population of the larger political order. Security against interference can be of great value when the population of the subunit has interests different from those of the majority in the federation. Such concerns were indeed central to Althusius, "the father of federalism" (Althusius 1995; Hueglin 1999).

b. Allow Institutional Experimentation Another classical argument for subunit autonomy is to allow room for institutional experimentation and innovation, "compass and room enough to refine the democracy" (Hume 1793, 514). "Experiments in living" (Mill 1962) allow citizens to learn from the experiences of other subunits.[8]

c. Secure Fit to Local Circumstances Third, local powers should be kept because they must address the "local circumstances and lesser interests" which the center unit may neglect or overrule because of the "great and national objects" (Madison 1961a; cf. Beer 1993, 124). Central governments and common legislation ignore local variations in preferences, while subunits can act on those preferences and hence provide a better fit of policies to local circumstances. Decentralized decision making allows for the creation of "club goods" or "internalities" for the subsets of individuals who prefer them and are prepared to pay for them (Musgrave 1959, 179–80; Olson 1969; Oates 1972; cf. Beer 1993, 182). However, as the federalists noted, there is a risk of majority tyranny both centrally and in subunits. So local government must also be restrained to curb "what pretends to be local self-govern-

---

[8] Thanks to Michael Doyle for this reminder.

ment, but is, too often, selfish mismanagement of local interests by a jobbing and borné, local oligarchy" (Mill 1969, 116). Of course, liberal contractualism will not allow considerations of economic efficiency to be the sole criterion for allocation of powers. Distributive standards must also apply – hence we need to know more about why such autonomy may violate equality.

An important application of this argument concerns federal orders that are created on the bases of preexisting political units. Subunit autonomy allows preexisting political units to maintain some control over institutional change in those areas where common policies are not required. Individuals' interest in maintaining legitimate expectations thus can support subunit autonomy.

This argument does not require that institutions or cultures remain unchanged, but rather, that the affected individuals control the speed and form of change. So this is an argument that will hold during transition, entering federal arrangements, but that may lose force over time. Moreover, the required local influence over decisions may often be secured by including subunits in central decision-making bodies through interlocking arrangements, rather than by granting them some powers.

This argument does not support the maintenance of unjust institutions or expectations in ways that prevent eradication of injustice. The concern to prevent subjection and to honor expectations may be overruled when other important interests are at stake. So it remains unclear why such autonomy should override egalitarian principles of justice.

d. Reduce Burdens of Decision Making A fourth reason for allocating some powers to subunits is to reduce the burdens of decision making. Good decisions will require much information when there are large local variations. If the only individuals affected by the decisions are in one subunit, local decision makers are likely to have a better grasp of affected preferences and alternatives (Smith 1954, 680). No clear benefit arises if outsiders are required to gather and reflect on such information; hence, their efforts and resources may be better employed elsewhere.

To conclude, there are some identifiable benefits for citizens under subunit autonomy, where they wield more political influence over the subunit agenda than they would have enjoyed under a unitary political order. But by assumption, the political decisions taken centrally – in a *unitary political order*, for short – ensure a more egalitarian distribution of benefits and burdens, as required by the arguments laid out above. It seems clear that this gain in political influence can sometimes be advantageous – even for those who are left economically worse off in such federal arrangements than they would be under a unitary political order. Let us call them the *subunit poor*. Their economic loss may be outweighed by the benefits provided them by more political power at the local level, due to some subunit autonomy.

5. Why Subunit Autonomy for Subunit Poor?

The arguments presented above suggest at least three main reasons why the subunit poor may prefer subunit autonomy to increased economic benefits.

a. Reduce Risk of Domination
The division of political agendas reduces the vulnerability of subunit citizens to the views of others. The immunity accorded by a split agenda allows subunits some protection against domination or intervention from other subunits. Such immunity may protect not only against ill will in the larger population, but also against incompetence or insufficient attention.

This argument not only holds for geographical units, but may also apply to minority cultural or religious groups living intermingled among others – thus supporting consociational arrangements.

b. Provide Increased Responsiveness to Own Interests
Second, subunit autonomy over certain issues allows *increased responsiveness* to each affected person's interests. The subunit poor will have more voting power on these issues, and this can be of value. This is important in policy areas where the subunit population has special interests or circumstances that make it important to shape institutions and policies accordingly. The fit between policies and circumstances can be at stake in central decisions that ignore local circumstances. Subunits with shared geography, resources, social institutions, culture, or other features make for similar interests and policy choices among members of the subunits. Added immunity and political power over such local issues for the subunit poor can be more important for their life plans and expectations than having somewhat more economic resources available under a unitary political order. The authority to shape institutions may be more important than a marginal increase in the resources to use *within* institutions that presumably fit the local circumstances less well. Even the economically worse off (within strict limits) may have reason to prefer democratically chosen policies and institutions within one subunit, such as a concern to maintain population in a region, desire to maintain traditional industries, and so forth. The alternative is to subject such decisions to centralized authority where a majority in the larger polity may overrule a local consensus. Indeed, the larger polity should have such powers insofar as the local costly choices can trigger redistributive obligations from the surrounding political order. An illustration can be seen in the German Federal Republic, in the redistributive obligations among the subunit Länder. The Basic Law, the constitution, warrants central legislation when required to maintain "uniformity of living conditions beyond the territory of any one Land." Recent debates concern why rich Länder should subsidize poorer Länder that refuse to reform their industries. A central issue is therefore what range of outcomes and policies

the subunit population should be responsible for, in the sense that they should bear the full economic burden of their collective choices.

This case for subunit autonomy, even at some economic cost, holds only in some circumstances. The political autonomy of the subunit must concern policies and institutions where local fit matters for individuals' interests and concerns. This leads to at least two constraints. First, the subunit's opportunity set must not be unduly limited by the subunit's relative share of resources. For instance, the subunit must be able to implement acceptable educational or health care arrangements. Second, these decisions should not systematically disadvantage a minority in the population. Subunit autonomy is problematic from the point of view of individuals whose interests systematically differ from the majority's in ways that matter, and whose interests would be better served by institutions and policies secured through majoritarian decisions in a *unitary political order*. If members of such minorities also are the *subunit poor*, they would be better off both in terms of institutions and in economic terms with central decisions, and it becomes difficult to defend local autonomy.

Note that this argument holds among individuals in a subunit with shared circumstances – be they resources, values, or existing institutions. Those similarly affected are more likely to comprehend the need and room for common policies. But this argument does not single out states as the only relevant subunits: States with multiple cultures or large natural variations may not satisfy these conditions. The arguments may also support nonstate units, such as cross-state regions, cultural minorities, or other groups who share institutions or practices (Føllesdal 1996, 2000b).[9]

c. Reduce Burdens of Responsiveness to Others
A third reason for allocating powers to subunits is to reduce each person's burdens of responsiveness. Subunit autonomy for decisions that solely affect individuals in that subunit relieves others from responsibility and the affiliated costs. Responsible decision making requires information gathering, consultations with affected parties, analysis of likely impacts, and the like. Each person avoids such tasks under subunit autonomy. It seems plausible that such reduction in responsibility may be worth paying for, in the sense that the subunit poor can be expected to forego some economic benefit precisely in order to gain nonmonetary resources otherwise spent deliberating about policy choices on behalf of others.

This argument from alleviating the burdens of responsiveness supports subunit autonomy only for certain issue areas, where the decisions only impact on members of the subunit. Several preconditions must be met. The individuals of the subunit must be able to make fair decisions through functioning democratic procedures against an acceptable allocation of background resources, and so forth. Furthermore, supplemental mechanisms for

---

[9] Thanks to Andrew Kuper for insisting on this point.

central intervention and support must presumably provide added safe-guards.

These three arguments suggest that the same interests that support claims to equal shares and restrictions on inequality can support claims to subunit autonomy over certain decisions. Autonomy may be preferred even at the price of economic equality – within strict limits stemming from the interest in avoiding misery and domination, and primarily concerning issues that do not affect other individuals.

6. Conclusion

By reflecting on "why equality?" and "why subunit autonomy?" I have sought to resolve some of the tensions between these norms within federal political orders.

Attention to the arguments for equality and autonomy indicates why various sorts of equality and subunit autonomy matter for individuals' interests.

The contractualist account of equal respect suggests that goods and burdens must be distributed among individuals across subunits in ways that avoid misery and domination, and so as to secure fair procedures and equal shares of the products of cooperation. Liberal contractualism still allows some distributive inequality among individuals in different subunits, insofar as such variations are unavoidable features of the immunity and autonomy required to protect against domination, and to ensure well-informed shaping of institutions and policies to local circumstances. The same interests that ground claims to equality often support subunit autonomy rather than a unitary political order. Thus our interest in equal shares of income and wealth may legitimately be weighed against our interest in enjoying more political influence over matters controlled by our subunit.

These reflections nevertheless pose an important challenge to federal orders based on states as subunits. As noted throughout, several arguments for decentralized legislative authority suggest that authority should be placed with substate regions or even with nongovernmental actors (cf. Howse 1995, 273–74). These implications are also argued on the basis of the "Principle of Subsidiarity" (Føllesdal 1998b). The case for *states* as the appropriate subunits remains to be made. Given pluralism of values and shared circumstances, both within and across state borders, claims that states should be privileged parties must be substantiated better than as yet. In defense of states as subunits, the main argument would appear to be that they have historically been the sites of political decision making, whose citizens' expectations have converged around shared institutions. As primary makers and implementers of policies, governments may remain the most plausible agents within federal orders. Yet the pluralism of cultures and values within states suggests that they may often be too large and heterogeneous for shared policies, as witnessed by regional unrest and regionally based political parties. Moreover, permanent minorities within states, such as migrant workers, cultural minorities, or the unemployed, have needs that are not always satisfied by states. From this point of view, a flaw of federal agreements is that they tend to perpetrate cleavages along state borders. This embedded partitioning may limit mutual respect, and reduce the interest in political participation beyond subunits, as witnessed in consociational arrangements (Lijphart 1979; cf. de Beus 1997). The political authority of preexisting states in emerging federations may thus not be legitimate in the long run. Which groups and organizations should be recognized as subunits with political power is an important question not addressed here. The arguments presented here suggest that the problem is not that subunits maintain unequal standards of living, for some such inequalities may be compatible with the equal respect of all. Federal arrangements may legitimately permit some economic inequalities for the sake of subunit autonomy, to the benefit of each person.

Acknowledgments

I am grateful for comments received at presentations at Humboldt Universität, Berlin, and at the Bielefeld conference on global justice, and to Andrew Kuper and Stefan Gosepath for extensive written comments.

References

Althusius, Johannes. (1995 [1603/1614]). *Politica Methodice Digesta.* Translated by Frederick S. Carney and with an introduction by Daniel J. Elazar. Indianapolis: Liberty Press.

Barry, Brian. (1989). *Theories of Justice.* Vol. 1 of *A Treatise on Social Justice.* Berkeley: University of California Press.

Beer, Samuel H. (1993). *To Make a Nation: The Rediscovery of American Federalism.* Cambridge: Harvard University Press.

Beitz, Charles R. (1979). *Political Theory and International Relations.* Princeton: Princeton University Press.

———. (1994). "Cosmopolitanism, Liberalism, and the States System." In *Political Restructuring in Europe: Ethical Perspectives,* edited by Chris Brown, 123–36. London: Routledge.

———. (2001). "Does Global Inequality Matter?" *Metaphilosophy,* 32:1/2.

Cohen, G. A. (1989). "On the Currency of Egalitarian Justice." *Ethics,* 99, 906–44.

Coleman, James. (1990). *Foundations of Social Theory.* Cambridge: Harvard University Press.

Dahl, Robert A. (1985). *A Preface to Economic Democracy.* Cambridge: Polity Press.

de Beus, Jos. (1997). "The Place of National Identity in a Well-Ordered Consociational Democracy." *Acta Philosophica Groningana* (Groningen), 24.

Dworkin, Ronald. (1978). "Liberalism." In *Public and Private Morality*, edited by Stuart Hampshire, 113–43. Cambridge: Cambridge University Press.

——. (1981a). "What Is Equality? Part 1: Equality of Welfare." *Philosophy and Public Affairs*, 10, 185–246.

——. (1981b). "What Is Equality? Part 2: Equality of Resources." *Philosophy and Public Affairs*, 10, 283–345.

——. (1987). "What Is Equality? Part 3: The Place of Liberty." *Iowa Law Review*, 73, 1–54.

Føllesdal, Andreas. (1991). *The Significance of State Borders for International Distributive Justice.* Ph.D. diss., Harvard University. UMI No. 9211679.

——. (1996). "Minority Rights: A Liberal Contractualist Case." In *Do We Need Minority Rights? Conceptual Issues*, edited by Juha Raikka, 59–83. The Hague: Kluwer.

——. (1998a). "Democracy and Federalism in the EU: A Liberal Contractualist Perspective." In *Democracy and the European Union: Studies in Economic Ethics and Philosophy*, edited by Andreas Føllesdal and Peter Koslowski, 231–53. Berlin: Springer.

——. (1998b). "Subsidiarity." *Journal of Political Philosophy*, 6:2, 231–59.

——. (2000a). "Global Justice as Impartiality: Whither Claims to Equal Shares?" In *International Justice*, edited by Tony Coates, 150–66. Aldershot: Ashgate.

——. (2000b). "Subsidiarity and Democratic Deliberation." In *Democracy in the European Union: Integration through Deliberation?*, edited by Erik Oddvar Eriksen and John Erik Fossum, 85–110. London: Routledge.

Habermas, Jürgen. (1991). "Justice and Solidarity: On the Discussion Concerning Stage 6." In *The Moral Domain: Essays in the Ongoing Discussion between Philosophy and the Social Sciences*, edited by Thomas E. Wren. Cambridge: MIT Press.

Hohfeld, Wesley Newcomb. (1964 [1919]). *Fundamental Legal Conceptions as Applied in Judicial Reasoning.* Edited by Walter Wheeler Cook. New Haven: Yale University Press.

Howse, Robert. (1995). "Federalism, Democracy and Regulatory Reform: A Skeptical View of the Case for Decentralization." In *Rethinking Federalism: Citizens, Markets and Governments in a Changing World*, edited by Karen Knop, Sylvia Ostry, Richard Simeon, and Katherine Swinton, 273–93. Vancouver: University of British Columbia Press.

Hueglin, Thomas O. (1999). *Early Modern Concepts for a Late Modern*

World: Althusius on Community and Federalism. Waterloo, Ontario: Wilfrid Laurier University Press.

Hume, David. (1793). *Essays and Treatises on Several Subjects.* Edinburgh.

Jordan, William. (1998). *The New Politics of Welfare.* London: Sage.

Kant, Immanuel. (1970 [1784]). "Idea for a Universal History with a Cosmopolitan Purpose." In *Kant's Political Writings*, edited by Hans Reiss and translated by H. B. Nisbet, 41–53. Cambridge: Cambridge University Press.

Lichtenberg, Judith. (1981). "National Boundaries and Moral Boundaries." In *Boundaries: National Autonomy and Its Limits*, edited by Peter G. Brown and Henry Shue, 79–100. Totowa, N.J.: Rowman and Allanhead.

Lijphart, Arend. (1979). "Consociation and Federation: Conceptual and Empirical Links." *Canadian Journal of Political Science,* 22, 499–515.

Macedo, Stephen. (1990). *Liberal Virtues: Citizenship, Virtue, and Community in Liberal Constitutionalism.* Oxford: Clarendon Press.

Madison, James. (1961a). *Federalist 10.* In *The Federalist,* by James Madison, Alexander Hamilton, and John Jay. Edited by Benjamin Wright. Cambridge: Harvard University Press.

———. (1961b). *Federalist 51.* In *The Federalist,* by James Madison, Alexander Hamilton, and John Jay. Edited by Benjamin Wright. Cambridge: Harvard University Press.

Mill, John Stuart. (1962 [1859]). *On Liberty.* Edited by Mary Warnock. Glasgow: Collins.

———. (1969 [1873]). *Autobiography.* Edited by Jack Stillinger. Boston: Houghton Mifflin.

Miller, David. (1995). *On Nationality.* Oxford: Oxford University Press.

Musgrave, Richard. (1959). *The Theory of Public Finance: A Study in Political Economy.* New York: McGraw Hill.

Norman, Wayne J. (1994). "Towards a Philosophy of Federalism." In *Group Rights*, edited by Judith Baker, 79–100. Toronto: University of Toronto Press.

Oates, Wallace. (1972). *Fiscal Federalism.* New York: Harcourt Brace Jovanovich.

Olson, Mancur. (1969). "Strategic Theory and Its Applications: The Principle of 'Fiscal Equivalence' – The Division of Responsibility among Different Levels of Government." *American Economic Review,* 59, 479–532.

O'Neill, Onora. (1989). *Constructions of Reason.* Cambridge: Cambridge University Press.

———. (1996). *Towards Justice and Virtue: A Constructive Account of Practical Reasoning.* Cambridge: Cambridge University Press.

Pettit, Philip. (1997). *Republicanism: A Theory of Freedom and Government.* Oxford: Clarendon Press.

260   ANDREAS FØLLESDAL

Pogge, Thomas W. (1989). *Realizing Rawls*. Ithaca: Cornell University Press.
——. (1992a). "Cosmopolitanism and Sovereignty." *Ethics,* 103, 48–75.
——. (1992b). "Loopholes in Moralities." *Ethics,* 89, 79–98.
——. (1994). "Cosmopolitanism and Sovereignty." In *Political Restructuring in Europe: Ethical Perspectives*, edited by Chris Brown, 89–122. London: Routledge.
Rawls, John. (1971). *A Theory of Justice*. Cambridge: Harvard University Press.
——. (1993). *Political Liberalism*. New York: Columbia University Press.
——. (1999). "Social Unity and Primary Goods." In *Collected Papers*, 359–87. Cambridge: Harvard University Press. First published 1982 in *Utilitarianism and Beyond*, edited by Amartya Sen and Bernard Williams, 159–85. Cambridge: Cambridge University Press.
Raz, Joseph. (1986). *The Morality of Freedom*. Oxford: Clarendon Press.
Riker, William H. (1993). "Federalism." In *A Companion to Contemporary Political Philosophy,* edited by Robert E. Goodin and Philip Pettit, 508–14. Oxford: Blackwell.
Scanlon, Thomas M. (1974). "Rawls' Theory of Justice." In *Reading Rawls,* edited by Norman Daniels, 169–204. New York: Basic Books. First published 1973 in *University of Pennsylvania Law Review,* 121, 1020–69.
——. (1982). "Contractualism and Utilitarianism." In *Utilitarianism and Beyond,* edited by Amartya K. Sen and Bernard Williams, 103–28. Cambridge: Cambridge University Press.
——. (1988). "Notes on Equality." Harvard University. Mimeograph.
——. (1997). *The Diversity of Objections to Inequality.* The Lindley Lecture. Lawrence: Department of Philosophy, University of Kansas.
Scharpf, Fritz W. (1985). "Die Politikverflechtungs-Falle: Europäische Integration und deutscher Föderalismus im Vergleich." *Politische Vierteljahresschrift,* 26:4, 324–50.
Sen, Amartya K. (1980). "Equality of What?" In *Choice, Welfare, and Measurement,* 353–69. Cambridge: MIT Press.
Skinner, Quintin. (1998). *Liberty before Liberalism.* Cambridge: Cambridge University Press.
Smith, Adam. (1954 [1776]). *An Inquiry into the Nature and Causes of the Wealth of Nations.* London: Dent.
Steiner, Hillel. (1994). *An Essay on Rights.* Cambridge: Blackwell.
Sunstein, Cass R. (1994). "Approaching Democracy: A New Legal Order for Eastern Europe – Constitutionalism and Secession." In *Political Restructuring in Europe: Ethical Perspectives,* edited by Chris Brown, 11–49. London: Routledge.
Temkin, Larry S. (1993). *Inequality.* Oxford: Oxford University Press.

——. (1995). "Justice and Equality: Some Questions about Scope." *Social Philosophy and Policy,* 12, 72–104.

Treaty on European Union. (1997). *Official Journal of the European Communities,* C 340, 10.11.1997.

van Parijs, Philippe. (1995). *Real Freedom for All.* Oxford: Oxford University Press.

Notes on Contributors

Charles R. Beitz is Professor of Politics at Princeton University. He is the author of the books *Political Theory and International Relations* and *Political Equality* and of numerous articles on topics in international political theory. His current research concerns the theory of human rights. He is the editor of the quarterly journal *Philosophy & Public Affairs*.

Rüdiger Bittner has taught philosophy at the universities of Heidelberg, Princeton, Hildesheim, and Yale and is currently professor of philosophy in Bielefeld, Germany. He has published in moral philosophy, theory of action, and aesthetics as well as on classical authors such as Kant, Nietzsche, Hobbes, and others. His book *Doing Things for Reasons* is forthcoming.

Simon Caney teaches political philosophy and international ethics in the Department of Politics at the University of Newcastle. He has published articles in philosophy and politics journals on liberalism, perfectionism, nationality, human rights, and international justice. Recent articles have appeared in the *Journal of Political Philosophy* and *Journal of Applied Philosophy*. He coedited *National Rights, International Obligations* with Peter Jones and David George, and is currently completing a book titled *Global Political Theory*.

Stéphane Chauvier is a lecturer of philosophy at the University of Caen (France). He is the author of *Du Droit d'être étranger. Essai sur le concept kantien d'un droit cosmopolitique* and *Justice internationale et solidarité*, and co-editor (with Alain Boyer) of *Libéralisme et republicanisme*. His latest book, *Dire "je": essai sur la subjectivité*, is forthcoming in September of this year.

Michael W. Doyle is director of the Center of International Studies and Edwards S. Sanford Professor of Politics and International Affairs at Princeton University. He is the author of *Ways of War and Peace*, *UN Peacekeeping in Cambodia*, and *Empires*.

Andreas Føllesdal is professor of practical philosophy at the University of Oslo and research professor at ARENA (Advanced Research on the Europeanisation of the Nation-State) at the Research Council of Norway. He publishes in the field of political philosophy, with a focus on issues of international political theory as they arise in the wake of changes in

Europe. He has written on such topics as the normative significance of state borders, minority rights, citizenship, distributive justice, federalism, subsidiarity, and deliberative democracy.

Rainer Forst teaches philosophy at Goethe-University in Frankfurt am Main. A translation of his *Kontexte der Gerechtigkeit* is forthcoming as *Contexts of Justice: Political Philosophy beyond Liberalism and Communitarianism.* He is the editor of *Toleranz* and is currently working on a book about the concept of toleration. Among his more recent publications in English are "The Basic Right to Justification: Toward a Constructivist Conception of Human Rights" (*Constellations,* 1999), "The Rule of Reasons: Three Models of Deliberative Democracy" (*Ratio Juris,* forthcoming), and "Toleration, Justice, and Reason" (*Reasonable Tolerance,* forthcoming).

Stefan Gosepath teaches philosophy at the Hochschule der Künste Berlin. He is the author of *Aufgeklärtes Eigeninteresse: Eine Theorie theoreti-scher und praktischer Rationalität,* coeditor of *Philosophie der Menschenrechte,* and editor of *Motive, Gründe, Zwecke: Theorien praktischer Rationalität.* He has published articles on rationality and political philosophy and is currently working on a book on the idea of equality.

Wilfried Hinsch is professor of philosophy at the University of the Saarland. He teaches moral and political philosophy and does research in these areas. His publications include the two books *Erfahrung und Selbstbewusstsein* and *Gerechtfertigte Ungleichheiten* (forthcoming), as well as several articles.

Andrew Hurrell is university lecturer in international relations and fellow of Nuffield College, Oxford. His major interests include international relations theory, with particular reference to international law and institutions, and the international relations of Latin America, with particular reference to the foreign policy of Brazil and U.S.–Latin American relations. Recent publications include *Regionalism in World Politics* (coedited with Louise Fawcett), *Inequality, Globalization and World Politics* (coedited with Ngaire Woods), and *Hedley Bull on International Society.*

Onora O'Neill is principal of Newnham College, Cambridge. She has written widely in ethics and political philosophy and on the philosophy of Immanuel Kant. She is particularly interested in the task of revising theories of justice to take account of the realities of a globalizing world. Her first book in this area was *Faces of Hunger: An Essay on Poverty, Justice, and Development;* her most recent book on these themes is *Bounds of Justice.*

Thomas W. Pogge teaches moral and political philosophy at Columbia University. His recent publications include "What We Can Reasonably Reject" (*Noûs* 2001), "Eradicating Systemic Poverty" (*Journal of Human Development* 2001), "Achieving Democracy" (*Ethics and International Affairs* 2001), "An Egalitarian Law of Peoples'" and "On the Site of Distributive Justice'" (*Philosophy and Public Affairs* 1994, 2000), "Human Flourishing and Universal Justice" (*Social Philosophy and Policy* 1999), "The Bounds of Nationalism'" (*Canadian Journal of Philosophy* 1997), "Creating Supra-National Institutions Democratically" (*Journal of Political Philosophy* 1997).

Leif Wenar is lecturer in philosophy at the University of Sheffield and, during 2000–01, a Laurance S. Rockefeller Visiting Fellow at the Princeton University Center for Human Values. His work on Rawlsian liberalism and private property rights has appeared in the journals *Ethics, Mind, The Columbia Law Review,* and *The Philosopher's Annual.* He is currently working on a book on the nature and justification of rights.

Véronique Zanetti has taught ethics and political philosophy at the universities of Bern and Fribourg (Switzerland). Currently she is writing a book on the ethical aspects of humanitarian intervention, with the support of the Swiss National Foundation for Scientific Research. Her publications include *La nature a-t-il une fin? Le probleme de la téléologie chez Kant; Critical Edition and Commentary on Kant's Schriften zur Aesthetik und Naturphilosophie* (coauthored with M. Frank); *Dworkin: A Debate* (coedited with S. Wesche); and several articles on the question of humanitarian intervention.

INDEX